Mindwatching

HANS J. AND MICHAEL EYSENCK

Mindwatching

Why People Behave the Way They Do

ANCHOR PRESS/DOUBLEDAY
GARDEN CITY, NEW YORK
1983

Copyright ©
Multimedia Publications, Inc., Willemstad (Curaçao),
Personality Investigations, Publications and Services Ltd., and
Michael Eysenck 1981

Anchor Press edition: 1983

Library of Congress Cataloging in Publication Data

Eysenck, H. J. (Hans Jurgen), 1916–
  Mindwatching.

  Includes bibliographical references and index.
  1. Psychology.   2. Psychology, Experimental.
I. Eysenck, Michael W.   II. Title.
BF121.E938   150
AACR2
ISBN: 0-385-17843-3
Library of Congress Catalog Card Number 81–43734

Printed in the United States of America

Photograph preceding title page copyright © Marvin E. Newman/Image Bank

To Fleur,
with love from her father and grandfather

Contents

Introduction

Psychology can claim to be regarded as the most important of all the sciences. After all, its subject matter is man himself, and nothing could be more interesting and important than that. More specifically, psychologists are mainly interested in the ways in which people behave in a wide variety of situations, ranging from conditions of great danger and stress to the peace and quiet of the research laboratory.

What do psychologists hope to learn from their study of behavior? Ultimately, the goal is to understand why people behave as they do, so that it will be possible to predict and change their behavior. The importance of such understanding to society can hardly be overemphasized. It is often necessary or desirable to change people's behavior in certain ways; examples that spring to mind include the drinking problems of alcoholics, the bizarre behavior patterns of neurotics and schizophrenics, the learning disabilities of many children, and the antisocial behavior of criminals.

It is, of course, already the case that psychologists have enriched our understanding of human behavior to the point at which major benefits to society have begun to accrue. Several of the chapters in this book, especially those in Section E, bear witness to the progress which has been made. For example, we show in Chapter 6 that research on conditioning and learning carried out in the laboratory has proved extremely useful in suggesting many of the techniques now used by behavior therapists to treat the mentally ill.

There is a sense in which everyone can claim to be a psychologist: we all attempt to predict and understand the behavior of other people.

Thus we expect Joe to be the life and soul of the party and Fred to be rather taciturn, and it comes as a great surprise if these predictions are disproved. In spite of these similarities between the concerns of psychologists and of lay people, there is the important difference that psychologists usually observe behavior under much more closely controlled conditions than the rest of us can in everyday life.

However, some people of a skeptical or cynical disposition doubt whether professional psychologists understand human behavior any better than the non-expert. They have discovered a virtually foolproof method of belittling the achievements of psychology. For them, most of the findings of psychologists are obvious and merely support common sense. Any findings which are not obvious, and which clearly contradict common sense, elicit the reply: "I don't believe that!"

The flaws in such a line of argument are fairly clear. It is a big mistake to assume that common sense has constructed a single, comprehensive theory of human behavior. An amusing game involves trying to find pairs of proverbs that express opposite meanings. For example, "Look before you leap" is the opposite of "He who hesitates is lost." Other examples are "Many hands make light work" compared with "Too many cooks spoil the broth," and "Out of sight, out of mind" versus "Absence makes the heart grow fonder." By judicious selection of the appropriate proverb, common sense has no trouble in "explaining" human actions, irrespective of what those actions actually are.

So common sense is not very helpful in shedding real light on human behavior. In many cases, only controlled experiments can reveal what is happening. For instance, one of the pairs of proverbs could be accounted for by means of the plausible hypothesis that "Out of sight, out of mind" is true when love is weak or nonexistent, whereas "Absence makes the heart grow fonder" is true when love is strong. This idea could be tested experimentally by measuring love in some way, and by relating the amount of love to an index of pining behavior during the separation.

What kinds of problems are psychologists interested in? In view of the fact that more than half a million psychological experiments have been reported in learned journals, it is easy to see that psychologists are interested in virtually every aspect of human and animal behavior. The junior author of this book, for example, is interested in the "tickling phenomenon": other people can tickle you, but you cannot tickle yourself properly. To his surprise he discovered a small but thriving literature devoted to tickling. While there are many reasons for the tickling phenomenon, it looks as if predictability is the most important: you know when and how you are going to tickle yourself, but not when and how someone else is going to tickle you.

By and large the experimental findings that psychologists find most interesting are those which are counter-intuitive, that is to say, surprising and quite unexpected. In this book, we discuss several of the most important, famous, and controversial experiments in the history of psychology. Most of them produced findings that were clearly counter-intuitive, and thus forced psychologists—and lay people—to reconsider their theoretical ideas.

A prime example of a counter-intuitive finding was that obtained by Stanley Milgram in his work on obedience to authority (Chapter 3). He asked people to administer electric shocks of increasing intensity to someone engaged in a learning task. It seems reasonable to assume that people would refuse to do this as the shock intensity increased to dangerous levels. In fact, Milgram found that many people were prepared to administer near-fatal shocks even to a man with a heart condition!

Heredity versus environment

One of the most important issues that psychologists have been interested in for many years is the relative importance of heredity and environment in determining the ways in which people think and act. Several of the chapters in this book, especially those in Section C, deal with various aspects of the so-called nature-nurture controversy. The first systematic work in this area was carried out by Sir Francis Galton, the brilliant Victorian scientist. While he is best known for his work on heredity, Galton had an extraordinarily wide range of interests. He was, for example, the man who coined the term "anticyclone" to refer to a meteorological condition in which a high-pressure area is surrounded by clockwise winds.

Galton realized the importance of twins to an understanding of the role played by heredity, and obtained information from 94 sets of twins. Of these, at least 35 pairs appeared to be identical, or monozygotic, twins produced by a single fertilized egg dividing in the womb. Such twins are essentially identical genetically, and must be distinguished from dizygotic twins, who are no more similar genetically than ordinary siblings.

Galton reported some amusing cases of confusion involving the identical twins. In five cases, a person engaged to an identical twin was never sure which was his or her future partner. In other cases, twins were even misled by their own reflection in a mirror, speaking to it in the mistaken belief that it was their twin.

Galton was much impressed by the general similarity of behavior of most of the twin pairs, and interpreted his findings in the following way: "There is no escape from the conclusion that nature prevails

Sharing the same sofa, two women who sixty-three years ago shared the same egg. There are about 30 million identical twins in the world. Photo: Multimedia Publications Inc. (Miki Koren).

enormously over nurture when the differences of nurture do not exceed what is commonly to be found among persons of the same rank of society and in the same country."

The obvious problem with Galton's endeavors is that the similarities within the pairs of identical twins observed by him may have been due in part to the fact that they were brought up in a similar environment. More telling evidence can be obtained if one considers identical twins brought up apart. If heredity is of major importance, such twins should act very similarly; if environmental forces are of crucial significance, dissimilarities in behavior should be the norm. Scientifically speaking, it is a pity that pairs of identical twins brought up in different homes are not very abundant, despite the existence of some 30 million identical twins in the world. At the last count, fewer than 100 pairs of identical twins separated at birth had been studied at all systematically.

— Interesting work on separated identical twins is currently being carried out at the University of Minnesota. Psychologists there have been surprised at the great similarities that exist between identical twins who have not seen each other for decades. For example, James Lewis, a security guard in Lima, Ohio, had not seen his identical twin, James Springer, a records clerk in Dayton, Ohio, for thirty-nine years. Each twin had married a girl called Linda, divorced her, and then married a woman called Betty. Lewis called his first son James Alan, and Springer called his James Allan. Even more amazingly, they had both spent holidays at the same beach in Florida (a stretch of sand only 300 yards long), and both had driven there and back in the same make of car (a Chevrolet). Furthermore, they both bite their fingernails to excess—they hardly have any nails left. They even have the same health problems: both suffer from tension headaches that start after lunch and turn into migraine; both have had two confirmed or suspected heart attacks; and both have hemorrhoids. Not surprisingly, Jim Lewis has referred to these coincidences—or are they coincidences?—as "spooky."

What do all these findings mean? David Lykken, one of the psychologists involved in the Minnesota project, draws the following provocative conclusions: "People get so upset when you suggest that the wiring diagram* can influence the mind. But to believe otherwise involves an assumption that mental events occur independently of the physical substrate. Clearly, many more aspects of our behavior are influenced by genetics than we have thought till now." Considerable support for this view will be discussed at several points in this book.

The experimental approach

Psychologists attach great importance to the use of controlled experimental methods in the pursuit of knowledge about human behavior, and tend to disregard information obtained in everyday situations. The reasons for this can be illustrated by taking as an example the interesting question of whether men or women are better car drivers. One way of attempting to answer the question is to look up car accident records. This approach indicates that women have more accidents, but less serious ones, than men.

However, these statistics should not be taken at face value. After all,

* The connections laid down in the genes.

women tend to drive at different times of day from men, they tend to spend less time driving than men, they are less likely than men to drive while drunk, and they often drive smaller cars which are easier to maneuver. In other words, real life is so complex that it is usually extremely difficult, if not impossible, to decide what is causing the results obtained. An experimental approach to the problem would involve taking men and women car drivers of the same age and with the same amount of driving experience and getting them to drive the same cars over the same driving course under the same conditions. The aim of controlled experimentation is to investigate the effects of one factor (sex of driver in this case), *while holding all other factors constant*. In real-life situations outside the laboratory it is seldom possible to do this, and so the correct interpretation of events is unclear.

Experimenter bias

While it is certainly true that properly controlled and rigorous experiments provide the best way of uncovering the secrets of human behavior, it is worth considering some of the difficulties which research may entail. Robert Rosenthal of Harvard University has emphasized the various ways in which the experimenter may unwittingly influence the results which he reports, a phenomenon known as "experimenter bias."

Mendel's famous pioneering work on genetics provides a probable case of experimenter bias. He expected that, when hybrid pea plants were self-fertilized, 75 percent of the offspring would show the dominant phenotype and 25 percent the recessive phenotype. That is almost exactly what Mendel reported; the snag is that later analysis revealed that his data were improbably good and precise.

The phenomenon of experimenter bias has been demonstrated many times in psychology. In one well-known case, experimenters were asked to count the number of head turns and body contractions made by planarians (flatworms). They were told to expect a lot of activity from half the worms, and very little from the remainder. In fact, all the worms were essentially identical. Nevertheless, the observers reported twice as many head turns and three times as many body contractions in the allegedly active worms than in the others.

Rosenthal has emphasized the point that experiments in psychology are, in part, social occasions. Although experimenters are told to treat their subjects in a consistent manner, they often fail to do so. There is evidence to suggest that chivalry is not dead, at least not in the psychological experiment. Male experimenters have been found to be more likable, pleasant, friendly, encouraging, honest, and relaxed when interacting with female subjects than with male subjects. In consequence, according to Rosenthal, "male and female subjects may, psychologically, simply not be in the same experiment at all."

There is a growing demand that psychological research should have immediate relevance to social problems; in contemporary jargon, the cry is for greater "ecological validity." While the requirement that psychology be socially relevant is one that appeals to many politicians, it is often exceedingly difficult to predict the long-term implications of research. It is generally agreed that Mendel's work on genetics has been of profound significance in several different ways, and yet his work was almost totally ignored for several decades after it had been published.

While we believe that it is a great mistake to finance research on the basis of its apparent social relevance rather than on its intrinsic merits, there is little doubt that much early research in psychology was perversely lacking in ecological validity. It was not unknown for theories of human behavior to be based almost entirely on rodent research. While some people may be "dirty rats," it is surely stretching things too far to assume that everyone is.

Psychologists no longer believe that experiments on rats will necessarily tell them something about human behavior. However, psychologists do still use college and university students as subjects in much of their research. Do students really behave similarly to other groups of people in our society? If they don't, isn't there the danger that theories based exclusively on research with students may not apply to most other people? Fortunately this danger seems to be more apparent than real. Typically psychologists who have done research on various nonstudent groups find that, though students tend to be more intelligent than most other groups of people, the similarities between students and other groups in patterns of behavior in the laboratory considerably outweigh the dissimilarities.

The ethical question

Psychologists are becoming increasingly concerned about ethical issues, especially where they concern the safety and well-being of subjects used in experiments. The problems involved can be difficult to resolve. If, for example, researchers want to study the effects of anxiety on task performance, they must obviously induce a state of anxiety in some of their subjects. There is a fine dividing line between producing modest levels of anxiety (which most people would regard as acceptable) and producing severe anxiety states (which would be quite unacceptable).

In an attempt to establish sensible and consistent ethical standards, the British Psychological Society and the American Psychological Association have both issued detailed recommendations on these matters, and many places of research have set up their own ethical committees to vet research proposals. Most psychologists argue that a certain amount of discomfort by subjects can be justified if the experiment is of sufficient value. However, psychologists often disagree about the importance of a particular piece of research. In particular, Zimbardo's research into prison conditions (Chapter 4) and Milgram's work on obedience to authority (Chapter 3) have aroused a storm of controversy because of the ethical problems which they pose.

About this book

One of our major concerns in writing this book is to demonstrate that the only way in which we can ever hope to obtain complete understanding of ourselves and our behavior is by integrating information from several different disciplines. The reason why this is necessary is that psychology as a science lies at the meeting point of several other sciences, including physiology, genetics, biology, anthropology, zoology, and sociology. While the task is a daunting one, it is likely that only someone who is expert in all of these sciences could ever realize the goal of truly understanding human behavior.

The structure of this book is based on the assumption that man can and should be looked at from several different perspectives.

Section A considers man as a social animal and group member. Other people are far and away the most important factors in our environment, and psychology must encompass that fact. The subject matter is similar to that of *sociology,* but social psychologists tend to be more inclined to adopt a scientific approach to social phenomena than sociologists. This section is entitled "Cautionary tales" because several of the chapters in it show how easy it is to misinterpret what is happening in social situations.

Section B considers man as a species that has developed from other species of animals. This approach obviously overlaps with the sciences of *zoology* and *biology,* and allows us to see how man has been molded by evolutionary forces. The emphasis is on primates such as monkeys and apes, because these species are more likely to provide us with relevant information about man than the rats and pigeons so beloved of certain psychologists.

Section C considers man from the inside, so to speak. This is traditionally, of course, the territory explored by researchers in *physiology,* but there are many psychophysiologists who believe (as we do) that physiology and psychology are intimately related. This section also

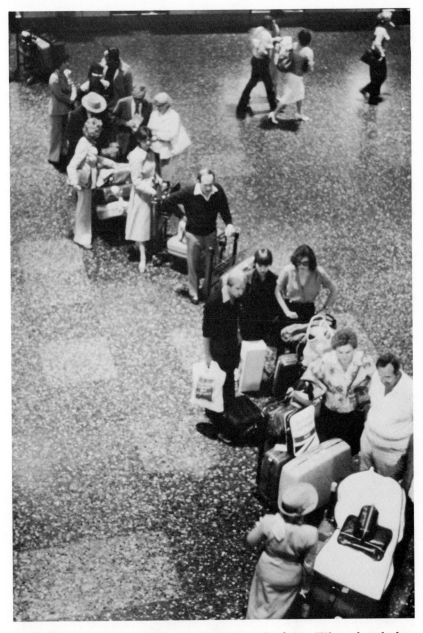

A well-behaved line waiting at baggage check-in. What do clothes, stances, luggage, hairstyles, and speech tell you about people? Photo: Multimedia Publications Inc. (Miki Koren).

deals with certain aspects of the nature-nurture controversy, and thus relates to the science of *genetics*.

Section D considers man as a fallible problem solver who has to cope with a complex environment. This requires the use of many psychological processes, including attention, perception, thinking, and memory. This section is perhaps the most purely *psychological* in the sense that other sciences do not usually study these processes in any detail.

Section E deals mainly with important *applications* of research in psychology to the society in which we live. The various chapters in this section demonstrate the great value of psychology in treating clinical conditions and criminals, in bringing up children, in improving our educational system, and even in understanding the roots of political ideology.

In sum, the hope is that psychology can make real progress by combining information from different scientific approaches. Several such approaches are discussed at length in this book, and we show how much progress has already been made. As yet, psychology is only a sturdy toddler; one day, it will grow to adulthood.

SECTION A

Cautionary tales

Very complicated psychological processes are involved when human beings get together. As psychologists have demonstrated many times (see Chapter 16 for details), other people provide us with a veritable flood of verbal and non-verbal information, and it can be extremely difficult to make sense of it all. Intriguingly, our impression that we have understood what is happening in a social situation is sometimes totally mistaken. Such errors form the basis for the research discussed in this section, and explain why it is entitled "Cautionary tales." Before discussing these social situations in more detail, let us consider various approaches that have been adopted toward man the social animal.

How social interactions are studied

Sociologists and social psychologists are both interested in people's social activities. However, while there is no absolute division between their interests, the former tend to be interested in large groups within society—political organizations, social classes, industrial concerns—whereas the latter are more concerned with small groups—twenty people or fewer.

In practical terms, sociologists are hampered by their inability to do anything but simply observe what is happening and attempt to guess why it is happening. They are not usually in a position to alter the way a large organization is run in order to explore the consequences. In other words, sociologists cannot carry out experiments in the normal sense of that word. This is not necessarily a crippling disadvantage, as the success story of astronomy demonstrates. Astronomers cannot directly affect the mysterious workings of the universe to see what happens, but they have been greatly assisted by major technological advances.

In contrast to sociologists and astronomers, social psychologists can very readily carry out experiments. They can set up small groups, they can manipulate the activities in which such groups participate, and they can even decide who is allowed to talk to whom and when. Some of the choicest fruits of their labor are discussed in the chapters that follow.

There has been some controversy about whether it is better to study man the social animal under controlled laboratory conditions or whether it is better to study him in his natural setting. We suspect that the quality of the researcher is much more important than the conditions in which he or she does the research. What does seem absurd, however, is the trend toward doing "imaginary experiments." The experimenter simply describes the setup of a hypothetical experiment and asks people how they would behave if they were to take part in such an experiment. Such imaginary experiments require much less time and money than real experiments, but they have little else to recommend them.

Does power corrupt?

Many social psychologists are interested in the effects of power and status on people's actions. After all, there are important status differences between the members of many social groups. This is especially clear at work, where the boss is regarded as the leader and everyone else plays a subordinate role. The potentially disastrous consequences of having powerful leaders are revealed clearly by a study of history, which is full of horrifying examples of leaders abusing their power, of followers slavishly obeying crazy commands.

On the face of it, it seems difficult to investigate such manifestations of power in the laboratory. Nevertheless Philip Zimbardo (Chapter 4) set up a mock prison at Stanford University, using respectable college students as mock guards and prisoners. He naturally assumed that they would behave in a civilized fashion. To his surprise the mock guards very rapidly started abusing their position of power over the pseudo-prisoners. In an even more celebrated and disturbing study at Yale, Stanley Milgram (Chapter 3) discovered that many people were prepared to administer near-lethal electric shocks to a hapless victim if ordered to do so by a figure of authority.

Since apparently normal and well-adjusted people were used in these studies, Zimbardo and Milgram both argued that abuses of power occur primarily because society has inculcated the notion that followers are expected to obey their leader, no matter what orders he may issue. In other words, abuses of power are inevitable in certain situations, and do not necessarily occur because leaders are sadists or psychopaths.

We believe that individual differences in personality are more important than Zimbardo and Milgram admitted. Only some of the people in these studies abused their positions, and neither Zimbardo nor Milgram really explains this aspect of their findings.

Labeling

One of the major lessons to be learned from the Zimbardo and Milgram studies is that people will often behave in aggressive and unpleasant ways largely because of the *situation* they find themselves in. Another line of exploration that has emphasized the importance of situation in determining social behavior concerns the diagnosis of people presenting themselves voluntarily at mental hospitals, discussed in Chapter 5. Rosenhan argued that psychiatrists would have a strong tendency under such circumstances to apply a psychiatric label to completely normal people, and that is exactly, and disturbingly, what he found.

Fortunately, Rosenhan's conclusion that we cannot tell the difference between the sane and the insane does not appear to be true, although it is worrying that the way in which we react to other people is so much affected by the labels applied to them. If you meet someone at a party you are almost certain to treat him differently if you are told he is a schizophrenic or a psychopath rather than a nurse. This is, of course, a sensible policy to adopt. But what if the label is wrong?

Passing the buck

One of the saddest phenomena of contemporary urban existence is the well-known tendency for bystanders not to get involved when there is an accident or other emergency. This has often been seen as a reflection of the generally uncaring and selfish attitudes of Western society. However, Darley and Latané (Chapter 1) have put forward convincing evidence that other factors are involved. In particular, they claimed, when we see other people not responding to an emergency we assume that nothing serious has happened and so fail to respond ourselves.

Beautiful is beautiful

One of the most interesting and important questions in social psychology concerns the reasons why people are attracted to one another. While people usually say that personal qualities such as friendliness, honesty, and warmth are what matter most, there is a lot of evidence (discussed in Chapter 2) that physical attractiveness is much more important than is generally supposed. Indeed, Michael Efran of the University of Toronto found that jurors were less certain about the guilt of attractive defendants and recommended much milder punishment for them. Naturally such amazing findings have provided ammunition for various groups of "uglies" set up in America to fight discrimination against the physically unattractive.

There is an important ethical point worth pondering as you read these chapters. Many of the most dramatic findings we discuss are the result of studies in which the participants were thoroughly deceived about major aspects of the experiment. In some cases, too, things were arranged so that the participants were almost bound to be embarrassed, frightened, or humiliated.

Most psychologists would argue that ends can justify means. In other words, if the findings of an experiment are important enough, they may justify a certain amount of discomfort on the part of the participants. This position makes some sense to us, but raises two awkward questions: (1) How much agreement is there on the relative importance of a particular experiment? (2) Is the amount of discomfort predictable *before* the experiment is carried out? There are no categorical answers to such questions yet. However, the British Psychological Society and the American Psychological Association have both issued guidelines on ethical principles in recent years.

1

Where has the Good Samaritan gone?

One of the recurring images of our time is that of someone being attacked and screaming for help in the middle of a large, impersonal city, their cries going unheard, and the onlookers doing absolutely nothing except calmly minding their own business. This apparent apathy has been used as evidence of the dehumanizing and uncaring attitude which modern cities produce in most of their inhabitants.

There have certainly been many real-life incidents that seem to fit this gloomy picture. A famous example was the case of Kitty Genovese, who was stabbed to death in the Queens area of New York City as she returned home from work at three o'clock in the morning. Yet there were thirty-eight witnesses who not merely saw but *watched* the murder from the windows of their apartments, and none of them attempted to intervene. Only one person took the relatively modest step of calling the police, and even that action was taken only after he had sought the advice of a friend in another part of the city.

When this horrifying story was given massive publicity in the New York *Times,* there were apoplectic reactions from readers, several of whom wrote letters demanding that the names of the onlookers be published so that they could be exposed to the public wrath they so richly deserved. Various noted psychiatrists put forward speculative explanations for the apathetic attitude of the witnesses to the murder. More interesting than the explanations themselves was that they had practically nothing in common. Dr. George Serban argued as follows: "It's the air of all New York, the air of injustice. The feeling that you might get hurt if you act and that whatever you do, you will be the one to suffer."

The victim's companions and a policeman are actively helping. Others demonstrate all shades of reaction from indifference to mild curiosity. Photo: Multimedia Publications Inc. (Israel Sun).

Dr. Ralph S. Banay suggested that the apathy of the bystanders was caused by confusion between fantasy and reality, a confusion engendered by an endless stream of television violence: "We underestimate the damage these accumulated images do to the brain . . . they were deaf, paralyzed, hypnotized with excitation. Fascinated by the drama, by the action, and yet not entirely sure that what was taking place was actually happening." According to this reading of the situation, some of the bystanders may have been expecting a bald-headed cop sucking a lollipop and calling himself Kojak to materialize and solve the problem.

In another incident in New York, this time in the Bronx, an 18-year-old switchboard operator was raped and beaten while alone in her office. She escaped briefly from her attacker, and ran naked and bleed-

A case of diffused responsibility: bystanders concerned but uncertain what to do. Photo: Multimedia Publications Inc. (Miki Koren).

ing into the street, screaming for help. Approximately forty people gathered and watched in broad daylight as the rapist tried to drag her back upstairs; not one of them came to her rescue despite her screams. She was finally rescued by two policemen who happened to be passing.

Then there was the case of Andrew Mormille, a 17-year-old boy who was stabbed in the stomach as he went home by train in Manhattan. In spite of the fact that his attackers promptly left the car, not one of the other eleven people in the car came to the assistance of the boy as he bled to death. A full-length feature film, *The Incident,* was based on this murder.

Are such cases truly representative or are they exceptional? Clearly, the press cannot always be relied on to provide unbiased coverage of events, and cases of bystander apathy are more newsworthy than cases where bystanders immediately take appropriate action.

But the point is that these particular incidents really did happen, however incredible they may seem. It occurred to two researchers at New York University at the end of the 1960s to ask the more significant question: "Are these cases of bystander apathy quite what they seem?" So they attempted to find an answer.

Key experiment   Diffusion of responsibility (John Darley and Bibb Latané)

John Darley and Bibb Latané[1,2] were intrigued by the Kitty Genovese case, and came up with an ingenious reason for the apparent apathy displayed by the bystanders. They pointed out that although it seems sensible to suppose that the greater the number of people who witness an incident, the more likely the victim is to receive assistance, this proved shockingly untrue in the Genovese case. With so many witnesses to the murder, surely someone should have gone to the girl's assistance.

Darley and Latané argued that, paradoxical though it may sound, a victim may be in a more fortunate position with just one bystander than with several, the reason being that responsibility for helping the victim falls firmly onto one person rather than being spread among many. In other words, when there are many observers of a crime or emergency there is a diffusion of responsibility. In addition, any potential blame for failing to help is distributed among many people, rather than attaching itself firmly to the sole observer.

Darley and Latané tested their ideas in a series of experiments in which the experimenter explained that he was interested in learning about the kinds of personal problems faced by college students when confronted with the pressures of an urban environment. To save any embarrassment about discussing personal problems in front of strangers, the students were told, they were to remain anonymous and would be placed in separate rooms. The experimenter told them he would not listen to their discussions, because the presence of an outside listener might prove inhibiting. Communication was to be by means of microphones, each subject hearing other people's communications through a pair of headphones. Subjects were led to believe that there were one, two, three, or six people in the discussion at any one time. In fact, in each "discussion" there was only one real subject—contributions from other "subjects" were tape-recorded.

The future "victim" spoke first in the discussion, saying that he was finding it difficult to adjust to New York City and to his academic studies. In tones indicating a feeling of some embarrassment, he mentioned that he was prone to seizures, especially when studying hard or having to take examinations. All of the other "subjects" then contributed in turn, after which the victim spoke again. His voice became loud and incoherent, finishing up as follows: "I-er-I-uh-I've got a-a one of the-er-sei—er-er-things coming on and-and-and I could really-er-use some help so if somebody would-er-er-help-er-er-help-er-uh-uh-uh [choking sounds] . . . I'm gonna die-er-er-I'm . . . gonna die-er-help-er-er-seizure-er . . . [chokes, then silence]."

The major interest was in seeing whether the real subjects would leave the room to go to the assistance of the student who was apparently having an epileptic fit. Of those subjects who thought they were the only person who knew the "victim" was having an epileptic attack, every single one left her room and reported the emergency. On the other hand, of those who believed that four other subjects had also heard the victim's pleas for help, only 62 percent responded. Since everyone heard the same tape recording of the emergency, it is clear that diffusion of responsibility occurred.

Of course, all this is rather academic from the victim's point of view. He doesn't care who helps him, as long as someone does. From his perspective, the important question is whether his chances are better with, say, five bystanders than with one. With five bystanders there are five times as many people available to help, but is this counteracted by the diffusion of responsibility effect? If the data are analyzed from the victim's standpoint, and timing is considered, it turns out that his chances of being helped within 45 seconds of the onset of the fit were about 50 percent with a single bystander, but 0 percent with five bystanders. In other words, help was more likely to be forthcoming, and more quickly, when there was only one bystander.

A further interesting observation made by Darley and Latané concerned participants' awareness of the factors determining whether or not they responded to the appeal for help. Subjects who believed there were four other bystanders and said they were aware of this fact when the epileptic seizure occurred, consistently claimed that it had had no effect on their own behavior.

Darley and Latané also considered the behavior of those participants who failed to report the emergency. In contrast to the stereotyped view of such people, they were by no means "apathetic." Most of them asked the experimenter if the victim was all right and being taken care of. Many showed various signs of nervousness (trembling hands, sweating palms) and actually seemed more emotionally aroused than the participants who reported the emergency. They had not decided *not* to intervene, it seemed, but were in an uncomfortable state of indecision.

Is it an emergency or not?

Of course, the number of bystanders is by no means the only factor that determines whether a victim will be assisted or not. As Latané and Darley point out, there are several stages involved in reacting to an

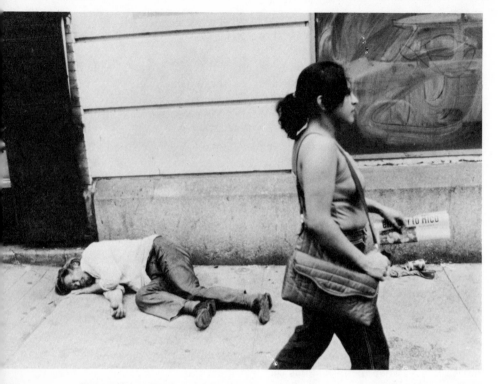

Bystanders decide whether the man lying on the pavement has had too much to drink or has had a heart attack. Photo: Multimedia Publications Inc. (Miki Koren).

emergency. First, the incident must be noticed and interpreted. The process of interpretation is vital, since many emergencies have an ambiguous quality about them—the man lying in the gutter may have had a heart attack or he may simply have had too much to drink. In the light of the chosen interpretation, the bystander must decide where his responsibility lies and determine what kind of assistance, if any, is warranted. Finally, he must act on his decision.

Latané and Darley quite rightly argue that the process of interpretation is especially important. Emergencies tend to occur very rarely, and most of us are ill-equipped to identify them or respond to them. So what sort of information do we use to clarify matters? Most of the time we take our cue from other people: if they look worried, it's an emergency; if they remain calm and unruffled, the incident can safely be ignored.

Latané and Darley looked at social influence in a simple study in which two girls started playing Frisbee in a waiting room at Grand Central Station in New York. When the Frisbee was thrown to a confederate, she either joined in enthusiastically or accused the girls of being childish and acting dangerously and promptly kicked the Frisbee back. If the confederate responded negatively, none of the other people in the waiting room joined in throwing the Frisbee; but if the confederate joined in, so did 86 percent of the other people present. Indeed, in the latter situation people wandered over from other parts of the waiting area to join in, and the girls' main problem was how to bring the Frisbee-throwing game to a halt.

. The importance of social influence on bystander intervention was demonstrated in a study conducted at Princeton University by John Darley and his associates. The participants were all asked to do some sketching, and were put in a room either alone or with one other participant. Participants sat either facing each other or back to back. While they were busy sketching, a workman in the adjoining room pushed over some heavy screens, which fell with a resounding crash. This was followed immediately by a cry of "Oh, my leg!" and a series of loud groans. Ninety percent of the participants who were on their own went to the assistance of the workman; 80 percent of the facing pairs of participants responded to the crash; but only 20 percent of the back-to-back pairs tried to help.

Now the really marked difference here is not between those who were on their own and those who were sketching in pairs. It was between the pairs who were facing each other and those who were sitting back to back. Why did seeing each other or not seeing each other make so much difference? The answer may be that the interpretation of an ambiguous event such as the sound of a crash is greatly affected by the reactions of other people. In the face-to-face situation each participant could see his partner's startled response to the crash, and so the interpretation that there was a genuine emergency was strengthened. Virtually all the people sitting face to face indicated that they thought the crash meant something was wrong; but only half of those sitting back to back interpreted the crash in this way. The behavior of other bystanders is thus crucial and can have very diverse effects. There have been numerous cases of mass panic, with every person in the crowd overreacting to an emergency, sometimes with disastrous results. On the other hand, if some members of a crowd indicate by their passive and unconcerned behavior that an event is *not* an emergency, the response of the rest of the crowd may be inhibited by the same process of social influence.

This negative effect of social influence was investigated by Latané and Darley in a study in which the subjects faced an ambiguous but potentially dangerous situation (smoke wafting into the experiment room through a small vent). The participants faced this situation alone, or with two other participants, or with two confederates of Latané and Darley who had been briefed to stare at the smoke for a moment, shrug their shoulders, and then totally ignore it.

Seventy-five percent of the solo participants went out of the room to report the possible emergency, compared with only 10 percent of those in the company of the confederates who ignored the danger. As the comedian and Harvard professor Tom Lehrer pointed out many years ago, people would rather die than make asses of themselves. And it was clearly the impassive behavior of the two confederates which affected the participants' reaction, because the smoke was more frequently reported when there were three genuine participants present, each reinforcing the others' apprehension.

The numbers game

In short it may be dangerous to rely on the old adage about there being "safety in numbers." If there are several bystanders in an emergency, they may be less inclined than a single bystander to do anything constructive. This may be because each of them feels it is not particularly his responsibility to intervene, or because the passive and controlled behavior of the other bystanders leads him to conclude that there is no emergency. The denial or diffusion of responsibility in a crowd seems to be more marked in women than men, presumably because it is culturally accepted that women let men take the initiative in emergencies.

Bibb Latané and his associates also asked people to clap or shout as loudly as possible, either on their own or in small groups of various sizes, and found that the sound of twelve hands clapping was not even three times as intense as the sound of two; and the same was true for shouting. They concluded that this could be evidence of the same social disease that affects groups of bystanders: social buck-passing.

Are there any circumstances in which the presence of other bystanders might help rather than hinder direct intervention? Perhaps the desire to gain the approval of others might sometimes lead a bystander to go to the rescue? In an experiment set up to examine this question, participants were led to believe that four other people in the experiment would either be aware or not be aware of how they reacted to overhearing a violent fight between another participant and an "intruder"—the incident ended in the intruder "escaping" with the other participant's tape recorder. Of the bystanders who thought their reactions would not be seen by the others 39 percent went to help, com-

"It's got nothing to do with me . . . Besides, I'm already late . . . Anyway, there are other people helping . . ." Photo: Multimedia Publications Inc. (Miki Koren).

pared with 74 percent of those who thought they were under observation. So the presence of other bystanders can have positive as well as negative consequences. Afterward, many of the participants who thought they were being watched claimed that this actually *inhibited* them from helping, which shows an interesting difference between their actual behavior and their conscious awareness.

So the presence of other bystanders can also make it *more* likely that people will help in an emergency, but only if the situation is interpreted as a genuine emergency. Leonard Bickman provided evidence of this by setting up an experiment in which individual participants heard a bookcase apparently falling on another participant, followed by a scream. When a confederate of the experimenter interpreted the crash and the scream as an emergency, the participant "bystander" offered assistance much faster than when the confederate suggested there was nothing to worry about. As expected, the confederate's interpretation of the incident influenced helping behavior by altering the bystander's own interpretation: 93 percent of the bystanders hearing the confederate say it was an emergency thought the victim had been hurt, against only 54 percent of those told it was not an emergency.

The victim: who gets helped?

Most liberal and egalitarian-minded individuals in our society would like to think that all kinds of people are likely to be assisted in an emergency. While such a uniformly caring society is certainly desirable, the available evidence indicates that bystanders are fairly selective in deciding whom to help.

One of the points that may have been important in the case of Kitty Genovese is that several of the onlookers thought the incident was "a lovers' quarrel," and most people's instinct in such circumstances is not to interfere. Lance Shotland and Margaret Straw of Penn State University arranged for a violent quarrel and fight between a man and a woman to take place in the presence of or within earshot of witnesses. The woman started screaming and pleading "Get away from me!" In order to establish the "relationship" between the two for the benefit of the bystanders, the woman screamed either "I don't know you!" or "I don't know why I ever married you!"

The tendency to intervene was tremendously affected by the presumed relationship between the attacker and the victim: 65 percent of the bystanders intervened when they thought the fight involved strangers, but only 19 percent did so when they thought the fight involved a married couple. The bystanders obviously believed they had witnessed a genuine fight, because 30 percent of the women witnesses feared sufficiently for their own safety to shut the door of their room, turn the lights out, and even lock the door.

There are probably several reasons why fewer people went to the assistance of the married woman. First, they thought a married woman would probably be embarrassed by the intervention of an outsider, whereas a woman attacked by a stranger wouldn't; second, they assumed that a woman attacked by a stranger would be more in need of help than a woman attacked by her husband; and finally, it occurred to them that the man would be more likely to offer violence to anyone who interfered if the woman he was attacking was his wife.

A recent survey published by the Law Enforcement Assistance Administration in Washington, D.C., showed that 60 percent of assaults are on total strangers. But when Shotland and Straw showed films of a vicious fight between a man and a woman, only one person in thirty guessed that the two people were strangers; the overwhelming majority assumed that a close relationship existed between them. Interestingly, newspaper interviews with witnesses to real-life aggression confirm that bystanders usually assume that men beat up only their nearest and dearest. In short, acts of aggression are less likely to be interrupted in large cities than in smaller communities, perhaps because the relationship between two fighting people is *less* likely to be known, and therefore more likely to be misinterpreted, in the larger community.

A further reason why onlookers are reluctant to get involved in a fight between people they assume to be married is that they feel the woman may be partly responsible for the attack on her. As a general rule, we have more sympathy for victims we believe to be blameless than for victims who appear to have "asked for it." The drunken bully in the bar who boasts of his great strength and then gets flattened is ignored as he lies writhing on the floor.

Irving Piliavin and his associates investigated this phenomenon by staging incidents in the subway in New York. A male "victim" staggered forward and collapsed on the floor lying face up. Sometimes he carried a black cane and appeared sober, and sometimes he smelled of alcohol and carried a bottle of liquor wrapped tightly in a brown bag. Less assistance was given when he was "drunk" than when he was "ill," probably because the "drunk" was seen as responsible for his plight, and because helping a smelly drunk who may vomit or become abusive involves greater "cost." Interestingly, however, provided there was one Good Samaritan who offered assistance, several more helpers were usually quick to materialize, irrespective, it seemed, of whether the victim was ill or drunk.

In an emergency, bystanders must of necessity act rapidly on the basis of relatively meager evidence. However, one fact about the victim that is immediately obvious is his or her race, and it is reasonable to assume that this might be one of the factors considered by the bystander. Samuel Gaertner of the University of Delaware has put forward the interesting theory that most whites in the United States would prefer not to think of themselves as the sort of people who would ignore a black victim's cries for assistance if the responsibility for helping was clearly theirs alone. However, he argued, if the situation allowed them to rationalize their prejudice, then prejudice would operate, but in a fairly subtle manner.

Gaertner investigated this hypothesis by arranging for a series of white female bystanders to witness a stack of chairs falling on a screaming girl, who was either black or white. The bystanders were either alone or with a calm, impassive confederate of the experimenter. All the bystanders who witnessed the incident on their own went to the assistance of the injured victim; her race did not affect their action. By contrast, 90 percent of those who were with the confederate lent a helping hand to the white victim but only 30 percent of them helped the black victim. In the latter situation, it was possible for them to rationalize their prejudice against the black victim simply by arguing that the incident was not serious or that it was not their particular responsibility to act. Incidentally, both in this study and in others, people who expressed unprejudiced views in questionnaires acted in just as biased a way as those who admitted they were prejudiced.

It has been clearly established that the nature of the victim is important in determining whether he or she will receive help. In addition to the factors already discussed—the race of the victim, the assumed relationship between attacker and victim, and the assumed responsibility of the victim for his or her misfortune—there is the physical attractiveness of the victim to be taken into account. A good-looking victim is more likely to receive help than a victim with a "port wine stain" birthmark on his face (see next chapter).

Why should the characteristics of the victim be so important? One theory is that the bystander decides whether or not to intervene on the basis of the "costs" associated with helping (possible physical harm, embarrassment) or the costs of not helping (self-blame and censure from others), and the "rewards" of helping (praise from self, victim, and others) or the rewards of not helping (continuation of other activities). In this delicate balance of profit and loss, the costs will be high if the victim is perceived to be unpleasant or disgusting. In another experiment it was found that if a participant "collapsed" in the subway, help was less likely to be offered, and was slower in arriving, when the victim had "blood" (red food coloring) dribbling out of his mouth, despite his apparently greater need of assistance. Presumably the cost of helping a "bloody" victim is greater because most bystanders have an inbuilt fear and revulsion at the sight of blood.

But of all the factors that have been found to affect bystanders' willingness to become involved, none has a more profound effect than the ambiguity or lack of ambiguity of the emergency. If it is obvious that someone is in desperate need of assistance, considerations such as the race of the victim, diffusion of responsibility, and social influence have relatively little effect—almost everyone rapidly and spontaneously does what he can to assist.

Russell Clark and Larry Word of Florida State University conducted an experiment in which bystanders either heard a maintenance man fall and cry out in agony or simply heard him fall but not cry out. In the former situation, unambiguously an emergency, every group of subjects, whether they were alone or in pairs or in groups of five, provided assistance. In other words, there was no evidence of diffusion of re-

Soldiers unhesitatingly help a wounded comrade. Photo: Rex Features.

sponsibility at all. If it was unclear whether the incident was an emergency or not, as in the latter situation, assistance was only one-third as likely to be offered. Typically bystanders in groups did not react at all in ambiguous situations.

The reason why ambiguity plays such a major role is that if a bystander interprets an ambiguous incident as *not* being an emergency, thinking of a suitable course of action and deciding to take on the responsibility of doing something become just too much trouble. In other words, the victim must be utterly convincing about the genuineness of his plight and his need for help.

Conclusions

One of the main implications of the various studies mentioned here is that the notion of the apathetic bystander is extremely misleading. In many circumstances, almost all bystanders will do whatever is possible to help an injured or distressed victim. But to understand bystander behavior one must take into account not only the alleged characteristics of the bystander but also the nature of the situation that faces him.

We should recognize that bystanders are often engaged in extremely complex problem solving under great stress and at very short notice. The problem of deciding whether an event is or is not an emergency, and what to do about it if it is, is difficult because most of us lack experience of emergencies. Admittedly, society does provide us with some rules, but many of these are mutually contradictory. On the one hand there is "Do unto others as you would have them do unto you." On the other hand there is "Don't poke your nose into other people's business" or, as the Bible says more poetically, "He that passeth by, and meddleth with strife belonging not to him, is like one that taketh a dog by the ears."

The bystander usually knows neither the victim nor the attacker, and he does not have the time to find out anything about them. He must respond on the basis of probabilities rather than certainties, and so he relies on the demeanor of other bystanders and the apparent worthiness of the victim as guides to action. In the circumstances, this is sensible behavior.

The bystander's problem is made worse by anxiety, a frequent disrupter of efficient patterns of behavior. For example, when soldiers were led to believe that one of their number had been badly hurt by explosives, they tried to take the appropriate course of action (mending a broken telephone in order to summon help) but anxiety made them much clumsier and slower than usual. In fact, bystanders are probably more deserving of praise than censure. For the most part, they cope surprisingly well with upsetting, complicated, and rapidly changing events.

2

Why some people get away with murder

The vast sums of money spent each year on makeup, cosmetic surgery, fashionable clothes, body padding, health farms, and the like indicate that most members of Western society attach great importance to personal attractiveness. Aristotle, who as usual managed to hit the nail on the head, argued that beauty was a greater recommendation than any letter of introduction. But does physical attractiveness really matter that much? Has it any significance other than in sexual and personal relations?

We all know that beautiful women are treated with much greater respect and reverence than unattractive women, at least by men, and one would expect social psychologists to have busied themselves looking at such an obviously important phenomenon. In fact, it is only quite recently that the whole idea that social interaction may be dramatically influenced by differences in attractiveness has received any serious attention. We do not know exactly why this should be so. However, it is interesting to note that American psychologists have devoted much effort to bolstering up the philosophy that anyone can do anything with hard work and application. It clearly runs counter to this outlook to emphasize the advantages that inheritance has conferred on extremely attractive people—it seems very unfair, not to say undemocratic, and ought not to be allowed.

Our ignorance was such only a few years ago that, someone said, we knew more about attractive stimuli for fish than for humans. People are, of course, more complicated than fish. While the three-spined stickleback can be relied on to become sexually excited when confronted with a red object, even a soggy piece of cardboard, human beings tend to be less predictable. This unpredictability is captured in the well-known saying "Beauty is in the eye of the beholder," and it is true that people in love find each other more physically attractive than the facts usually warrant. But it is also the case that different people asked to sort a set of photographs of different faces into those of greater and lesser attractiveness will tend to agree with each other's verdicts. The film industry capitalizes on this broad agreement when it invests in film stars of unusual physical attractiveness, even though their acting ability may be mediocre.

The short and the tall

It has usually been assumed that physical attractiveness is more easily identified and is more important in women than in men. It seems, though, that height is a valued characteristic in men in Western society. As the distinguished American sociologist M. P. Feldman put it, "American society is a society with a heightist premise: to be tall is to be good and to be short is to be stigmatized." To support his contention, Feldman noted that every American President elected this century was the taller of the two major political candidates, and it is certainly hard to imagine an unusually short man being thought of as "presidential timber." We must beware of attaching too much importance to this finding, however; apparently, the successful presidential candidate is nearly always hairier than his defeated opponent, suggesting that King Kong might be an outstanding candidate.

In passing, it is intriguing to compare the different reactions to the debates between John Kennedy and Richard Nixon during the 1960 presidential campaign. Those listening on radio thought more highly of Nixon's contributions to the debates, whereas those watching the debates on television gave the edge to Kennedy. The difference probably reflected the greater physical attractiveness of Kennedy; there may also be some truth in the notion that Nixon's "five o'clock shadow" caused him to lose the election by a whisker!

When a "Mr. England" was introduced to a number of classes of college students in America, he was referred to as someone varying between relatively low status ("Mr. England, a student from Cambridge") and high status ("Professor England from Cambridge"). Afterward, the students were asked to estimate the man's height to the nearest half inch. As Mr. England climbed the academic ladder of success, he gained a total of five inches in the eyes of the students. This confirms the idea that height in men is valued. Even more surprising are the results of a survey of recent male graduates of the University of

Hugh Hefner and playmates: a preponderance of blondes. Photo: Rex Features.

Pittsburgh. This revealed that the tallest students (6 feet 2 inches and over) received an average starting salary at least 12 percent higher than those who were under 6 feet.

Faces

Since the characteristics of the face are a major part of physical attractiveness in both sexes, it is interesting to consider which facial features are most important. This can be done by asking people to rate eyes, mouth, nose, etc., for attractiveness and comparing the results with ratings of overall facial attractiveness. It has been found that the attractiveness of a face is most affected by the expression, followed by the mouth, complexion, eyebrows, eyes, hair, chin, and nose in that order. The relative unimportance of the eyes, the "mirrors of the soul," seems astonishing; but this is explained by the further finding that the eyes are downgraded in importance by women who wear glasses. For those who do not wear glasses, the eyes are the major determinant of facial beauty.

Another way of considering facial beauty is to argue that it is determined more by the total combination or pattern of parts of the face than by the attractiveness of each element in isolation. This notion,

which has much to recommend it, was expressed in poetical fashion by
Alexander Pope:

> 'Tis not a lip, or eye, we beauty call,
> But the joint force and full result of all.

Bodies male and female

Jerry Wiggins of the University of Illinois started his investigation of
physical attractiveness in women by suggesting that men can be divided
into three broad categories on the basis of their particular predilec-
tions: breast men, buttocks men, and leg men. He presented to his
subjects nude female silhouettes of various shapes and sizes; overall,
relatively large breasts, long legs, and small buttocks were most popular. It will come as no surprise to those familiar with the "philosophy"
of Hugh Hefner that large breasts were especially favored by readers of
Playboy, who tend to date frequently and to have "masculine" interests. Small breasts were preferred by men with fundamentalist religious
beliefs suffering from mild depression.

The stereotyped muscle man with an Atlas physique (broad chest
and small buttocks) has often been presented as the ideal male body.
Whether women agree seems doubtful. A survey in *Cosmopolitan*
asked 100 women to name the male body characteristic they found
most sexually arousing. Only one woman attributed sexual arousal to
muscular chests and shoulders, whereas 39 women selected the male
buttocks. Rating studies using various male profile silhouettes suggest
that women prefer men with only moderately large chests, large legs,
and small buttocks. Some women preferred relatively small men; these
women tended to be reserved in manner but of high social status,
which could be good news for jockeys.

Self-images

Do we see ourselves as others see us where our level of physical attractiveness is concerned? While it is certainly true that there is usually
some correspondence between an individual's self-report of his or her
physical attractiveness level and the opinion of external observers,
agreement between the two assessments is often surprisingly poor.
Many people see themselves as much less pretty or handsome than they
actually are, and this tendency may well be more marked in the young.
Among girls of 10 or 11, it was found that three-quarters seriously
believed themselves to be the least physically attractive girl in their
class at school.

One of the factors affecting attractiveness was identified by the American Country and Western singer Mickey Gilley. In one song he gets to wondering "Ain't it funny, ain't it strange/The way a man's opinions change/When he starts to face that lonely night," and follows this up with: "All the girls get prettier at closing time./They all get to look like movie stars." In a study conducted in a number of bars on a Thursday evening, a group of psychologists found that the people in each bar rated members of the opposite sex as more physically attractive at midnight than at 10:30 P.M., which offers some support to this hypothesis.

Key experiment   Attractiveness and jury decision making (Michael Efran)

Some of the most thought-provoking and disquieting work on physical attractiveness was that initiated by Michael Efran[1] of the University of Toronto in 1974. He, like everyone else, was well aware that physical attractiveness is much desired and valued by most cultures and societies, and that it confers various benefits on those lucky enough to be especially handsome or beautiful. The fascinating issue which Efran set out to explore was: Just how far do the advantages of being physically attractive go? Can beautiful people get away with murder?

Many lawyers suspect that juries and judges tend to be more lenient when the accused person (the defendant) is attractive rather than ugly, but less lenient when the victim of a crime is physically attractive. In a famous case in 1857, Madeleine Smith, the young, vivacious, and beautiful daughter of a prosperous Scottish architect, was accused of murdering her lover, Pierre L'Angelier, by the administration of arsenic. While this was shocking enough, Scottish society was even more outraged when it became clear from her diaries that she thoroughly enjoyed sexual activity. In spite of the fact that she was the only person to gain from his death (he had threatened blackmail if she would not marry him), and that she was known to have purchased arsenic on three separate occasions, the jury returned a verdict of "not proven." It is easy to imagine how her beauty helped to save her from the gallows. A final point: three eminent authorities decided not to allow into evidence L'Angelier's pocketbook, which would have greatly strengthened the prosecution's case. Were they, too, entranced by Miss Smith's obvious charms?

It is useful to consider our stereotype of criminals. If you close your eyes and form an image of a typical criminal, it is likely that he will be rather ugly or abnormal in appearance. Sir Francis Galton, the gifted Victorian scientist, claimed that "coarse and low types of face" are prevalent among the criminal classes, and demonstrated this by means of composite portraiture, in which several faces are superimposed. Certainly, his portraits of thieves and men serving long sentences for murder and other crimes of violence look pretty unpleasant; however, he seemed disappointed when he had to admit that convicts produced composites "with no villainy written on them."

It seemed to Efran that the decisions of juries might very well be swayed by the physical attractiveness of the defendant. His initial investigation involved asking a large number of students whether they believed that jurors should be influenced by the defendant's physical attractiveness; he also asked them whether the defendant's character and past history should be considered. There was a striking difference in the answers given to the two questions: 79 percent believed that jurors should be influenced by the defendant's character, whereas only 7 percent believed that physical attractiveness should play a role in judicial decisions.

Given that most people are firmly convinced that the looks of the accused are irrelevant, it should presumably prove very difficult (or even impossible) to find evidence of juries being affected by the defendant's appearance. In fact, Michael Efran found it was quite straightforward. Mock juries, some of them consisting of men jurors only and some of women jurors only, were set up, and the jurors were asked to imagine that they were the student members of a student-faculty court hearing the case of a student accused of cheating in an examination. The evidence was rather inconclusive, since the accused had been seen conversing with another student during the examination, but the conversation had not been overheard. The accused was sometimes male, sometimes female, and an attractive or unattractive photograph was given to the jurors. Their task was to decide on the certainty of guilt and also on the severity of punishment to be meted out if the accused were found guilty.

Efran's most important findings concerned the effects of the defendant's physical attractiveness on the jurors' decisions. Despite their expressed belief that physical attractiveness should not matter, the jurors were less certain about the guilt of attractive defendants and recommended much milder punishment for them. The tendency to bend over backward to be lenient to an attractive defendant was especially marked when the defendant was a pretty girl and the jurors were all young men.

This study by Efran, like most good studies, suggests more questions than it answers. The main one is whether real juries confronted with a real case make decisions in the same way as simulated juries considering a hypothetical case. If they do, then there are obvious reasons for concern, since the notion that every person is equal before the law is deeply rooted in our legal system. Clearly, most people would find it objectionable if pretty or handsome criminals were to escape their just deserts while plain and ugly innocents languished in prison.

In one ingenious study, two experimental juries were formed; they watched actual trials along with the real jury. The real jury was less likely to favor conviction of the defendant than the judge or either of the experimental juries. If the consequences of a guilty verdict are likely to be extremely serious, juries may become more cautious. However, since most people are not aware that the defendant's attractiveness may be influencing their verdict, we cannot assume that attractiveness does not affect the decisions of real juries.

It is clearly worrying that unattractive people tend to be more harshly treated by juries than attractive people. However, most of the available research suggests that physical attractiveness has little or no effect on juries when serious crimes are involved.

A further question arising out of Efran's study is whether the attractiveness of the victim also affects the decisions of juries. Billy Thornton of the University of Maine considered the emotive crime of rape, and looked at the influence of the physical attractiveness of the rape victim on the decisions of a group of simulated jurors. In line with sex stereotypes, women jurors were more likely to convict the defendant than were men jurors. The attractiveness of the victim did not affect the jury's assessment of the credibility of her testimony or the extent of her responsibility, but the accused man was given a longer sentence when the victim was pretty rather than homely.

In another study, an attempt was made to make the simulated trial situation more realistic. The jurors listened to a one-hour tape recording of a case involving automobile negligence, and there were slides showing the plaintiff and the defendant. When the plaintiff was unattractive and the defendant attractive, only 17 percent of the verdicts were in favor of the plaintiff and an average of only $5,500 was awarded to the plaintiff; when the plaintiff was attractive and the defendant unattractive, the respective figures were 49 percent and $10,000. Unto him that hath shall be given . . .

One of the puzzling features of the bias shown toward or against defendants and victims because of their relative good looks or lack thereof is to decide exactly why this phenomenon occurs, especially since most people claim that they personally would not let mere appearance affect their assessment of guilt or innocence. Possibly we are more lenient to beautiful women than to plain Janes because we regard them as possessing generally desirable qualities and so assume they will be less likely to transgress in the future than their unattractive sisters.

This notion that attractive women are treated leniently only because we expect them not to err again can be tested by focusing on crimes which very good-looking people might be expected to be more likely to commit again than unattractive people. For example, suppose that a woman ingratiates herself with a middle-aged bachelor and persuades him to invest a sizable sum of money in a nonexistent company, and that this leads to charges of larceny and of obtaining money under false pretenses. We would probably all agree that middle-aged bachelors are more readily parted from their money by attractive women than by plain women. If it is easier for a beautiful woman to obtain money by deception, then she may be more likely to repeat the trick in the future than an unattractive woman. Reasoning thus, the simulated jurors punished the glamorous larcenist more severely than the unglamorous one, sentencing her to an average of five and a half years in prison, as compared with four years.

In spite of this finding, it is patently obvious that in most circumstances attractive adults tend to be given the benefit of any doubt. According to Karen Dion, this tendency has its origins in early childhood. She gave female students a brief written account of the undesirable behavior (physical aggression toward another child or toward an animal) of a child of 7. The child was seen as being more culpable if it was unattractive, and its transgressions were regarded as more undesirable than when committed by an attractive child. When the reported aggression was severe, the female students were more inclined to attribute a chronic antisocial disposition to the unattractive child than to the attractive child, and they also felt that unattractive children were more likely to commit a similar offense at some time in the future than good-looking children.

It could be argued that the physical attractiveness of a defendant affects the workings of justice only in those cases where the evidence is ambiguous and unclear. However, these are exactly the cases which tend to come to trial, since defendants usually plead guilty if the evidence against them is overwhelming. Would it be constructive to forewarn jurors about the possible bias caused by the attractiveness or otherwise of defendants and victims? When jurors serving in a case of negligent homicide made an explicit commitment to be impartial, they actually gave socially and physically unattractive defendants *less* severe sentences than generally attractive defendants. It therefore appears that alertness to bias may produce a "reverse" biasing affect.

The handicaps of being unattractive

It has been convincingly demonstrated many times that physically attractive people are believed to be superior to unattractive people in all kinds of ways. They are considered more perceptive, confident, assertive, happy, amiable, humorous, flexible, friendly, exciting, intelligent, and talented than unattractive people, and there is some evidence that they regard themselves in a relatively flattering light. In addition, attractive people have many more dates than unattractive people, their opinions are more valued, and the world in general is more helpful to them.

All in all, then, what is beautiful is good. However, there is one major exception to this view, perhaps caused by feelings of jealousy. Unattractive women do *not* rate beautiful women as having more socially desirable personalities than plain women. They regard beautiful women as being vain, egotistical, incompetent as parents, status-seeking, snobbish, and out of touch with those less privileged than themselves. They also see attractive women as being more likely to have extramarital affairs and also more likely to ask for a divorce.

In general, however, the beautiful people of this planet inhabit a more pleasant, forgiving, and supportive social world than plain people. The conditions which face the unattractive are less easy to adapt to. Amerigo Farina and his associates at the University of Connecticut carried this idea to its logical conclusion and investigated whether physical unattractiveness might indirectly contribute to mental illness. The first problem they encountered when they tried to test this theory in a mental hospital was a certain amount of hostility from the hospital staff, some of whom felt it was rather offensive to try to demonstrate that people who are emotionally unstable and unable to adjust to society are ugly as well.

Farina discovered that female mental patients do indeed appear to be much less attractive than female shoppers or university employees. Of course, it could be argued that mental patients are either less able or less inclined to groom themselves than other people. However, the least physically attractive of the patients had more previous admissions to a hospital than the more attractive ones, had spent more days in the hospital during their current stay, and were more likely to be diagnosed as seriously disturbed or schizophrenic. The less attractive patients were also judged to be less pleasant, and they interacted less with other people and were visited less frequently.

Obviously it would be ludicrous to assume that physical unattractiveness is the only or even a major factor in mental illness. What is plausible, however, is that people who already have problems (anxiety, social incompetence) might find them exacerbated if they have to cope with the additional problem of being physically unattractive.

If problems in coping with society are greater for the physically unattractive, then in some circumstances the use of cosmetic surgery should prove helpful. In one study carried out in New York, cosmetic surgery was made available to prisoners suffering from a variety of disfigurements (knife and burn scars, tattoos, injection scars from drug abuse). Among those not addicted to heroin, cosmetic surgery almost halved the incidence of recidivism (return to prison within one year of release) seen in prisoners whose disfigurements remained untreated. Fifty-six percent of prisoners receiving no surgery returned to prison, compared with only 30 percent of those who had received surgery. Cosmetic surgery was particularly helpful to those with facial disfigurements, and seemed to provide impetus for the offenders to seek to change other aspects of themselves.

Boy meets girl

One situation in which everyone knows that physical appearance plays a leading role is dating. However, judging by what people say, looks are by no means as important as other attributes. Students of both sexes claimed that the most important attribute of a potential date was personality, followed by their character, then their looks, then (much farther down the list) their intelligence.

It is interesting that people often seem blissfully unaware of the true extent to which physical attractiveness in others affects their actual behavior. This seems to apply in many situations, including dating.[2] A Computer Dance was organized for new students at the University of Minnesota, with a computer allegedly being used to match couples according to interests and personality. When the dance had been in full swing for nearly three hours, all the students were asked how much they liked their dates, whether they wanted to go out with them again, and so on. For both men and women, the only important factor in determining how much they liked their dates was their physical attractiveness. Personality counted for little, and those whose academic performance was good were liked less than those who were poor academically.

Perhaps looks count for more on first meetings than when people know each other better. As George Bernard Shaw put it, with his customary Irish flair, "Beauty is all very well, but who ever looks at it when it has been in the house three days?" Shaw may be right about beauty becoming less important as familiarity increases, but he is wrong to suggest that it ever becomes irrelevant. Some cynics have claimed that dating is a form of trading: each person tries to make social interaction as profitable as possible, profit being defined as the rewards gained from the interaction minus the costs that must be paid. Thus a girl who is worth traveling five miles to see would need to be

unusually attractive to warrant a fifty-mile trip. If physical attractiveness constitutes a "reward," then the point of equilibrium will tend
to occur when two people are of approximately equal attractiveness.
Indeed, engaged and married couples do tend to be similar in physical
attractiveness, although there are exceptions. Sophia Loren is rather
more beautiful than her husband Carlo Ponti, but he provides other
kinds of "rewards," in the form of talent and wealth, to maintain the
balance. The trade-off is virtually equal.

This matching of attractiveness of couples seems reasonable enough
from some points of view, but rather puzzling from others. Since nearly
everyone values extremely attractive individuals of the opposite sex
most, why do unattractive men tend to marry ugly women, and vice
versa? The answer seems to be that our choice is determined not so
much by what we want but by what we can get. There is no point in
trying to climb Everest if you have no climbing equipment.

Sociologists have noted that attractiveness facilitates social mobility.
Working-class girls who marry "above themselves" are much more
physically attractive than those who do not. These upwardly mobile
girls seem to cast their nets more widely and selectively than their
peers: they are far less likely to "go steady" with one boy at school,
and report far less sexual activity during their school days (10 percent
versus 70 percent for non-mobile girls), presumably because they can
have enough boyfriends without allowing sexual intercourse.

Another social advantage of physical attractiveness is its instant
"halo" effect. If a man is seen in the company of beautiful women, he
tends to go up a notch in our estimation, and likewise with a woman
accompanied by a handsome man. On the other hand, we tend to un-

*Ponti and Loren: an alliance between two very different talents, but the
rewards are fairly equal. Photo: Rex Features.*

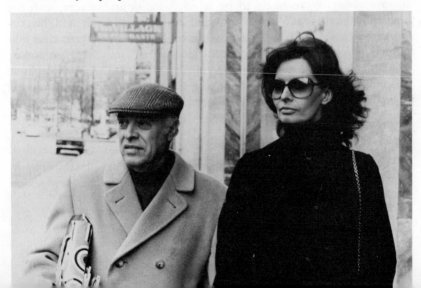

dervalue someone who goes out with unattractive members of the opposite sex.

The right face for the right job

Finally, physical attractiveness often plays a decisive part in the job market. Several laws have quite properly been passed in both Britain and the United States to prohibit job discrimination on the basis of race and sex. Perhaps rather more insidious, because less well recognized, is job discrimination on the basis of the applicant's physical attractiveness. Robert Dipboye and his associates at the University of Tennessee asked college students to evaluate the qualifications of twelve applicants for the job of trainee sales manager. The students were given a brief description of the applicants' qualifications and a photograph, and were most inclined to hire a physically attractive man with high qualifications. When they were asked to select just one candidate, 11 percent picked the well-qualified unattractive man, but 35 percent chose the well-qualified attractive man. The students were then asked to assume that they had hired each applicant, and to suggest an appropriate starting salary. Higher salaries were given to the highly qualified, to men, and to the most physically attractive.

It might be argued that professional interviewers would be less likely than amateurs to allow physical attractiveness to influence their decisions about an applicant's suitability for a job. Dipboye considered this possibility in a study in which college students and professional interviewers evaluated several applicants for the position of head of a furniture department in a large store in a city. Attractive applicants were nearly always preferred to unattractive applicants of equal educational achievement, and this was just as true of professional interviewers as of amateur students.

An interesting exception to the notion that physically attractive people are always more likely to be selected for desirable jobs than the physically unattractive was discovered by Thomas Cash and his coworkers. They found that attractive men had an advantage over unattractive men when applying for "masculine" jobs (car salesman, shipping clerk) but not when applying for "feminine" jobs (telephone operator, office receptionist). Similarly, attractive women were preferred to unattractive women for feminine jobs but not for masculine jobs.

Conclusions

There is a general feeling that physical attractiveness plays an important role in first encounters between men and women, but few people realize just how far-reaching its influence really is. Physically attractive people are treated more leniently than unattractive people by juries, they are less likely to become mentally ill, they are more socially mobile, and they are more likely to impress potential employers. It seems unfair that the attractive should enjoy all these important advantages. The first step in remedying the situation is to establish the facts, which is what we have done, of necessity briefly, in this chapter. Then comes the task of making as many people as possible aware of the potential dangers in discriminating against the physically unattractive.

3

The dangers of obedience

Virtually all societies develop hierarchical structures in which certain people are given power and authority over others. In our society, for example, parents, shop stewards, headmasters, and managers are invested with varying degrees of authority. The relationship between authority figures and their subordinates is almost bound to give rise to moral conflict. This is powerfully illustrated by the story of Abraham, commanded by God to kill his son Isaac. Abraham's dilemma was that he felt love for God and for his son, and yet he was placed in a position where he was apparently required to betray one or the other of them. How far was his obedience to God supposed to go?

A similar conflict is involved when soldiers at war are ordered to kill defenseless civilians, as happened in the Vietnam War when Lieutenant Calley ordered the massacre of civilians at My Lai. Calley's defense rested on the assertion that he had been following the orders of his superiors—in other words, simply "doing his duty." The soldier's conflict is between the requirements of army discipline and respect for human life.

How do people resolve the conflicts they face when authority figures issue such commands? The problem is one that psychologists have tried to study, and their answers have given us much valuable, and unexpected, information about human nature.

Key experiment   Obedience to authority (Stanley Milgram)

The most important and best-known work on obedience to authority was carried out by Stanley Milgram[1,2] at Yale University between

1960 and 1963. The impact of his work was such that he was awarded the Socio-Psychological Prize of the American Association for the Advancement of Science in 1964.

One of the many fascinating aspects of Milgram's work is that the results he came up with surprised both himself and his professional colleagues, not to mention the general public. In fact, his work almost entirely escaped one of the most common complaints leveled at psychological research, namely that the experimental findings merely confirm common sense. Anyone unfamiliar with Milgram's work may find it interesting to guess how much obedience to the authority of the experimenter was shown by the great variety of individuals of different ages and occupations who participated in the following study.

Imagine that you have arrived at Yale University to take part in a study of learning and memory. You go into a room and are met by a 31-year-old high school biology teacher, the experimenter, whose demeanor is rather stern throughout the experiment. The other person in the room is also there to take part in the experiment. He is a rotund, 47-year-old accountant of Irish-American stock, mild-mannered and likable.

The experimenter tells you that he is interested in the effects of punishment on learning. It is decided by drawing lots that the accountant will be the learner and you will be the teacher. You all go into an adjacent room, where the learner is strapped into an "electric chair" apparatus and an electrode is attached to his wrist. Electrode paste is then applied "to avoid blisters and burns." You are told that the electrode is connected to a nearby shock generator unit.

You then go to another room, which has a shock generator unit. It has thirty lever switches, each labeled with a voltage between 15 and 450 volts. Groups of four switches of increasing voltage have the following verbal designations: Slight Shock, Moderate Shock, Strong Shock, Very Strong Shock, Intense Shock, Extreme Intensity Shock, and Danger: Severe Shock. The final two lever switches are simply designated XXX.

You are told to administer a shock to the learner every time he gives a wrong answer on the learning task, and you are instructed to "move one level higher on the shock generator each time the learner flashes a wrong answer." You are also told that although the shocks can be extremely painful, they cause no permanent tissue damage. You yourself are given a sample shock of 45 volts to show you that the equipment is working.

As the learning task proceeds, the learner makes a number of errors, and is given progressively more intense shocks. After receiving shocks of 75, 90, and 105 volts, he merely grunts. At 120 volts, he shouts to the experimenter that the shocks are becoming painful. At 150 volts, he shouts, "Experimenter, get me out of here! I won't be in the experiment any more! I refuse to go on!" At 180 volts, he yells, "I can't stand the pain," and by 270 volts his response becomes an agonized scream. Thereafter, there are shrieks of agony, and vehement refusals to go on with the experiment or provide answers to the learning task. When the 300-volt shock is reached, he pounds on the wall. If you, the "teacher," say at any point that you don't want to continue the experiment, the experimenter tells you that you must.

What would you do in this unpleasant situation? What do you imagine other people would do? Stanley Milgram put these two questions to groups of psychiatrists, students, and middle-class adults. When predicting their own behavior, absolutely everyone predicted that they would defy the experimenter and refuse to continue with the experiment either when the shock reached 300 volts or, typically, much earlier. Perhaps because people tend to have a more flattering opinion of themselves than of other people, there was a tendency to believe that other people would be less reluctant to prolong the suffering of the

Authority figures throughout history have brutalized and dehumanized their enemies. Hitler did so on an unprecedented and barbaric scale. Photo: Barnaby's Picture Library.

learner. For example, psychiatrists at a leading medical school predicted that 3.73 percent of subjects would still obey the experimenter at 300 volts, and that only one in a thousand would go on to the 450-volt stage.

Most people unfamiliar with the actual results would predict that only the occasional psychopath or sadist would be likely to keep on administering intense electric shocks to an obviously distraught and unwilling subject. In fact, Milgram found that 62 percent of the people exposed to the conditions just described continued to obey the experimenter, and continued to the 450-volt level. In fact, there were 500 times as many individuals prepared to administer the maximum shock than was predicted by the group of eminent psychiatrists.

Milgram's findings obviously run counter to common sense and appear to indicate that people are prepared to go to rather extreme lengths in order to remain obedient to the commands of a higher authority. On the face of it, this seems an extraordinary and very puzzling finding, and one without much obvious relevance to everyday life. However, it is worth remembering how people at work act toward their superiors. People in authority quite frequently say or do something that is obviously wrong or inadequate, and yet there is a universal reluctance among subordinates to challenge their decisions. If anyone *does* challenge a decision, he or she is likely to experience a certain amount of anxiety.

While you were reading the description of the experiment, you may well have wondered about the ethics of conducting an experiment in which extremely painful electric shocks are administered to the "learner." The Milgram study has, indeed, been attacked on ethical grounds, not because of the damage done to the learner, but because of its effects on the "teacher." In fact, the learner was working in liaison with the experimenter and did not actually receive any shocks at all. The drawing of lots was rigged so that the mild-mannered accountant would always be the learner and the subject would always be the teacher.

But the effects of the experiment on the teachers were dramatic. For example, a 46-year-old encyclopedia salesman passed from nervous laughter to such violent convulsions that the experiment had to be halted. As one observer reported: "I observed a mature and initially poised businessman enter the laboratory smiling and confident. Within twenty minutes he was reduced to a twitching, stuttering wreck, who was rapidly approaching a point of nervous collapse. He constantly pulled on his earlobe, and twisted his hands. At one point, he pushed his fist into his forehead and muttered, 'Oh God, let's stop it.' And yet he continued to respond to every word of the experimenter, and obeyed to the end."

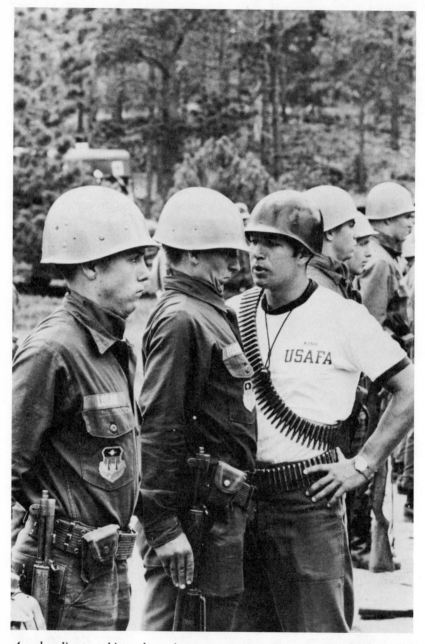

A subordinate taking abuse from a superior. How much will he take? How much does his duty as a soldier require him to take? Photo: Rex Features.

This was not an exceptional case. Many people had fits of nervous laughter, sweated, groaned, trembled, and dug their fingernails into their skin. Not surprisingly, there was considerable public concern and even outrage about the morality of exposing people to such conflict. Should psychologists really be permitted to reduce anyone to a "twitching, stuttering wreck"? Mightn't a person's self-image be permanently affected by the realization that he had been prepared to go to such extreme lengths to obey the authority of the experimenter? Furthermore, it was argued, Milgram's subjects placed their trust in the experimenter and assumed he would act in a careful, responsible manner; wasn't this trust abused by putting the subjects through such a degrading experience? Finally, the success of the experiment depended on deception—the actual situation was not what it appeared to be.

Confronted with this hornet's nest of moral problems, Milgram put forward a number of reasonable counter-arguments to justify the research he had carried out. He pointed out that there was a full debriefing at the end of the experiment, with all the participants being told that the learner had not actually received any dangerous electric shocks; the true purpose of the experiment was also explained to them. Of those who took part, 84 percent stated they were glad to have been in the experiment, 15 percent indicating neutral feelings, and only one person in a hundred expressed negative feelings. Further questioning revealed that four-fifths of the participants felt that more experiments of this sort should be conducted, and 74 percent said they had learned something of personal importance as a result of taking part. Many participants said that they would be more wary in the future about assuming that authority figures should always be obeyed.

Milgram also argued that what critics of his work really objected to was the unflattering picture it drew of human nature rather than the deception or methodology involved. Would the Milgram study have been the subject of public outrage if all the participants had disobeyed the experimenter at the first sign of discomfort from the learner? The evidence suggests not. Several people were given a description of the Milgram study; some were told that most of the participants were obedient to the experimenter, and the rest that most of them were disobedient. They rated the experiment as more harmful and as providing a worse experience when there was a large measure of obedience. Although many psychologists worry about the ethics of deception, and argue that it is in principle wrong to mislead people who take part in experiments, few lay observers felt that the morality of the Milgram study had anything to do with whether or not the participants were deceived.

The most frightening implication of the Milgram study is that half the population of North America is either sadistic or psychopathic, or both, which is clearly absurd, whatever we see on our television screens or read in the newspapers. In fact, when similar studies were carried out in Rome, South Africa, Australia, and Munich, the level of obedience to the experimenter was rather greater than that obtained by Milgram. Indeed, 85 percent of the people who were tested in Munich were discovered to be fully obedient to the experimenter.

Since over half the population in most countries is apparently prepared to administer very strong electric shocks to other people, then most of the obedient participants in Milgram-type studies must be quite ordinary people. The case of Adolf Eichmann, tried and convicted for ordering the deaths of many thousands of Jews, is relevant here. The prosecution attempted to depict Eichmann as a sadistic monster, which seems reasonable enough in view of the enormity of his crimes. In actual fact, his actions were in many ways those of an uninspired bureaucrat who simply sits at his desk and tries to carry out his job competently.

Let us consider just three of Milgram's "ordinary" obedient participants. One was a 39-year-old social worker, referred to by Milgram as Morris Braverman; he had a bald pate, a rather serious demeanor, and gave the impression of being intelligent and concerned. As the shocks increased in intensity, he started to snicker; gradually his suppressed laughter became more insistent and disruptive, apparently triggered off by the learner's screams. At times, he even rubbed his face in an attempt to hide his laughter. Afterward, he seemed to find his own behavior rather bewildering: "My reactions were awfully peculiar . . . my reactions were giggly, and trying to stifle laughter. This isn't the way I usually am . . . And my reaction was to the situation of having to hurt somebody. And being totally helpless and caught up in a set of circumstances where I just couldn't deviate and I couldn't try to help. This is what got me."

Another obedient participant was a housewife whom Milgram called Mrs. Elinor Rosenblum. Mrs. Rosenblum was proud of the fact that she had graduated from the University of Wisconsin a little over twenty years previously. She did volunteer work once a week with groups of juvenile delinquents and was active in the local Girl Scout organization. She constantly referred to her social achievements and had a pleasant but rather verbose manner. During the experiment, she kept muttering that she was shaking, but nevertheless went on to administer the 450-volt shock. When she was asked what was the highest level of sample shock she would be prepared to experience, she became indignant: "Fifteen volts. I don't even think it's necessary. Fifteen, if I were to get any, and I wouldn't even want that. I don't think it's necessary."

The pope—supreme moral authority for Roman Catholics—has created acute moral and social conflicts by prohibiting artificial contraception. Photo: Rex Features.

The "victim" in Milgram's experiment being wired up to the shock generator.

In an adjacent room the "teacher" gives himself a mild electric shock to convince himself that the apparatus really works.

The victim's screams are heard through the dividing wall.

Another "teacher" forces the victim's hand onto the shock plate. Photos © 1965 by Stanley Milgram. From the film Obedience, *distributed by the New York University Film Library.*

She described how she had felt during the experiment in the following words: "Every time I pressed the button, I died. Did you see me shaking? I was just dying here to think that I was administering shocks to the poor man." It did not seem to dawn on her that there was something inconsistent about being prepared to administer a shock to someone else that was thirty times more intense than the shock she was reluctantly prepared to tolerate herself.

One of the most striking cases of total obedience was that of Pasqual Gino, a 43-year-old water inspector of Italian descent. He continued through to the end of the series of shocks. When the learner stopped providing answers on the learning task, he said, he reasoned to himself as follows: "Good God, he's dead; well, here we go, we'll finish him. And I just continued all the way through to 450 volts." He was relieved to discover that the learner was still alive at the end of the experiment, but indicated that he wouldn't have been concerned if the learner had been dead, as he was simply carrying out a job.

What the Milgram experiment did very successfully was to create a conflict situation in which some forces push the subject toward obedience and others prompt him toward disobedience. In our culture there is a lot of emphasis on the necessity of obeying authority, on the grounds that an efficient and well-organized society can only exist if there is a fairly stable hierarchy in which some people are given power and authority over others. Most societies attempt to ensure obedience by moving the obedient individual up a niche in the hierarchy. This is a doubly ingenious ploy, because the individual is rewarded for his obedience and feels motivated to climb to the next niche, and the hierarchy itself is preserved and strengthened. In the Milgram study, the experimenter represents an authority figure. His authority is enhanced by wearing a special coat, by being associated with Yale University, and by his aura of expertise in human behavior and his presumably detailed knowledge of the experiment being carried out. In everyday life, we place responsibility for our health in the hands of our doctor, we go to an accountant for financial advice, and so on. Of necessity we rely heavily on the opinions of various authority figures, and this is what Milgram's subjects were doing.

On the other hand, the "learner" in the Milgram study does everything he can to persuade the subject to stop administering the shocks to him. He screams, he begs the subject to stop, and in some cases he even says he has a heart condition. The participants, however, cannot satisfy both the experimenter and the "victim," and it is this conflict that causes the tension and the nervous laughter.

It follows from this analysis of Milgram's experiment that obedience to the experimenter could be reduced either by increasing the obviousness of the learner's plight or by reducing the authority of the experimenter. Milgram looked at a series of four situations in which the "learner" was brought progressively closer, in a psychological sense, to the subject administering the shocks. In the Remote Feedback situation, the victim could be neither heard nor seen, though he did pound on the wall at one point. In the Voice Feedback situation (this was the situation described at the start of this chapter), the victim could be heard screaming but could not be seen. In the third situation (Proximity), the victim was only 1½ feet away from the subject and could therefore be seen as well as heard. The fourth situation (Touch-Proximity) was identical to the third, except that the subject had to force the victim's hand onto the shock plate in order to administer shocks above the 150-volt level.

Milgram found that the closer his subjects were to the victim, the more concerned they were about him and the more reluctant they were to obey the experimenter. Sixty-six percent of subjects were obedient in

The Ayatollah Khomeini: absolute power, while it lasts . . . Photo: Rex Features.

Charles Manson, a mass murderer who wielded appalling power. Photo: Rex Features.

the Remote situation, 62 percent in Voice Feedback, 40 percent in Proximity, and 30 percent in Touch-Proximity. It is obviously easier to ignore the consequences of one's actions when the victim is neither audible nor visible. In other words most people would find it easier, psychologically, to drop a bomb from 20,000 feet and possibly kill thousands of people than to kill one person cold-bloodedly with a knife.

What happens if steps are taken to reduce the influence of the experimenter? To answer this, Milgram compared one situation in which the experimenter sat only a few feet away from the subject with a second situation in which, after giving the initial instructions, the experimenter left the laboratory and gave his orders by telephone. The comparison had dramatic results: 65 percent of subjects were obedient in the first situation but only 22.5 percent in the second. However, if the experimenter returned to the laboratory after the subject had refused to give higher-intensity shocks when ordered to do so by telephone, he was often able to persuade the subject to revert to obedience. Some subjects found an interesting and ingenious way of minimizing conflict: they sabotaged the experiment by assuring the experimenter on the telephone that they were raising the shock intensities as instructed but kept on administering the lowest level of shock.

Throughout these experiments the subjects appear to have been pulled in opposite directions by the experimenter and by the victim. If the suffering of the victim was emphasized or the authority of the experimenter reduced, the level of obedience was much less. But if the victim's plight was *not* forcibly brought to the subject's attention, and the experimenter was perceived as a valid authority figure, obedience became the norm.

Many critics of Milgram's work argued that unexpected findings might have been due to the setting of the experiment, since Yale University is a reputable and distinguished institution. Indeed, several subjects remarked that it was this very fact which gave them confidence in the integrity of the experimenter. Men will happily expose their throats to a man with a razor blade in a barber's shop but not in a shoe shop. Most women will not undress fully in the presence of a complete stranger of the opposite sex but are prepared to do so for a gynecological examination.

So Milgram tried to find out how important the setting was by moving his apparatus to a three-room office suite in a ramshackle commercial building in a poor neighborhood. The study was allegedly carried out by Research Associates of Bridgeport, a private firm which claimed to be conducting research for industry. He discovered that moving the experiment from the elegance of Yale University to a run-down office building made some difference, but not as much as might have been expected. Forty-eight percent of the Bridgeport subjects were prepared to administer all the shocks compared with 65 percent of the Yale subjects.

Not surprisingly, it was the unexpected behavior of the obedient subjects which attracted the lion's share of attention from the experts (and others) and stimulated various other experiments. Most subsequent researchers found that between one-third and one-half of participants do not obey—they defy the authority of the experimenter. Are disobedient people different from obedient people? For example, one might imagine that men would be more likely to administer intense shocks than women—after all, they are supposed to be more aggressive. On the other hand, women tend to be more yielding than men on many tests of compliance, and so might be readier to obey the experimenter. In fact, Milgram found no difference in obedience between male and female participants. What he did discover was that obedient women became much more nervous and concerned than obedient men. But when ordered to administer genuine electric shocks to a puppy in a Milgram-type study, only 54 percent of male participants did so, as against 100 percent of female participants, who were prepared to give the most severe shock to the howling and yelping dog.

How does one explain these astonishing findings? As yet, all we can reasonably say is that not enough work has been done to enable psychologists to predict who will be obedient and who will be disobedient. Typically, however, better-educated people are more likely to be disobedient, perhaps because they do not regard the experimenter as so intimidating. People who have spent a number of years in one of the armed forces are more likely to be obedient, suggesting that the effects of service discipline are very long-lasting.

Common sense suggests that people with an authoritarian personality are more obedient than those of a more liberal disposition (see Chapter 22). Milgram tested this, and found that obedient subjects had much more pronounced authoritarian attitudes than defiant subjects on a test of fascist tendencies (the "F Scale").

Obedience: abdication of responsibility

Of all the questions raised by Milgram's dramatic work, the most engrossing is whether or not his findings are relevant to some of the atrocious war crimes of this century. Milgram obviously feels that they are, citing evidence from interviews with former members of SS concentration camp personnel and Gestapo units. Two themes reiterated again and again were the dehumanizing of the victims of such crimes and the "helpless cog" attitude of those responsible for committing them.

One of the main features of Nazi Germany was the systematic devaluation of the Jews over a period of more than a decade by means of vehement anti-Jewish propaganda. This was reinforced by excluding

Jews from German citizenship and, ultimately, denying them the status of human beings. On a vastly reduced scale, many of Milgram's obedient subjects harshly devalued their victims. One subject justified himself by saying that the victim "was so stupid and stubborn he deserved

A stark moment in the long agony of the Holocaust. Photo: C. Dvorjak.

to get shocked." When Milgram asked some of the participants in his study to think of five words to describe the learner's personality, obedient subjects gave fewer positive and more negative words than disobedient subjects.

The "helpless cog" attitude was exemplified by Adolf Eichmann. At his trial for his part in the extermination of the Jews, his main defense was that he was merely a little cog in the machinery that carried out the directives of the German Reich. Personal responsibility for one's actions is easier to evade if one belongs to an organization in which responsibilities are divided and duties highly specialized.

Wesley Killam and Leon Mann of the University of Sydney compared obedience in two groups of subjects, one group playing a "transmitter role" (ordering someone else to administer the shocks to the learner in the Milgram experiment) and the other playing an "executant role" (directly administering the shocks). The transmitter group, at one remove from administering the shocks, was twice as obedient as the executant group, which seems to mirror what happens in society generally.

Obedience: a fatal flaw?

The potential implications of his work made Milgram profoundly pessimistic about the future: "The capacity for man to abandon his humanity, indeed the inevitability that he does so, as he merges his unique personality into the larger institutional structures . . . is the fatal flaw nature has designed into us, and which in the long run gives our species only a modest chance for survival." He even went so far as to claim that an individual's conscience ceases to operate when he or she is responding to the dictates of authority. Under such circumstances, the individual enters an "agentic" state, viewing himself as merely the instrument of the authority figure.

Is this pessimism justified? There are some reasons for supposing that it isn't. Certainly the analogy drawn between the Milgram situation and Nazi Germany is imprecise and even misleading. Milgram's experiment was presented to the participants in a way that emphasized its positive, culturally desirable values, such as increasing our knowledge of human learning and memory. By contrast, the avowed goals of Nazi Germany were morally vile, in spite of the attempt to portray them as a purification of the Aryan race and the creation of a higher civilization. Another difference is that Milgram's subjects were obedient only when the experimenter kept a close watch on them, whereas minute-by-minute surveillance was largely unnecessary in the conditions which prevailed in Nazi Germany.

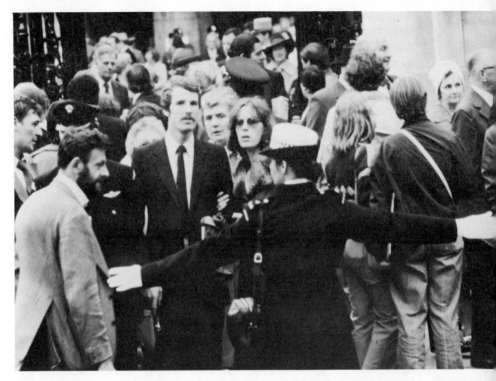

Power being exercised in quite a different way: a policewoman direct-ing traffic. Photo: Multimedia Publications Inc. (Miki Koren).

Milgram's idea that people obeying an authority figure overrule or simply forget their own consciences may have been true of some of the people in charge of Nazi concentration camps, but it was certainly not true of most of his subjects. It would indeed have been disturbing if the subjects had whistled and looked relaxed and happy while adminis-tering severe electric shocks. The obvious tension and unease of most of the obedient subjects clearly revealed that they had not lost sight of moral issues. Their moral confusion was shown by a disinclination to look in the direction of the learner, a fact that hardly suggests sadistic pleasure in inflicting pain.

Another reassuring finding emerged when Milgram put two stooge subjects in with each genuine subject, all performing the teacher role. When the two stooge subjects quit the experiment halfway through, 90 percent of the real subjects followed suit and also disobeyed the experi-menter. While there were many people in Nazi Germany who strongly disapproved of what was happening, subjects in the Milgram experiment had little idea whether other people would approve of them for disobeying, although they knew the experimenter would not approve. In a sense, then, Milgram loaded the dice by depriving his subjects of any effective moral support that might have had the effect of strengthening their desire to disobey.

Misinterpretations

Finally, we return to the vexed question of why outside observers so spectacularly overestimate likely levels of disobedience to authority. An interesting view on this was put forward by Stephen West and his associates. They argued that "actors" (anyone actively involved in a situation) and external observers frequently have very different perceptions of the causes of behavior in any given situation. The attention of the actor is focused on the environment from which he selects information to guide his actions, whereas the attention of the observer is focused on the actor and his behavior. In consequence, the actor tends to attribute the causes of his behavior to his environment, whereas the observer attributes the actor's actions to characteristics of the actor. For example, if you ask different people why a particular person robbed a bank, they will probably tell you he is a shady, antisocial, and thoroughly disreputable character. If you ask the robber himself, he will probably say that he had a tip-off that the bank was easy to rob or that he needed the money. Similarly, we say we go to parties because we know interesting people or because we get lots of invitations, but we tend to say other people go to parties because they are sociable or extroverted.

According to West's analysis, people underestimate obedience in the Milgram situation because they tend to ignore the authority of the experimenter. They ask themselves what kinds of people would be obedient, and conclude that only sadists would go along with the experimenter.

Amazingly, West persuaded a number of people to take part in the burglary of an advertising firm; their job was to act as inside lookouts and microfilm the firm's records. Those who took part said they agreed to do so because of the amount of money involved and the allegedly foolproof nature of the plan. External observers, on the other hand, put their dubious behavior down to their character, describing them as outgoing, unintelligent, poor, insecure, unhappy, untrustworthy, unsophisticated, and impulsive. No doubt you will already have thought of some choice adjectives to describe experimental psychologists who try to persuade young college students to embark on a career in industrial espionage.

Conclusions

Extremely powerful conflicts can arise when people are ordered to perform immoral acts by an authority figure, and these conflicts can produce almost intolerably high levels of tension. Obedience is more likely when the individual is more involved with the authority figure than with the victim; disobedience is more likely when the individual witnesses the plight of the victim in some way. Milgram's work poses a number of moral issues from the point of view of both experimenter and subject. It is instructive to compare the experimental findings of Milgram and others with the horrific reality of Hitler's Germany, but the analogy should not be taken too far.

4

The Stanford prison experiment: Zimbardo's hell

One of the most notorious experiments in the history of psychology—because of what it appeared to reveal about human nature and the way in which it was set up—was an attempt to discover exactly how and why being in prison is such a degrading experience. There is clearly a lot wrong with the prison system in Western societies. The rising incidence of prison riots (at Hull and Parkhurst in Britain and San Quentin in America, to take three grim examples) is a sign that something is seriously wrong.

But while there is a general feeling that some reform of the prison system is called for, there is no agreement about what kind of reform is necessary or desirable, mainly because people have different ideas about the reasons for the current problem.

Reforming the system is all very well, but the problems must be correctly identified first. At least three major components of the prison system need to be considered: the guards, the prisoners themselves, and the organizational structure and physical environment of the prison. Are the guards to blame for the current climate of unrest? We know that it is primarily those of a somewhat aggressive or sadistic disposition who choose to become guards in the first place. The second possibility is that prisoners, being naturally subversive and antisocial, tend to create an unsavory atmosphere whatever their environment. The third possibility is that it is the prison itself, with its cold, forbidding atmosphere and rigid power structure, which is mainly responsible.

A plausible case can be made for any or all of these factors causing·

What's wrong with the prison system—the guards, the prisoners, or the organizational structure of prisons? Photo: Rex Features.

trouble within our prisons; yet it is extremely difficult to prove. What can psychologists contribute toward an understanding of the malfunctions in the prison system? It was Philip Zimbardo of Stanford University who came up with an ingenious experiment designed to explore these failings. Many critics have accused him and his colleagues of overstepping the mark in their pursuit of scientific knowledge, by degrading and humiliating the participants. But until the experiment began they could not have predicted what would happen. The Zimbardo experiment has now gone down as one of the most famous, some would say infamous, in the annals of psychology.

Key experiment   The mock-prison study (Philip Zimbardo, Craig Haney, Curt Banks, and David Jaffe)

Philip Zimbardo and his co-workers at Stanford University were interested in determining the causes of the dehumanization that is so prevalent in prisons. Suppose that ordinary members of society were persuaded to act as guards and prisoners in a mock prison which mimicked the environment and day-to-day running of an actual prison? If the mock prison failed to produce the hostility and alienation of a real prison, this would surely suggest that the personality characteristics of the guards or the prisoners, or both, are the vital ingredients in the unpleasantness found in a real prison. On the other hand, if the behavior observed in the mock prison was very similar to that in a real prison, this would suggest that it is the environment of a prison which is the crucial factor in producing unpleasantness.

The experiment started on August 14, 1971, in Palo Alto, California. The quiet of a Sunday morning was shattered by a screeching squad car siren as police swept through the city picking up the participating college students from their homes in a surprise "mass arrest." All of the "suspects" were charged with a felony, warned of their constitutional rights, spread-eagled against the police car, searched, handcuffed, and taken away in the back seat of the police car to the police station. The whole operation was carried out so realistically, thanks to the cooperation of the Palo Alto City Police Department, that the alarmed mother of one 18-year-old student arrested for armed robbery exclaimed, "I felt my son must have done something; the police have come to get my son!"

On arrival at the police station, each suspect was fingerprinted and identification forms were prepared for his "jacket," or central information file. He was then left on his own in a detention cell. Later in the day, each suspect was blindfolded and taken to the "Stanford County Prison," where he was stripped naked, skin-searched, deloused, and issued with a uniform, bedding, and basic supplies. The uniform worn by the prisoners consisted of a loose-fitting muslin smock with an identity number on the front and back, no underclothes, a light chain and lock around one ankle, rubber sandals, and a cap made from a nylon stocking.

The prison warden gathered the prisoners together and told them about the sixteen basic rules of prisoner conduct, starting with "Prisoners must address the guards as 'Mr. Correctional Officer,'" and ending with "Failure to obey any of the above rules may result in punishment."

The "guards" had been told beforehand that their task was to "maintain the reasonable degree of order within the prison necessary for its effective functioning." They were given only minimal guidance about the way they were expected to behave, except that they were specifically prohibited from using physical aggression. They were clearly distinguishable from the prisoners by their uniform, which consisted of a plain khaki shirt and trousers, a whistle, a police nightstick, and reflecting sunglasses.

The guards and prisoners were selected from among a total of 75

*A "prisoner," blindfolded for the journey to "Stanford County Prison,"
with one of the "guards." Photo: Philip Zimbardo.*

respondents to a newspaper advertisement asking for male volunteers
to participate in a psychological study of "prison life" for $15 a day
over a period of two weeks. The 10 prisoners and 11 guards who actually took part in the experiment were among those respondents judged
to be the most stable (physically and mentally), the most mature, and

the least inclined toward antisocial behavior. The majority of them were middle-class students.

The prisoners and guards were to live within the confines of the "Stanford County Prison," which was situated in the basement of the psychology building at Stanford University. This mock prison was deliberately designed to be as unpleasant as possible. There were three small cells (9 feet by 6 feet), with three prisoners assigned to each. As in a real prison, the windows were barred, and in addition to guards there was a warden, a superintendent (Zimbardo), a parole board, and a grievance committee. All the participants had agreed to take part in spite of having been told that those assigned to play the prisoner role

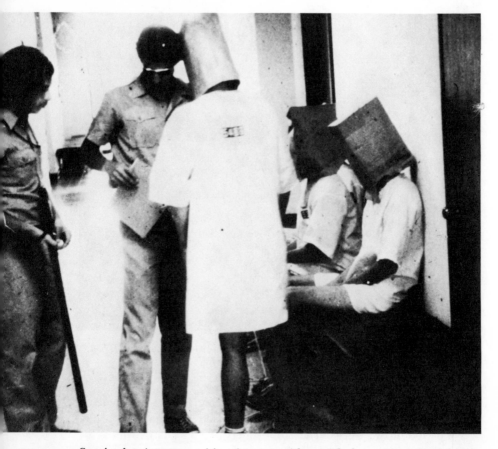

Stanford prisoners waiting in a corridor with bags over their heads. Photo: Philip Zimbardo.

The symbols of impersonal authority, reflecting sunglasses and a night-stick. Photo: Philip Zimbardo.

could expect to be under surveillance, might be harassed, and might have some of their basic rights curtailed during imprisonment.

The happenings within the mock prison were so unpleasant and po-tentially so dangerous that the entire experiment had to be brought to a premature end after six days rather than the scheduled fourteen. Vio-lence and rebellion broke out within less than two days of the start of the experiment. The prisoners ripped off their clothing and their iden-tity numbers, shouted and cursed at the guards, and barricaded them-selves inside the cells. The guards put down the rebellion violently, using fire extinguishers, transformed the prisoners' rights into "privi-leges," played the prisoners off against one another, and systematically harassed them. One of the prisoners showed such severe symptoms of emotional disturbance (disorganized thinking, uncontrollable crying and screaming) after only one day that he had to be released.

On the third day a rumor spread through the prison about a mass es-cape plot. This led the superintendent and the guards to take various repressive and preventative steps. On the fourth day, two more pris-oners displayed symptoms of severe emotional disturbance and were released; a third developed a psychosomatic rash all over his body and

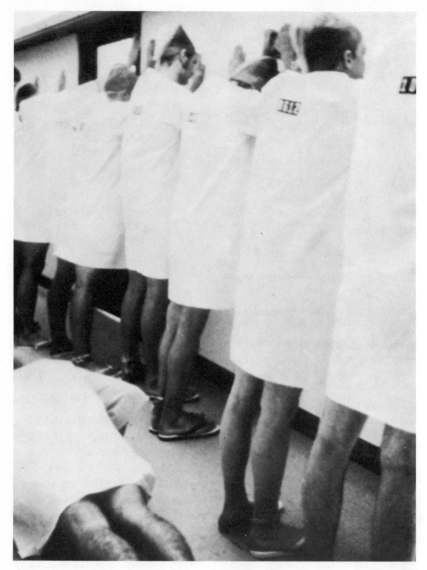

More harassment of prisoners by the Stanford guards: forced push-ups and prolonged standing in uncomfortable positions. Photo: Philip Zimbardo.

was also released. As time passed, some of the guards seemed to derive great satisfaction from exercising power and behaving in a sadistic manner. A particularly interesting observation was that the use of force, harassment, and aggression by the guards increased steadily from day to day, in spite of the fact that prisoner resistance declined and evaporated. The guards also manifested more indirect displays of power as time went by, such as rapping their sticks against their hands or against the furniture, walking with a swagger, or adopting extravagant postures. The prisoners, on the other hand, began to slouch and keep their eyes fixed on the ground.

What seems to have led to the experiment being abandoned was a comment made by Christina Maslach, Zimbardo's fiancée. She had gone to the prison to help interview the prisoners. While she was there she saw a line of blindfolded prisoners shuffling along under guard to the toilet. Miss Maslach burst into tears and exclaimed, "It's awful what you are doing to those boys!" Naturally, Philip Zimbardo's heart melted at these words, and the experiment was officially halted the next morning.

Perhaps the most vivid accounts of what it was like to take part in such a dehumanizing experience were the diary entries of those directly involved. Before the experiment one of the guards wrote in his diary that he was a pacifist and so unaggressive that he could not imagine maltreating any other living being. By the third day, he appeared to be thoroughly enjoying the power to manipulate people. Before the prisoners received visitors, he warned them not to complain unless they wanted the visit to come to an abrupt end. What he really liked, he said, was having almost total control over everything that was said and done.

On the fifth day, problems arose because a new prisoner refused to eat his sausage. The guard's diary entry at this point reads as follows: "We throw him into the Hole ordering him to hold sausages in each hand . . . We decide to play upon prisoner solidarity and tell the new one that all the others will be deprived of visitors if he does not eat his dinner . . . I walk by and slam my stick into the Hole door . . . I am very angry at this prisoner for causing discomfort and trouble for the others. I decided to force-feed him, but he wouldn't eat. I let the food slide down his face . . . I hated myself for making him eat but I hated him more for not eating."

As we have already noted, the guards became increasingly brutal and aggressive during the course of the experiment and ignored the warning not to use physical force. However, Zimbardo and his colleagues reported that there were differences in behavior among the guards, and only about a third of the guards, they felt, were so consistently hostile and degrading as to be described as sadistic.

On the other hand, the prisoners became progressively more passive as the days passed and sank into a state of depression and helplessness. Perhaps the reason for this was that they began to realize there was very little they could do to improve matters or control the environ-

One of several Stanford prisoners who ripped off their clothes and barricaded themselves inside their cells in protest. Photo: Philip Zimbardo.

ment. As the old saying goes, "There's no point in banging your head against a brick wall."

Despite its premature end Zimbardo's experiment showed that brutal, ugly prison situations can develop even when upright citizens play the parts of prisoners and guards. The dehumanization which occurred in the Stanford experiment could hardly be attributed to the "deviant personalities" of those involved; the most natural explanation was that it was the prison environment which was mainly responsible for the participants' behavior. In Zimbardo's own words, his study revealed "the power of social, institutional forces to make good men engage in evil deeds."

But how similar was the mock prison to a real prison? The evidence from those with firsthand experience of real prisons is somewhat mixed. Prisoners in the maximum security wing of Rhode Island Penitentiary said that they recognized the reactions of the mock prisoners as corresponding to the confused and overemotional reactions of many first offenders. A remark by one ex-convict throws some light on the passivity of the mock prisoners: "The only way to really make it with the bosses [in Texas prisons] is to withdraw into yourself, both mentally and physically—literally making yourself as small as possible. It's another way they dehumanize you. They want you to make no waves in prison."

What the critics said

The associate warden at San Quentin was predictably skeptical about Zimbardo's experiment when he was interviewed on television. Asked whether it was relevant to the prison system, he replied that it was worthless, biased, and methodologically unsound; but he was basing his judgment on a brief news article he had read. Subsequently, Zimbardo's right to visit any of California's prisons was refused by the Superintendent of the Department of Corrections. This action suggests, at least to the cynical mind, that officialdom was frightened because Zimbardo had got it right.

The most weighty attack came from Boston psychologists Ali Banuazizi and Siamak Movahedi, who argued that the participants in the Stanford Prison Experiment were not in a social situation that was functionally equivalent to that of a real prison; all they were asked to do was to play the roles of prisoners and guards, and since they had strong stereotypes of how guards and prisoners behave in a real prison, they simply engaged in conscious role-playing based on these stereotypes. It was therefore to be expected that the results would show how accurate the stereotypes were. In this connection, it is interesting to note that most of the guards, when questioned about their aggressive behavior, argued that they had "just played the role" of a tough guard.

Banuazizi and Movahedi examined some of these ideas by asking people to fill in a questionnaire giving a description of the Stanford Prison Experiment followed by a series of questions. Eighty-one percent of those questioned guessed fairly accurately what the experimenter was trying to prove; one respondent, for example, wrote: "He believes that people are pushed about, put down, and humiliated in jails."

The vast majority of respondents (90 percent) predicted that the mock guards would be oppressive, hostile, and aggressive. Such a wide consensus suggests that there is a familiar stereotype concerning the behavior of prison guards. There was less agreement about the probable reactions of the mock prisoners. Approximately 30 percent thought the prisoners would be rebellious and defiant, another 30 percent guessed they would be passive and docile, and most of the others thought they would probably fluctuate between both extremes.

So, as these data indicate, the mock guards may simply have been pretending to conform to the cultural stereotype of the aggressive, unpleasant prison guard, and did not "really" get involved in the part they were playing. However, it is less clear whether the mock prisoners' behavior can be so readily accounted for by the stereotype argument; there are no cultural expectations concerning the typical behavior of prisoners.

Banuazizi and Movahedi also pointed out that, in spite of some broad similarities between the functioning of the mock prison and that of real prisons, there were also a number of differences. For example, some of the mock guards said they were willing to work overtime for no extra pay, which implies a far greater dedication to duty than prison guards, or any other group of workers, are likely to demonstrate in this inflationary age.

It is certainly true that the behavior patterns exhibited by those engaged in role-playing reflect many different things, including what the role-player would like to do, what he feels is socially desirable, and what he thinks the experimenter expects him to do. In this connection, Banuazizi and Movahedi were correct when they criticized Zimbardo for assuming that his results could be explained fairly simply. But their own explanation of Zimbardo's results was not totally adequate either. Was the passivity, depression, helplessness, and even psychological dysfunction displayed by the prisoners merely a remarkable piece of acting designed to please the experimenters? Even if severe emotional disturbance can be simulated, psychosomatic rashes presumably cannot.

The strongest evidence against the idea that Zimbardo's subjects were merely "acting out" culturally defined roles is that extreme versions of these roles were observed mainly toward the end of the experiment. If Banuazizi and Movahedi were correct, why was full-blown stereotyped behavior not manifest from the beginning? Furthermore, the physical abuse and harassment shown by the guards seem to have gone quite a long way beyond what would have been expected from mere playacting. While acting is most likely in the presence of an audience, Zimbardo actually found that harassment of prisoners was greater when individual guards were alone with solitary prisoners or out of range of the recording equipment.

A close examination of the data collected by Zimbardo suggests that there was undoubtedly some playacting during the early stages of the study, with stereotyped expectations helping to determine the participants' behavior. However, it is worth noting that real prison guards during the early days of their employment are also likely to be "role-playing." As the experiment progressed, the participants seem to have become increasingly involved in the roles assigned to them; in other words, they became noticeably less and less self-conscious.

The aspect of the Stanford Prison Experiment which worried people most was whether it was morally acceptable to expose the participants to such degradation and hostility. Can one really justify a study in which four participants had to be released because of "extreme depression, disorganized thinking, uncontrollable crying, and fits of rage"? Was it reasonable for Zimbardo to stand by while the guards forced the prisoners to clean toilets with their bare hands, hosed them with fire extinguishers, and repeatedly made them do push-ups, sometimes with a guard standing on their back?

Professor Harris Savin of the University of Pennsylvania, for instance, described the mock prison as a "hell" and compared Zimbardo to used-car salesmen and others "whose roles tempt them to be as obnoxious as the law allows." He concluded as follows: "Professors who, in pursuit of their own academic interests and professional advancement, deceive, humiliate, and otherwise mistreat their students, are subverting the atmosphere of mutual trust and intellectual honesty without which, as we are fond of telling outsiders who want to meddle in our affairs, neither education nor free inquiry can flourish."

Zimbardo's defense

In his reply, Zimbardo argued that psychological research is morally justified if the gains—new knowledge, for instance—outweigh the losses.[1] He claimed that the "losses" suffered by the participants did not persist after the end of the study. This was ascertained by means of

Prisoners forfeit the right to privacy and to dress, eat, exercise, and work as individuals. Photo: Rex Features.

questionnaires sent to the participants several weeks after the study, several months later, and then at yearly intervals. An attempt was made to minimize the negative effects of the study by holding day-long debriefing sessions, in which the moral conflicts posed by the study were made explicit.

Zimbardo admitted that there was a lot of suffering during the course of the experiment, but pointed out that all of the participants signed a formal "informed consent" statement, which specified that there would be an invasion of privacy, loss of some civil rights, and harassment. He also pointed out that any professional psychologists who felt unhappy about the study could have lodged a complaint with the American Psychological Association Ethics Committee. In fact, only one inquiry was addressed to the committee within two years after the study took place, and that was from Zimbardo himself.

In perspective

On the positive side, most of the participants reported that they had learned valuable things about themselves. Some of the participants volunteered to give up part of their summer holiday to work in local prisons, and most of them became advocates of penal reform. Another possible benefit of the study was the influence which it had on the public at large. For example, one citizens' group used the results of the study in a legal action to prevent the construction of a huge new prison in Contra Costa County, California, in favor of smaller, community-based facilities.[2]

The moral position adopted by Zimbardo is one in which the ends do justify the means and in which research is evaluated by considering the benefits and costs involved. This accords with the view of most psychologists and was expressed in the following words by the American Psychological Association Committee on Ethical Standards in Psychological Research: "The general ethical question always is whether there is a negative effect upon the dignity and welfare of the participants that the importance of the research does not warrant." Even so there are difficulties.

The first point to consider is this: it is all very well to justify research on the basis of likely benefits and costs, but we do not always know what the consequences are going to be until *after* the experiment has been carried out. Zimbardo claims that the high costs of his prison experiment, in terms of degradation and physical assault, surprised him. Nevertheless, an earlier and smaller version of the main experiment had been carried out under Zimbardo's supervision at Stanford University, with many of the same disquieting results.

Secondly, one person's assessment of the benefits and costs of a piece of research may not agree with someone else's. Many people would disagree with Zimbardo, arguing that the suffering of the participants was not justified by the information gained.

Immanuel Kant and others have argued that ends *cannot* justify means. There should be no exceptions to a moral principle, regardless of the consequences. But rigid following of such principles can have extremely unfortunate consequences. If a madman with a gun asks you where your mother is because he wants to shoot her, would you tell him, for the sake of sticking to the principle "Always tell the truth"? The inflexible and unrealistic nature of such a moral position has limited appeal.

Implications for prison reform

In spite of the criticisms, the Stanford Prison Experiment obviously produced thought-provoking and striking results. What is it about the organizational structure of prisons that produces such unfortunate effects on the morale and behavior of the inmates? Zimbardo argued that one relevant factor is that prisons are designed to maximize anonymity. All prisoners are put into standard uniforms, required to have hair of a standard length, and are fed standard meals on standard plates at standard times. Of course their personal identity is under siege.

However, it was the power structure within prisons which Zimbardo identified as being the most important factor: "Power is the most important variable in social psychology and the most neglected . . . The great discovery of American behaviorism, namely that responses that are reinforced will increase in frequency, is but a technological footnote to the primary issue of who controls the reinforcers."

Within the prison system it is, of course, the guards who exert the power. Typically, they expect the prisoners to obey all the prison rules, but they don't reward them for their obedience. But if prisoners disobey the rules, that *is* noticed, and is followed by punishment. In such circumstances, the best a prisoner can hope for is that the guards will behave predictably, so that he knows how to behave in order to avoid punishment. When actual prisoners are asked, "What are the characteristics of a good guard?" most say they prefer guards who "go by the book" and don't make exceptions.

The fact that prisoners are relatively unable either to control their environment or to obtain rewards by acting in certain ways may be of crucial importance. Laboratory research has indicated that such circumstances produce an apathetic state known as "learned helplessness," which seems to have much in common with the passivity and unresponsiveness of Zimbardo's mock prisoners. Perhaps prisoners would be more contented with their lot if they were praised and rewarded for following the prison rules, rather than simply punished for disobeying them. Such an approach has been adopted with some success in the "token economies" discussed in Chapter 21.

Conclusions

Philip Zimbardo set up a mock prison to investigate the failings of the prison system. He found that responsible citizens, when asked to play the part of prison guards, acted in a degrading and dehumanizing way toward other responsible citizens playing the part of prisoners. This suggested that it is the environment and power structure of a prison rather than the sadistic nature of the guards or the antisocial nature of the prisoners which lead to the horrors of prison. More specifically, prison power structures require the guards to punish the prisoners for violating the rules, and the prisoners are not allowed to control their environment to any significant extent. However, Zimbardo's work did not actually disprove alternative explanations, and there is evidence that criminals do differ in personality from the normal population (as we shall see in Chapter 21).

As well as providing new information about the prison system, the Stanford Prison Experiment also raised important ethical issues. According to Zimbardo, research should be judged by the criterion of whether the benefits exceed the costs. In a study in which the costs included several days of utter misery and degradation for some of the participants, the benefits would need to be very substantial indeed. Many people feel that Zimbardo's study was a clear case of the costs greatly exceeding the claimed benefits, and that the study should not have been carried out, or should have been halted sooner.

5

Who says who is mad?

One of the great controversies among psychiatrists and clinical psychologists concerns the nature of mental illness. The dominant view is that there are important similarities between mental and physical illness and that methods of treatment should take account of that fact. The treatment of physical illness begins with the doctor identifying the nature of the illness. Arriving at a correct diagnosis (the medical term for classification of illness) is the most crucial part of a doctor's work. Having satisfied himself that he has discovered the true nature of the physical ailment, the doctor is in a position to prescribe the appropriate form of treatment.

In the same way, it is often assumed that psychiatric disorders are accompanied by symptoms which point to a particular diagnosis (schizophrenia, for example, or manic-depressive psychosis), which is then used to guide treatment. Of course, it is often a lot harder to diagnose correctly a problem when it is of a mental rather than a physical nature: even non-medically qualified people recognize warts and broken legs when they see them. The complexity of the problem was well illustrated by one study in which three psychiatrists all interviewed the same male patients and found they could agree on the appropriate diagnosis in only 20 percent of the cases.

A very strong reaction against the idea that mental illness should be viewed in medical terms has developed over the past twenty years or so. People such as Thomas Szasz and R. D. Laing have claimed that mental illness is a myth. In essence, they argue, anyone allegedly suffering from mental illness is simply behaving in ways which deviate

What is acceptable on stage would seem bizarre in real life. Photo: Multimedia Publications Inc. (Sergio Trippodo).

from those which are expected. Society reacts to this deviant behavior with disapproval and tends to apply a semi-permanent label of mental illness to the person concerned; and once that person has been labeled as mentally ill, society expects him to behave in accordance with the label. Thus we expect and even encourage people labeled "schizophrenic" to behave in bizarre and unpredictable ways, just as we expect those labeled "comedians" to be witty and amusing. As a result, psychiatrists and others involved in the business of diagnosing or labeling mental patients are actually creating fresh problems for the people they are meant to be supporting and helping.

The importance of labels was memorably expressed by Laing. He claimed that if someone labeled a scientist said, "All men are machines," he might receive a Nobel Prize. In contrast, if someone labeled a schizophrenic said, "I am a machine," he would promptly be locked away in a psychiatric hospital.

This challenge to psychiatric orthodoxy has already brought about a number of changes in psychiatric rehabilitation schemes. In California, some of the ideas of people like Szasz and Laing were used in the formulation of the Lanterman-Patris-Short Act. The effect of this act was to make it more difficult to commit patients to mental hospitals, and still more difficult to keep them there for long periods.

The bitter personal disputes between those who subscribe to the medical model of psychiatric disorders and those who believe that psychiatric diagnoses are purely in the minds of the observers has probably succeeded in creating more heat than light. An ingenious attempt to evaluate the relative merits of these two diametrically opposed positions, however, was made a few years ago by David Rosenhan; the repercussions of his work are still with us today.

Key experiment   Can we detect insanity? (David L. Rosenhan)

David Rosenhan of Stanford University was extremely interested in the various approaches that have been adopted toward the treatment of psychiatric disorders. In particular, he wondered whether it is really as simple to distinguish between normality and abnormality as is implied by the medical model. In murder trials, for example, it is not unusual for eminent psychiatrists for the defense to contradict equally eminent psychiatrists for the prosecution on the issue of the defendant's sanity. Rosenhan also pointed out that what is regarded as normal in one culture may be viewed as dangerously abnormal in another. Finally he came up with a clever way of trying to determine how well we are able to distinguish between the normal and the abnormal, or between the sane and the insane.

He wondered what would happen if a number of entirely sane people attempted to gain admission to a mental hospital by pretending to have one of the symptoms of insanity.[1,2] Would these sane individuals be classified as insane? If they were admitted to the mental hospital, would the staff realize that a mistake had been made?

The answers to these and other questions were obtained in a study in which eight normal people, five men and three women, attempted to

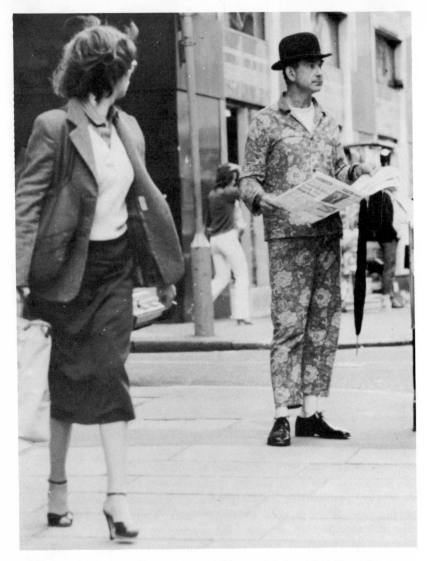

Double take. Photo: Multimedia Publications Inc. (Miki Koren).

gain admission to twelve different psychiatric hospitals. They consisted of a young psychology graduate, a pediatrician, a psychiatrist, three psychologists, a painter, and a housewife. The twelve psychiatric hospitals were located in five different states on the east and the west coasts. They also varied considerably, ranging from relatively new to old and shabby, and from good staff-patient ratios to severe understaffing.

Each of the eight participants phoned the hospital asking for an appointment. Upon arrival at the admissions office, each of them complained of hearing voices (these voices were often unclear, but appeared to be saying "empty," "hollow," and "thud"; they sounded unfamiliar but were of the same sex as the participant).

The only important elements of deception were the claims about hearing voices and falsification of the participants' names and occupations; the significant events in each participant's life were described as they actually happened. All of these sane people were judged to be insane, and all of them were admitted to the hospital, apparently on the basis of their hallucinations. One of them was diagnosed as suffering from manic-depressive psychosis; the others were diagnosed as schizophrenic.

As soon as these pseudo-patients had been admitted to the psychiatric ward, they stopped simulating signs of abnormality, although several experienced a brief period of nervousness and anxiety, because they felt they would immediately be exposed as frauds, which would be highly embarrassing.

While they were in the psychiatric ward, the pseudo-patients indicated that they were fine and no longer experienced any symptoms. In general, they behaved in a friendly and cooperative way. The only unusual aspect of their behavior was that they spent a fair amount of time writing down their observations about the ward, its patients, and the staff. To begin with, these notes were written secretly, but as it gradually became clear that no one took much notice, the note-taking was done quite openly.

The hierarchical structure of the various psychiatric hospitals was such that those of greatest professional status had the least to do with their patients (and pseudo-patients). The average daily contact of the pseudo-patients with psychiatrists, psychologists, and doctors was 6.8 minutes. In view of this general lack of careful observation by those in authority, it is not surprising that the pseudo-patients were not released very quickly. The actual length of hospitalization ranged from 7 to 52 days, with 19 days being the average.

The fact that all the pseudo-patients were released within a few weeks of admission may suggest that the psychiatric staff discovered that the pseudo-patients had been sane all the time. However, this was not the case. All the pseudo-patients were discharged with a diagnosis of "schizophrenia in remission," indicating that the deception had not been detected.

Interestingly, several of the real patients became suspicious about the pseudo-patients. The first three pseudo-patients were placed in wards containing a total of 118 patients, 35 of whom voiced their doubts. They said things like "You're not crazy. You're a journalist, or a pro-

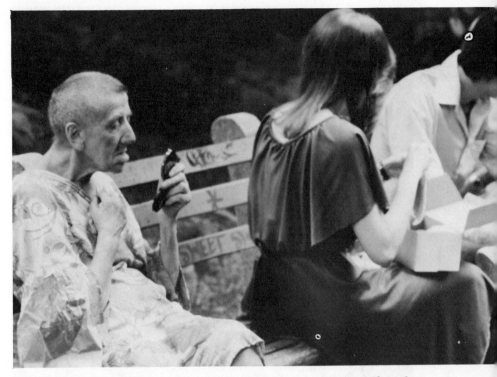

Eccentricities of appearance get noticed. But are they significantly more abnormal than going jogging at the crack of dawn or keeping your life's savings under a mattress? Photos: Multimedia Publications Inc. (Miki Koren).

fessor. You're checking up on the hospital." However, most of them were reassured by the pseudo-patients' insistence that they had been sick before they came into the hospital, though they felt fine once they had been admitted. Nevertheless, a few of the bona fide patients continued to voice the opinion that the pseudo-patients were sane.

If we accept these findings at face value, they suggest that the distinction between the sane and the insane is so blurred that it is entirely possible for the sane to be mistaken for the insane, at least by psychiatrists. Rosenhan wondered whether he could show the opposite effect, namely the insane being regarded as sane. He used as his testing ground a research and teaching hospital. The staff there had heard about the study just described and had informed Rosenhan that they would not have proved so gullible.

The first thing that Rosenhan did was to tell the staff of this hospital

What's normal in some contexts is an arrestable offense in others.
Photos: Multimedia Publications Inc. (Miki Koren).

that one or more pseudo-patients would attempt to gain admission at some time during the following three months. Each staff member was asked to observe all patients who presented themselves for admission or in the ward and say whether they thought they were pseudo-patients or genuine patients.

Judgments were obtained on a total of 193 patients admitted for psychiatric treatment. Forty-one genuine patients were judged with great confidence to be pseudo-patients by at least one staff member. Nineteen patients were suspected of being frauds by one of the psychiatrists and another staff member. In fact, none of Rosenhan's pseudo-patients sought admittance during this time. Apparently, then, mental hospital staff do sometimes think that people committed to their care are sane.

Rosenhan's main conclusion, which is tremendously important if it is true, was as follows: "It is clear that we cannot distinguish the sane from the insane in psychiatric hospitals." Part of the problem may be that, under normal circumstances, doctors and psychiatrists are more inclined to call a healthy person sick than a sick person healthy. It is obviously dangerous for a doctor to fail to take appropriate action when a sick person asks for treatment. A psychiatrist who refuses to hospitalize someone who has suspicious symptoms and asks to be hospitalized may face legal action if the patient subsequently commits suicide or murder, so it is natural for him to err on the side of caution.

If psychiatrists become too cautious, however, they may start to apply the labels of mental illness to normal people. This could be extremely damaging for those concerned because society deeply distrusts the mentally ill. While there is more tolerance now than in the past, when the mentally ill were thrown behind bars in asylums or burned as witches, mental illness is still stigmatized. Remember Thomas Eagleton, who was compelled to step down as George McGovern's running mate in the 1972 presidential campaign because of a short period of mental illness many years previously?

The other main points made by Rosenhan concern the rather degrading conditions experienced by some of his pseudo-patients during their stay in the hospital. Rosenhan himself saw one patient being beaten for having approached an attendant and saying, "I like you." It was customary for the morning staff to wake the patients by shouting, "Come on, you m——f——s, out of bed!"

On several occasions, the pseudo-patients approached a staff member with courteous requests for information. Nurses and attendants simply ignored the request and moved on with head averted 88 percent of the time, compared with 71 percent of the time when the request was addressed to a psychiatrist. Even when the pseudo-patients did receive a reply, it was often unhelpful. If the pseudo-patient said, "Pardon me, Dr. X. Could you tell me when I am eligible for grounds privileges?"

the doctor would often respond along the lines: "Good morning, Dave. How are you today?" and then move away without waiting for an answer. Such treatment is hardly likely to restore the shattered self-esteem of the mentally ill.

Since Rosenhan seemed to be suggesting that most psychiatrists were wasting their time and couldn't tell the difference between the normal and the abnormal, it was only to be expected that his study would be greeted with a storm of protest.[3] This was exactly what happened, and the letters pages of *Science* (in which Rosenhan published his original study) were soon smoldering with criticism.

One of the main attacks on Rosenhan's work was that it was illogical of him to argue that because the process of psychiatric diagnosis did not seem to work very well with pseudo-patients, psychiatric diagnoses are *never* of value. The weakness of this line of argument was most forcibly expressed by Seymour Kety: "If I were to drink a quart of blood and, concealing what I had done, come to the emergency room of any hospital vomiting blood, the behavior of the staff would be quite predictable. If they labeled and treated me as having a bleeding peptic ulcer, I doubt that I could argue convincingly that medical science does not know how to diagnose that condition."

Another point made by several psychologists and psychiatrists concerned Rosenhan's condemnation of psychiatrists for diagnosing schizophrenia on the extremely slim evidence of a single symptom (i.e., auditory hallucinations). Of course, a further relevant factor is that the pseudo-patients indicated voluntarily that they wanted to be admitted to a mental hospital. How many normal, sane people are desperately keen to be allowed to live a severely restricted life surrounded by extremely abnormal people? It is perhaps not unreasonable for the staff of a psychiatric hospital to suspect that something *is* seriously wrong with anyone asking to be admitted.

Rosenhan claimed that there is one well-recognized difference between physical and mental illness: people usually recover from the former, whereas the latter is supposed to be lasting. Indeed, when they were discharged from the hospital his pseudo-patients were diagnosed as having schizophrenia in remission; they were *not* deemed to be entirely normal. However, it certainly does not follow from this that being discharged after less than three weeks in the hospital means that the staff were remarkably alert and perceptive. It is known that schizophrenics often have short periods of remission during which they seem perfectly normal. As a result, a fairly lengthy period of observation is required before one can be certain whether or not recovery has taken place, and so 19 days as an average period before discharging "schizophrenics" was not unreasonable.

A diagnosis of schizophrenia in remission may sound as if the psychiatrists still had serious doubts about the mental health of the pseudo-patients ("in remission" simply means "without signs of ill-ness"). Apparently no suggestions were made about continuing serious problems. In fact, one-third of released schizophrenics require rehospi-talization within one year, and 50 percent require it within two years; accordingly, the diagnosis can be construed simply as a matter of pru-dence.

One of the things which Rosenhan found particularly distressing was that the sanity of the pseudo-patients was not discovered, in spite of the fact that they behaved perfectly normally while they were in the psychi-atric hospital. However, there are several reasons for doubting whether the pseudo-patients really did behave as they would normally. Since six of the pseudo-patients were clinically or professionally trained, it would presumably have been "normal" for them to discuss medicine and psychology with their professional peers, which they did not. It would also have been "normal" for them to have told the staff that they had only wanted to gain admittance to the hospital as part of an exper-iment, but they did not do this either.

A related, and potentially more serious, problem is that the pseudo-patients may unwittingly have acted in ways that conformed to their psychiatric diagnosis, and thus lengthened their stay in the hospital. This could have occurred because they knew a good deal about the purpose of the study and its probable outcome (indeed, one of the pseudo-patients was Rosenhan himself).

But perhaps the most persuasive reason for not agreeing with Rosenhan's claim that we cannot distinguish between the sane and the insane in psychiatric hospitals is that many of the real patients made precisely that distinction.

In 1975, Rosenhan replied to the growing army of his critics by suggesting that they were allowing their emotions to run away with them: "One can have little difficulty understanding those who fight mightily, even angrily, to retain current beliefs. Those beliefs were not earned without sweat in training, research, and on the clinical firing line."

Other studies of psychiatric assessment

Rosenhan also pointed out that there is growing evidence that psy-chiatric diagnoses can quite easily be distorted. In one study, Temerlin played a tape-recorded discussion between a doctor and an interviewee to groups of psychiatrists and clinical psychologists. Some of those lis-tening were given a prior suggestion by the doctor that the interviewee "sounds neurotic but is actually quite psychotic." The interviewee in fact gave "healthy" responses to several of the questions relevant for a diagnosis. In the absence of the prior suggestion, everyone agreed that the interviewee was not psychotic. However, 60 percent of the psychiatrists and 28 percent of the clinical psychologists given the suggestion rated the interviewee as psychotic.

The study by Temerlin certainly shows that psychiatric diagnosis can be a complex and unreliable process. What is not so clear is whether the psychologists and psychiatrists were simply misled by the prior suggestion. If an expert, who knows much more about a patient than you do, offers an opinion about that person, is it not sensible to heed what is said?

In some related work, S. Langer and R. P. Abelson videotaped an interview in which the discussion concentrated on a client's work history and on the difficulties he experienced at work. The videotape was seen by two groups of well-trained psychiatrists and psychodynamic psychologists who were told that they were observing either a job interview or a psychiatric interview. In spite of the fact that everyone saw the same videotape, those who thought they had watched a job interview rated the client as much better adjusted than did those who thought they had seen a psychiatric interview.

Once again, the message seems to be that psychiatric assessment is often biased and unreliable. One would of course expect real job applicants to be better adjusted than the average psychiatric patient, in which case information about the kind of interview (job or psychiatric) is relevant and ought to have some influence.

The key point here can be illustrated by imagining that you are a soldier on guard at an army camp somewhere overseas. While on duty, you hear a sound and see the vague outline of a figure. If you know that the local inhabitants are basically friendly and that the enemy is not in the immediate vicinity, you'll simply ask the other person to identify himself. On the other hand, if the local people are mostly hostile and enemy forces are known to be close, you'll probably shoot first and ask questions afterward. In other words, you take the entire situation into account in making your decision. Similarly, it is a reasonable assumption that people who ask to be admitted to a psychiatric hospital are far more likely to be mentally ill than average members of the public. Rosenhan implies that it is wrong for psychiatrists to take account of this fact when reaching a diagnosis, because it automatically biases them in favor of deciding that the person requesting admission *is* mentally ill. It makes more sense to argue that psychiatrists are right to use all the information available to them.

Rosenhan does seem to be making a valid point, though, when he points out that psychiatrists should be more careful about applying psy-

The latest in skinhead chic and an Eskimo woman chewing leather to make it supple. Transplant both of them into different cultures and both might be labeled insane. Photos: Multimedia Publications Inc. (Israel Sun), left; Pixfeatures, right.

chiatric labels to patients. The label not only affects the way other people regard the individuals concerned; it can also affect those individuals' opinions of themselves and how they interact with others. In one experiment, male outpatients with a psychiatric history were led to believe that a confederate of the experimenter had been informed either of their actual psychiatric history or that they were patients with a physical illness. Although the confederate was not in fact told anything about the patients' conditions, mental or physical, he rated patients as much more tense and anxious when they thought their psychiatric history had been revealed.

Schizophrenia: myth or fact?

In spite of the criticisms of Rosenhan's study, it could still be argued that schizophrenia is something which exists in the mind of the observer rather than inside the patient. In other words, if an individual acts counter to society's *idea* of what is normal, then he is abnormal, and what one culture may regard as normal may be regarded as completely abnormal in another.

An American anthropologist, Jane Murphy, studied various ideas about normality during a field study in which she spent considerable time with two very different non-Western groups, the Yupik-speaking Eskimos on an island in the Bering Sea and the Egba Yorubas in Africa. The Eskimos use the word *nuthkavihak* to indicate that a person's soul or mind is out of order. *Nuthkavihak* manifests itself in various ways, including talking to oneself, screaming at people who don't exist, believing oneself to be an animal, drinking urine, making strange grimaces, and threatening people. There is an obvious closeness between the concept of *nuthkavihak* and schizophrenia; another significant similarity is that *nuthkavihak* is never used to describe a single phenomenon, but rather is applied to a pattern in which three or four of the symptoms exist together.

The Yorubas have a word, *were,* which can be translated as "insanity." The typical symptoms of *were* include hearing voices, laughing when there is nothing to laugh at, asking oneself questions and answering them, taking a weapon and suddenly hitting someone with it, and defecating in public and then walking around in the feces.

It is very striking that these two primitive groups of people, very different from each other and from Western society, should nevertheless identify a state of insanity or craziness that corresponds so well to the Western diagnosis of "schizophrenia." Since most other non-Western groups also have a concept akin to that of schizophrenia, one is on very flimsy ground if one defines schizophrenia primarily in terms of society's response to unusual modes of behavior.

A major criticism of Western society is that it displays a great deal of intolerance toward the mentally ill. Are the Eskimos and Yorubas more tolerant than we are of those suffering from *nuthkavihak* and *were?* Not at all. The Eskimos sometimes place an insane person in an igloo with bars across the opening through which food can be passed; they physically restrain insane people when they become violent; and they force them to return home if they run away. In Nigeria, the Yoruba healer of the insane frequently has between twelve and fifteen patients in custody at any one time. Those who are inclined to run away are usually shackled, and various herbal concoctions are administered to them to calm them down.

Many people have argued that the complex and competitive nature of Western society plays a substantial part in causing schizophrenia. In fact, the evidence suggests otherwise. The number of people who suffer from schizophrenia is a little less than 1 in every 100; this is true of the two primitive groups just considered and several Western groups as well. The figure is much higher in America because the American standard for schizophrenia is more lenient. The United States–United Kingdom diagnostic unit found that the same patients were diagnosed as schizophrenic five times more frequently by American psychiatrists than by British.

If schizophrenia is *not* something that is merely in the minds of observers, how should it be regarded? The remarkable similarities in definition, treatment, and incidence of schizophrenia across very diverse societies suggest that schizophrenia is relatively unaffected by environmental conditions. This naturally suggests that genetic factors might be important. Other evidence strongly supports this notion. Let us consider pairs of identical twins in which at least one member of the pair is schizophrenic. What is the probability that the *other* twin will also be schizophrenic? The answer is in the region of one chance in two, which is an amazingly high probability in view of the relatively low incidence of schizophrenia in the population at large. However, it could be argued that this is really a reflection of environmental influences—it must be very disturbing to grow up in a family in which the other sibling is mentally distraught. This argument sounds plausible, but it does not explain a further finding: where one of a pair of identical twins is schizophrenic the probability of both twins being schizophrenic is also one in two *even if the twins are separated shortly after birth.*

Conclusions

Many people (not all of them schizophrenics) are of two minds about the value of Rosenhan's work. Few would deny, however, that he was successful in highlighting the dilemma facing psychiatrists. If, on the one hand, a psychiatrist fails to hospitalize and apply psychiatric labels to those seeking admission to psychiatric hospitals, he runs the risk of prosecution if anyone he turns away commits suicide or murder. On the other hand, if a psychiatrist gives a psychiatric diagnosis to someone who is not really suffering from mental illness, that person will almost certainly be stigmatized by society and probably suffer a drastic change in his self-image as well. There are differing views on the relative costs of turning away a schizophrenic person and admitting a sane one. Overall Rosenhan may be right that psychiatrists are too willing to risk admitting people who are sane.

The readiness of psychiatrists to diagnose schizophrenia on the basis of only *one* of the major symptoms of schizophrenia (i.e., hallucinations) certainly lends support to the view that they err on the side of caution. However, several psychiatrists expressed great surprise at this aspect of Rosenhan's findings, pointing out that complaints about auditory hallucinations would usually be dealt with by outpatient psychiatric care.

While Rosenhan's work is provocative and ingenious, his major conclusions must be rejected. There is overwhelming evidence that the sane *can* be distinguished from the insane with a fair degree of accuracy, except perhaps under the very unusual conditions of Rosenhan's experiment. Furthermore, schizophrenia is not simply society's way of labeling and controlling those who exhibit deviant behavior. As Seymour Kety pithily remarked, "If schizophrenia is a myth, it is a myth with a strong genetic component."

SECTION B

What can we learn from animals?

Most people, even if they have only a smattering of knowledge about psychology, have heard of Pavlov's experiments with dogs, and possibly of Skinner's work with rats and pigeons. Nevertheless, the general public has always been skeptical about the relevance of animal experiments to an understanding of the human psyche, and at one time their suspicion that psychologists were so obsessed with carrying out experiments on animals that they had little time or energy left to study human beings would certainly have had some foundation.

However, contemporary psychologists are well aware of the dangers of assuming that what is true of other animal species is necessarily true of man. Man is not an unusually complicated sort of rat or dog. Why, then, do researchers continue to carry out so many animal experiments? There are many reasons, and it will be useful to discuss some of the main ones.

1. In medical research it is standard practice to try out new drugs on animals before using them on human patients. While this procedure cannot guarantee that humans will not receive harmful drugs, it clearly helps to minimize the risks. Psychological methods of treating neuroses and psychoses can also be dangerous; it is merely a sensible precaution to do initial tests on animals where this is feasible (Chapter 6).

2. In many cases animal experiments have proved a fertile source of ideas for changing and improving human behavior. Given that the differences between man and other animals are such that some of these ideas turn out to be relatively fruitless, the overall picture is nevertheless highly encouraging.

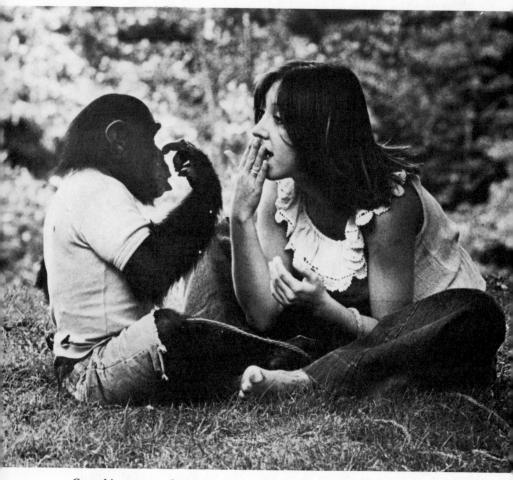

Can chimpanzees learn language? Photo: Susan Kuklin.

3. Some experiments cannot be carried out with human beings on ethical grounds. For example, no psychologist would contemplate separating a mother and child for long periods of time in order to investigate the importance of the mother to the child's development. However, such experiments have been carried out with chimpanzees (Chapter 8). 4. Animal experiments can also be justified if they enable us to satisfy our natural curiosity about the world around us. For example, it is fascinating to see whether chimpanzees can learn language (Chapter 7). It would be even more fascinating, of course, if chimpanzees ever got

to the stage of being able to tell us something about how the world looks to a chimpanzee.

The chapters in this section deal with some of the most informative and thought-provoking animal experiments ever carried out. In Chapter 6, for example, we discuss work on "avoidance learning" in dogs. Dogs will continue to jump across a barrier to avoid an electric shock, even when the shocks are discontinued. This apparently senseless behavior resembles the sort of behavior seen in people suffering from obsessive-compulsive neuroses. But the real value of this work with dogs was that it suggested a new method of treatment for people afflicted with such neuroses, which turned out to be considerably more effective than any previous treatments—a case of informed animal research helping to alleviate human suffering.

Common sense suggests that we are most likely to obtain valuable information from animal experiments if we use species as similar to ourselves as possible, that is to say, monkeys, apes, and chimpanzees. Herbert Terrace (Chapter 7) addressed himself to one of the most important and controversial questions in the whole field of animal research: can chimpanzees learn a recognizable language? The answers he found have major implications for theories of language acquisition in humans. Noam Chomsky, doyen of the science of linguistics, believes that human infants are only able to master language because the human brain is "pre-wired" to make the appropriate grammatical transformations. According to him, other species are not pre-wired in this way and should therefore lack the ability to acquire language. The possibility of language acquisition by chimpanzees has been looked at by other researchers, of course, but Terrace's work is the most thorough in the field so far, and of especial value because it compares the social, physical, and emotional development of young chimpanzees with that of human children.

Another aspect of the human condition which has been gainfully studied using animal models is the problem of maternal deprivation. The consequences of a child receiving inadequate mothering are far-reaching and of great social significance. What does a mother provide that is so essential to a child's normal development? What can be done to mitigate some of the sad consequences of maternal deprivation? In Chapter 8 we discuss Harry Harlow's answers to these and other fascinating questions, based on his work with rhesus monkeys.

All in all, the chapters in this section prove convincingly that there is a lot we can learn from animal experiments.

6

The gentle art of conditioning

There are three very pertinent questions which psychologists get asked over and over again and which they sometimes find difficult to answer. The first is: "What is the use of psychology?" Medicine is obviously useful because it enables us to cure patients suffering from a great variety of physical disorders. Physics is obviously useful because the laws of physics govern everything we do. And biology, botany, geology, chemistry, and so forth are obviously useful for much the same reason. But of what possible use is psychology? Psychologists constantly disagree with one another, found schools, and generally indulge in philosophical arguments that seem to have little relevance to practical affairs. There is more to this objection than many psychologists like to admit, but we believe there is an answer.

The second question is a little more involved: "Psychologists spend hours running rats through mazes, making dogs salivate to the sound of bells, and generally making animals do fairly unnatural things like pressing pedals with their feet, in order to please the experimenter (and obtain food). Surely all this has little relevance to the behavior of human beings? After all, humans possess language, intelligence of a high order, and the benefits of culture transmitted over thousands of years. Animals don't, so what can we learn from animals that we couldn't learn much better from humans? Psychologists seem to know far more about the behavior of rats than about the behavior of humans, yet their proper business is man and not other animals." Here again there is much truth in the objection; again we hope to show that there is some method in the apparent perversity of the researchers.

The third question is this: "Much of the work done by psychologists on dogs, rats, hamsters, pigeons, and so on seems to be cruel and involves giving electric shocks and other painful treatment to innocent, defenseless animals. This should not be allowed. It may be necessary to tolerate vivisection and other cruel practices for medical purposes, if they provide the only means of finding better methods for treating diseases, but in psychology such practices seem to be used merely for the purpose of satisfying aimless curiosity." Again, one can only say that to some degree psychologists have been guilty in this respect. But the objection is certainly not valid for all types of psychological work. As we illustrate later in this chapter, this and the other two criticisms do not necessarily apply to everything psychologists do.

The experiments we are about to describe may also help to scotch another objection, one often voiced by psychologists themselves: "Psychologists carry out experiments in laboratories, and then use the results to make far-reaching deductions about the everyday lives of people at work, at play, or in their homes. But isn't the very act of conducting an experiment in a laboratory, and using very refined apparatus, unrealistic? Isn't the artificiality of the laboratory likely to affect the behavior of the subjects to such an extent that nothing of general value can be deduced from experiments? The subjects of experiments are mostly students; are they really representative of the man in the street? Can we learn anything from the behavior of students in laboratory situations about the behavior of ordinary people in ordinary situations?"

There is a famous group of experiments on animals which illustrates very neatly what we can learn from animals about ourselves, and how valuable such knowledge is in laying the foundation for important advances in human welfare. This group of experiments concerns "avoidance learning" and "response prevention," and the key experiment we have chosen as an example is not in this case a single experiment, but an amalgam of a whole series of studies done on dogs, rats, and other animals. What is important is not so much the detail of each experiment, but the general methodology and findings. But first of all, the terms "avoidance learning" and "response prevention" require a brief explanation.

Avoidance learning

Imagine a large laboratory room, divided into two compartments by a barrier across the middle; this barrier is low enough for dogs to jump over quite easily, but it can be raised so that they cannot cross it at all. Both compartments—let us call them A and B—have metal rods on the floor which can be electrified independently so as to give the dogs a mild shock to the soles of their feet. A similar arrangement can be made for rats, using a simple box divided in two (hence the term "shuttlebox," which psychologists often use to describe this particular arrangement).

The experiment itself is a very simple one involving "avoidance learning," i.e., training the dog to respond to a stimulus that he learns to associate with an electric shock. The stimulus might be a flickering light. We will assume that the dog is in portion A of the shuttlebox; the flickering light is put on, and ten seconds later the floor in this portion of the box is electrified, giving the dog a mild shock; very soon he jumps across the barrier into section B, where he is safe for a while. After a few minutes the flickering light comes on again, and after ten seconds the floor of section B is electrified; the dog jumps back into A, which is now safe. This continues for a while, the dog jumping from A to B and from B to A, until he learns to jump not when he gets a shock but when he receives the "conditioned stimulus," i.e., the flickering light which heralds the shock. Most dogs (and rats) learn this habit pretty quickly, and will continue to jump in response to the conditioned stimulus, even when it is not followed by the unpleasant sensation of an electric shock. In other words, they have become "conditioned" to adopt an avoidance habit which is functionally useless; they jump to the signal even though there is no longer an electric shock to avoid. If this type of conditioning occurred in human subjects, we would probably label them as "neurotic." As we shall shortly see, there are other important similarities between human neurosis and conditioned avoidance learning in dogs.

As with human neurosis, the avoidance habit is extremely strong, and very difficult to break. Many methods have been tried to make dogs conditioned in this way unlearn the habit of jumping when the flickering light shows, but most of them do not work at all well. One might assume that electrifying the floor in the part of the shuttlebox the dog is jumping *into* would break the habit of responding to the light. But receiving a shock when he lands does not put the dog off at all; on the contrary, he jumps all the more enthusiastically, even though he is punished with a shock every time he lands. This again is fairly typical of human neurotic behavior, which is not usually eliminated by any form of punishment, however severe.

Obsessive-compulsive neuroses

Before describing how this habit may be changed, let us consider a typical human neurosis which is very similar to avoidance learning,

*TV watching, perhaps the most common (and undiagnosed) addiction.
Photo: Lisa Mackson.*

namely the obsessive-compulsive neurosis. Typically, a patient suffering from this type of neurosis shows a very strong fear of being contaminated, of coming into contact with germs, dirt, or other substances; he tries to reduce this fear by cleaning and washing himself and by avoiding all contact with certain substances. This cleaning-washing behavior gradually increases in frequency, until he spends an inordinate amount of time cleaning himself, washing himself, polishing handles of doors, chairs, tables, vacuuming the floor, and so on. In the end cleaning behavior becomes so obsessive that it takes up practically all the patient's waking hours. He loses his job, has no social intercourse with friends or relatives, and, if he is married, probably loses his wife as well. A disorder of this kind is obviously extremely serious, and until work on "response prevention" was done with dogs there seemed little hope of curing it. Psychiatrists tried many different methods of treating obsessive-compulsive neurosis, including psychoanalysis, electric shock treatment, psychotherapy, leucotomy (a brain operation in which parts of the prefrontal lobes are severed from the rest of the brain; see Chapter 11). None of these treatments has proved effective, and none of them achieves results which are any better than spontaneous remission (the improvement often observed in neurotic disorders with the passage of time even when no treatment has been given). However, although spontaneous remission is quite powerful in most neurotic disorders, it is exceptionally weak in obsessional and compulsive disorders; only one patient in three recovers on his own or is much improved even after a period of five years, a poor rate of improvement compared with that for anxiety neurosis or reactive depression, where the rate of remission is something like 70 percent after two years.

Few people who have not come into contact with obsessive-compulsive neurotics can have any idea of just how debilitating the disorder is. Here is a description of fears and rituals which obsessed a 19-year-old boy, as told by his elderly father: "When George wakes in the morning, usually at 11 A.M., he feels that his hands are contaminated and so he cannot touch his clothing. He won't wash in the bathroom because he feels that the carpet is contaminated and he won't go downstairs until he is dressed. Consequently, I have to dress him, having first cleaned his shoes and got out a clean shirt, underwear, socks, and trousers. He holds his hands above his head while I pull on his underpants and trousers and we both make sure, by proceeding very cautiously, that he doesn't contaminate the outside of his clothing. Any error or mishap, he will have to have clean clothes because he must avoid at all costs passing on the contamination to others. George then goes downstairs, washes his hands in the kitchen, and thereafter spends about twenty minutes in the toilet. This is quite a palaver. He has to roll up his shirt and vest to make sure they do not touch the toilet seat and has to check that he does it properly. I then have to stand at the doorway and supervise him, my main function being to give reassurance that he has not done anything silly to contaminate his clothing. Thankfully he is now managing on some occasions to cope in the toilet without my close supervision but I still have to be on call so that I can help him if he starts to panic for any reason. Incidentally, I have to put newspapers down on the floor of the toilet and change them daily to make sure that his trousers never come into contact with any contaminating substances. If he only wants to urinate, then my task is made easier. I simply have to check his trousers and boots for splashes, sometimes getting down on my hands and knees with a flashlight. I am forever telling him how ridiculous I think these rituals are, especially because I never ever find anything wrong. George never flushes the toilet because he feels that his clothing could be splashed, so one of my duties is to pull the chain and to cope with the frequent blockages which occur because of George's excessive use of toilet paper. Recently he has been checking that there are no pubic hairs on the floor and he asked me to get down on my hands and knees to check the floor meticulously. Basically he has to be completely sure that there is no contamination around because if he is not sure then he will start to worry and rumi-nate about it later on. He has to be completely sure and therefore needs a second opinion. As soon as he has zipped up his trousers I have to march in with a pad soaked in antiseptic and give the zip a quick once-over. When he washes his hands after toileting, he meticu-lously scrubs each finger and methodically works his way up as far as his elbow. I used to have to watch him at every step of the way, but now he only calls me in on occasions. Sometimes he will have washed and dried his hands and then decide that he is not sure whether he washed them properly. At this stage I usually have to supervise him so that when he is finished he is absolutely certain that the job has been done perfectly without missing a square inch of contamination."

The story goes on and on like this all through the day, but it would be tedious to continue. It takes little imagination to realize that a per-son so afflicted cannot have an ordinary life and that the disorder is grossly disabling.

Why do people like George behave like this? The evidence strongly suggests that it is in order to reduce their anxiety, which would other-wise be unbearably painful. It is easy to show that this theory is along the right lines; when they are prevented from cleaning themselves their anxiety mounts; sometimes they become visibly terrified. When they are allowed to wash and clean themselves, their anxiety visibly de-creases; there are also psychophysiological methods of measuring the decline of anxiety.

There are obvious similarities between the case of the dog jumping in response to the flickering light (although objectively he has nothing to fear because the electricity supply has been disconnected) and the obsessive-compulsive patient cleaning himself (although objectively there is no danger of contamination). The dog jumps and the young man washes himself because such actions relieve fear and anxiety, even though in both cases the fear and anxiety are unnecessary.

Response prevention

Both in dogs and in humans neurotic disorders can go on for months or even years without any improvement, despite all attempts to cure them. Yet one method *has* been found fruitful in the case of the dogs; and the question arises whether this method can also be used with human patients.

This method has been called "response prevention."[1,2,3,4] Essen-tially, it works as follows. When the flickering light is put on and the dog tries to jump into the "safe" area, the barrier is raised so high that he simply cannot jump over it. The fact of being prevented from jumping causes the dog to be "flooded with emotion" (the term "flooding" has become widely used to describe this method of treatment). He will yelp, howl, bark, run around the cage wildly, and may even urinate and defecate in his fear. After a while, however, his emotion clearly decreases in intensity, and after half an hour or so he is apparently reconciled to his fate, particularly as he has not received any electric shock. Repeat the treatment a few times and the dog is permanently cured; the flickering light can be put on, but he will not attempt to jump across the barrier.

Psychologically, of course, this makes sense. If we may anthropomorphize for a moment, the dog was jumping in the belief that if he didn't jump he would receive an electric shock; by means of our response prevention technique we have managed to demonstrate to him that he will not receive a shock for not jumping, and that consequently his fears are unfounded. The dog now gets the point and acts upon his new experience. Previously fear made it impossible for him to "test reality"; we have forced him to do that, and now he can act in a more rational fashion.

Key experiment

Can we use the "response prevention" technique with human patients, and does it have the same effect? The answer is yes to both questions. Naturally experimenters have used slightly different methods of proving the point, so we will just give a fairly generalized description of the procedures used (a detailed description of these procedures is given by S. J. Rachman and R. J. Hodgson in their book *Obsessions and Compulsions*).[5]

First, the psychologist explains the details of the treatment to the patient and obtains his informed consent (without the active cooperation of the patient the treatment will not be successful, and in any case the patient has the right to know what is going to be done to him and why). The patient must also have the right to refuse if he doesn't like what the therapist is proposing.

Having agreed, the patient is brought into a room which contains little besides a table, two chairs, one for the psychologist and one for the patient, and a container filled with some dirt or other material that the patient is known to think "contaminating." The therapist then puts his hand into the dirt in the container, and persuades the patient to do likewise. Now comes the crucial point: the patient is urged not to go and wash his hands (as he would normally do in order to reduce his anxiety), but rather to sit still and tolerate the very strong emotions of fear, anguish, and anxiety that threaten to overwhelm him. Being "flooded" with emotion is an unpleasant experience, but the emotion gradually subsides, and after half an hour or so the patient can tolerate the situation with a degree of composure that he would have thought impossible at the beginning.

This, essentially, is the kernel of the procedure now widely employed by clinical psychologists in the treatment of obsessive-compulsive disorders; of course, the process has to be repeated a number of times, but the treatment is short. Between twenty and thirty exposures of this kind are usually required.

What typically happens in cases of this kind is that the discomfort suffered by the patient and the patient's urge to clean himself both follow a very similar course. The ritual serves to reduce urge and discomfort. But when the patient is prevented from carrying out his ritual of cleaning and washing, the level declines more or less constantly with time; after about an hour urge and discomfort drop to roughly the level they would have reached had the patient been allowed to perform his ritual, and the decline continues until the final point is reached in about three hours. Thus our theoretical account of what happens during response prevention treatment is a fairly accurate mirror of the actual behavior and feeling of the patient.

We must now ask two questions. First, does the treatment actually work? And second, do patients suffer relapses after being cured? The answer to the first question is simple. Yes, the treatment works in something like 80–90 percent of cases, and it does so within a very short time; usually fewer than twenty supervised exposures are necessary to produce either a complete cure or a very considerable reduction in the number of rituals carried out. The treatment works, and works well. Until quite recently, obsessive-compulsive patients were received with dismay and hopelessness in most psychiatric institutions, because nothing could be done for them. Now they are warmly welcomed and doctors are only too eager to try out these new methods in the almost certain hope of being able to cure them. This tremendous change has come about in just a few years, and all because of a new approach directly learned from psychologists' experiments with dogs.

But what happens once a patient is cured, or very much improved, and the treatment ceases? Freud would have called such treatment "purely symptomatic," meaning that one may have dealt with the symptoms but not with any underlying "disease" or "complexes." According to Freud, such symptomatic treatment is useless; it leads inevitably to relapses or symptom substitution (i.e., the growth of new symptoms), assuming that the original symptom was successfully abolished. It is one of the tenets of psychoanalytic doctrine that symptoms are merely the outward indication of a very complex underlying

Every year thousands of animals are experimented on in psychological research laboratories. Here a dog undergoes behavior-modifying brain surgery. Photo: Multimedia Publications Inc. (Israel Sun).

disorder. Unless one cures this underlying disorder, the symptoms either cannot disappear or will be replaced by others. It is this "disease model" of obsessive-compulsive disorders which is most fashionable among psychiatrists. Psychologists, on the other hand, believe that the disease model is inapplicable to behavioral disorders. They maintain that in the case of behavioral disorders one is simply dealing with faulty learning or conditioning patterns; so the patient needs not medical treatment but some form of reeducation or reconditioning. Instances of relapse or symptom substitution would provide crucial evidence for the disease model, but is such evidence available? What actually happens to patients after successful response intervention treatment?

The answer is very simple. Although many patients have been followed up over several years, no relapses have been observed, and nothing in the way of symptom substitution—exactly the opposite of what Freud predicted. What is usually found instead is a continued improvement in the mental health and behavior of the patient, even in areas not treated. The work record of many patients improves considerably, and so does their general happiness, their marital satisfaction, and so forth. This is a very important finding, and it is paralleled by similar findings in other types of neurotic patients treated by other methods of behavior therapy.

Why does the treatment fail in certain cases? The answer seems to be that it fails for those patients who find the degree of fear and anxiety induced at the beginning of the treatment too painful to bear. In such cases it should be possible to prescribe tranquilizers or other drugs to reduce these extreme levels of discomfort, though one should emphasize that the disorder cannot be treated by medication.

There are other possible ways of dealing with this recalcitrant 10 or 15 percent of patients who do not respond well to response intervention treatment, but it is still too early to say whether any of these new methods will be successful. Meanwhile let us rejoice that a disorder previously impossible to treat has now yielded to psychological investigation and innovation and can be treated with great success in a very short time.

The value of animal psychology

Now, let us return to the objections to psychology quoted at the beginning of this chapter. What good does psychology do? Well, in this case at least it has enabled large numbers of people suffering from distressing mental disorders to receive treatment that restores them to a healthy and happy life; that is something of which we can be proud. We purposely chose only one example to illustrate this point; behavior therapy has had many similar success stories. Considering its triumphs and its extreme youth (the term itself was coined barely twenty years ago, and the movement itself is hardly older than that), we can expect many more advances in the future. So, it becomes increasingly difficult to argue that psychology is neither practical nor useful in this modern world.

What about the value of animal experiments? Again, our jumping dogs clearly demonstrate the importance of animal work in understanding some of the mechanisms which govern human behavior. They also suggested methods for changing and improving it. Work on response prevention in animals antedated the use of the technique on obsessive-compulsive patients. In retrospect, it is doubtful whether the technique would have been considered for use with humans without previous experience with animals. Indeed, would psychologists have had the courage to use it, in the face of acute dismay and discomfort on the part of their patients, had they not known from animal experiments how successful it could be? None of this proves, of course, that human beings are simply larger, more complicated versions of rats and

A dog trained to jump through hoops in response to a conditioned stimulus. Photo: Multimedia Publications Inc. (Israel Sun).

dogs—no psychologist would subscribe to such a view. What such a body of research demonstrates is that we share certain similarities with rats and dogs as far as our nervous system is concerned, and that it is possible to exploit these similarities. It does not follow that because there are certain mechanisms in rats and dogs, the same mechanisms are present in humans—it would be simple-minded to believe that, and animal psychologists are particularly wary of making such analogies. It is simply suggested that, where possible, similarities should be exploited and that before we try out new methods on human beings, we should try them out on animals. The methods which work with animals will not necessarily work with humans, but there are many procedures we would feel ethically compelled to reject in work with humans unless we could be sure, from experience with animals, that they stood a good chance of being successful. This is precisely the view taken by medical researchers testing new drugs or exploring new theories in physiology and neurology. It is difficult to see why psychologists should be expected to adopt a different attitude.

Last, we must face the question of the cruelty involved and the degree to which we are justified in using animals in experiments. This is not a scientific question but an ethical one and, as in most ethical problems, it is not a matter of black and white but of various shades of gray. There are rights and wrongs, advantages and disadvantages on both sides, but we believe that in cases like the one just described the relatively slight pain and discomfort suffered by the animals involved can be justified in terms of the ultimate benefit to human beings who are themselves suffering. Others may disagree. You, the reader, must decide for yourself. In matters like this there are no convenient or categorical answers.

Conclusions

In summary, then, we find that an apparently trivial experiment in animal psychology can have far-reaching consequences for human happiness and for the treatment of certain neurotic disorders hitherto considered untreatable. We also see that such experiments, particularly when applied to humans, have important theoretical consequences; they indicate that psychoanalytic theory is, in fact, mistaken about certain disorders and that simpler behavioristic accounts of neurotic illness are more likely to be correct. Finally, such experiments suggest that it may be wrong to condemn animal experiments as irrelevant to human behavior. We may yet learn a good deal from rats and dogs that will help us to understand and beneficially influence human learning and behavior.

We shall return to the uses of conditioning in Section E.

7

The chimp who grew up as a child

Some of the most interesting experiments in the history of psychology have concerned chimpanzees, our nearest animal relatives. Most investigators have focused on one big question: can chimpanzees acquire the skills of language? But there is an even larger question: do young chimpanzees have the potential to grow up and develop in the same way as human children? An ambitious recent study by Herbert Terrace of Columbia University examined the socialization of a young chimpanzee and the development of his personality over a period of four years, far longer than the experimental period required for any of the other experiments described in this book.

Why teach chimps to talk?

Before discussing Terrace's work in detail, let us consider some of the background. For example, why is it important to know whether chimpanzees can be taught language? The simplest reason is that we have a natural curiosity to explore the unknown, even when the cost is astronomically high (one has only to think of the manned landings on the moon). The idea that we might be able to communicate properly with another species, and so make contact with a point of view wholly outside our experience, is intrinsically fascinating.

A second good reason was expressed by Terrace: "The opportunity to observe how the addition of language, as we know it, would influence the culture of a group of chimpanzees might provide a priceless glimpse of what life was like at the dawn of human civilization."

Of all the primates, Homo sapiens *has the longest development period relative to gestation and lifespan. Photo: Multimedia Publications Inc. (Sergio Trippodo).*

A third reason for seeing whether chimpanzees can master language is that the success or otherwise of such an endeavor may help to resolve a bitter theoretical controversy about the human learning of language. The famous behaviorist B. F. Skinner claims that humans learn language in much the same way as rats learn to press a lever for food: any kind of behavior that is followed by reward or reinforcement will be repeated. If Skinner is right, then there is no obvious reason why chimpanzees should not learn language, provided their attempts at language are suitably rewarded.

There seems to be some merit to Skinner's point of view. When a human infant makes a sound that is recognizable as a word, or as an approximation of a word, the parents usually show their approval verbally ("Good girl!") or physically (hugs and kisses), presumably reinforcing the infant's behavior. However, when communication between a mother and her child during the first year of life is looked at closely, it turns out that the mother rewards virtually all of the baby's vocalizations, rather than just those which resemble adult speech.

There have been numerous critics of Skinner's position, most of whom claim that he has proposed a grossly oversimplified account of the learning of language. The psycholinguist Noam Chomsky has argued that the sheer variety of sentences that children produce and their ability to create new sentences cannot be explained by simplistic ideas about reinforcement. Chomsky contends that the human brain is "pre-wired" to make the various grammatical transformations that occur in any language; others have referred to this capacity to learn language as the "language acquisition device." The existence of such an innate capacity would certainly help to explain the remarkable ability children have to produce grammatically correct sentences many years before they have had any formal training in grammar.

A head for language

Some psychologists have argued that the ability to use this innate language acquisition device depends on the specialization which gradually develops in the two hemispheres of the brain. Normal children start to talk during their second year, after which their language skills improve rapidly until the age of five; thereafter, these skills develop more slowly until puberty. The development of brain specialization closely parallels the pattern of language learning. Brain specialization is virtually complete at puberty; until then children learn language easily, but thereafter it is difficult to learn a *second* language and the learner tends to speak it with a foreign accent. Before puberty, children readily learn to speak second languages perfectly.

Chomsky and his followers have assumed that the innate capacity to acquire language is found only in humans. Accordingly, since chimpanzees do not have the benefit of a language acquisition device, they should be out of their element when it comes to mastering language. So, on the question whether chimpanzees can learn language, Skinner's position tends toward an affirmative answer and Chomsky's toward a negative. Who is right?

There is no doubt that the earliest attempts to impart the rudiments of language to chimpanzees produced results favoring Chomsky: they were almost unmitigated failures. Keith and Katharine Hayes spent six years trying to teach a female chimpanzee called Vicki to speak English words. At the end of that time, Vicki could say only four words: "momma," "poppa," "up," and "cup." Her teachers had to push her lips and mouth into the correct positions at first, but she eventually learned to position her lips and mouth with her own hands to produce the sounds.

Why did this attempt fail? Undoubtedly part of the reason is that it is not at all natural for chimpanzees to make much use of their vocal cords. If they are left undisturbed, chimpanzees are usually silent. Furthermore, they are physically able to produce only about 12 distinct sounds (compared to about 100 for humans).

Chimp sign language

A major breakthrough occurred when Allen and Beatrice Gardner of the University of Nevada in Reno saw a silent presentation of a film made by Keith and Katharine Hayes. Even without the sound track, the Gardners were able to tell what Vicki was saying simply by watching the gestures that accompanied her sounds. This led them to wonder whether it might not be easier to use gestures than sounds, especially since chimpanzees in captivity spontaneously use a variety of begging and other gestures.

In June 1966 the Gardners began training a one-year-old female chimpanzee. They called her Washoe after the name of the county in Nevada where they lived. Washoe demonstrated the proverbial imitativeness of apes in many ways. For example, during the tenth month of the study she bathed one of her dolls in the way the Gardners usually bathed her. She filled her little bathtub with water, dunked the doll in the tub, then took it out and patted it dry with a towel.

This capacity for imitation was extremely useful when it came to teaching Washoe the American Sign Language, a gesture-based language often learned by deaf people. She managed to learn 4 signs or words during the first seven months of teaching, 9 more in the following seven months, and 21 in the next seven-month period. After three and a half years, Washoe had learned to express a total of 132 words, and the Gardners estimated that she understood about three times as many signs as she could express. She was also able to combine words in sensible ways.

There have been some other notable studies. David Premack of the University of California invented an artificial language using plastic chips. He was so successful with his "star" chimpanzee, Sarah, that she was eventually able to manipulate the chips to produce a complicated sequence such as "Mary give apple Sarah."

It is tempting to argue that work done over the past ten years or so has demonstrated convincingly that chimpanzees can learn language, and many people have been so tempted. However, as the work of Terrace shows, this may have been a too hasty judgment.

Key experiment   Project Nim (Herbert Terrace)

When he first met the male chimpanzee he intended to train, Herbert Terrace was a 37-year-old bachelor teaching at Columbia University. It

Nim using and reacting to sign language. His face has the typical chimp curious/interested expression in all except the third picture. In this picture Nim's face expresses excitement, unlike the cat, which looks distinctly uncomfortable. Photos: H. S. Terrace, Columbia University.

was December 2, 1973, and the chimpanzee was just two weeks old. Terrace decided to call him Nim Chimpsky (a pun on Noam Chomsky). In contrast to the key experiments discussed in other chapters, this one lasted nonstop for nearly four years.[1]

Terrace felt that chimpanzees in other studies had too often been brought up in a relatively sterile and unsocial environment. As a result, the main motivation such chimpanzees had for using language was to obtain food and water. Terrace was determined that Nim Chimpsky would be brought up in an environment resembling the loving and sociable atmosphere surrounding a human child. This approach had the advantage that language on Nim's part would develop as a result of social interactions, exactly as happens with human children. So it would also be possible to study the social development of Nim as well as his linguistic progress.

Terrace was by no means convinced that chimpanzees had really acquired language in the way claimed by earlier investigators. He felt that what the chimpanzees had learned could often be dismissed as unnatural tricks. You can teach pigeons to peck at discs of different colors in a certain order to obtain food (for example, they might peck at the discs in the order white, red, blue, and green), but no one would regard that as evidence that pigeons can construct sentences. Nor would it prove anything if we superimposed the word "please" on the white disc, "teacher" on the red disc, "give" on the blue disc, and "food" on the green disc, and the pigeon "spoke" to us by pecking in the right order: "Please teacher give food." Terrace hoped that this sort of problem could be obviated by resisting any temptation to teach Nim language as if it were a party trick. Language learning was to be part of socialization.

The story of Terrace's experiment with Nim really divides up into two parts: Nim's general social development and, more specifically, his acquisition of language.

The socialization of Nim

Nim Chimpsky was the son of Pan and Carolyn, who were regarded as the most intelligent and stable animals in a chimpanzee colony in Oklahoma. He spent most of the first eighteen months of his life in the large house owned by W. E. R. and Stephanie LaFarge. Their New York household consisted of Stephanie, her second husband, W.E.R., three children from her previous marriage, W.E.R.'s four children from an earlier marriage, and a schoolteacher friend of the family.

During his first four months in the LaFarge house, Nim slept for 15–18 hours a day at the foot of Stephanie and W.E.R.'s bed. Just like a human infant, he had his diapers changed every few hours, was burped after feeding, tossed in the air, hugged, and held protectively by each of his caretakers.

Nim was even more childlike than a child in many ways. His emotional reactions, for example, seemed to be much stronger than those of a child, especially when he realized that one of his caretakers was unhappy. On one occasion when Jennie (one of the children in the household) was crying, Nim leaped into her arms and stared intently into her eyes. He then touched her cheeks very gently and tried to wipe away her tears.

Sometimes the way in which Nim reacted to W.E.R. was strangely reminiscent of the Oedipus complex. One afternoon when Stephanie and W.E.R. were taking a nap, W.E.R. reached over to put his arm around Stephanie. In an instant, Nim stood up and bit him. (It has often been observed in chimpanzee colonies that an infant male chimpanzee will attack his father when he copulates with his mother.)

Nim's development was in certain respects more rapid than that of human children. He could crawl by the end of his second month, and stand a month later if he had something to grasp. By the time he was twenty months old, he was toilet-trained, and would regularly use his potty.

His behavior at bedtime was fairly similar to that of a human child. When he started to sleep on his own during his fifth month, he screamed or whimpered for a few minutes when put to bed; however, letting him hold on to a bottle or a pacifier was usually all that was needed to calm him down.

When Nim was almost a year old, he started using four rooms at Columbia University as both a nursery school and a day-care center, returning to the LaFarges' at night. He was so mobile and energetic that the rooms had to be thoroughly chimp-proofed to prevent him from escaping. Initially, his teachers tried using a chain lock together with a dead-bolt lock, which Nim managed to open. After that they tried spring-loaded hooks which required considerable dexterity to open. Nim still managed to escape occasionally into the main part of the psychology department. (Contrary to popular belief, it was actually quite easy to pick Nim out from among the psychologists.)

A common source of worry, and disagreement, among Nim's teachers and caretakers was how Nim should be disciplined when he did antisocial things like biting and snarling. Should he be put in a small, dark room for a while when he was naughty? Should he simply be ignored? When one caretaker suggested a particular form of discipline, one of the others would usually say, "You can't do that to *my* chimp!"

Moments from the loving, companionable teacher-pupil relationship which Laura Petitto established with Nim. Photos: Susan Kuklin.

Eventually Nim's teachers and caretakers discovered that the most effective way of disciplining him was to walk away from him while indicating "you bad" or "I not love you" in American Sign Language. His typical reaction to this was immediately to stop what he was doing and run quickly to his caretaker, signing "hug" or "sorry."

By June 1975 Nim had become so boisterous and difficult to manage that it became necessary to move him from the LaFarge house. Among other things, he had broken several valuable objects as a result of his ability to jump on any piece of furniture or hang from the light fixtures. Fortunately, Columbia University owned a twenty-one-room mansion, Delafield, half of which they rented inexpensively to Terrace. There Nim was allocated five rooms for his exclusive use.

While he was at Delafield, Nim often behaved in the mischievous way that young children do. On one occasion, he had heard Carol (one of his teachers) preparing a bowl of cereal for his lunch in the nearby observation room just before she left. A few minutes later his next teacher, Laura Petitto, left him on the diaper-changing table on his own while she went into the classroom to prepare for his next activity. When she went into the observation room to collect the bowl of cereal for him, it was missing. Nim was still lying on the diaper-changing table, but with an exaggerated expression of innocence. She looked severe and signed "where bowl?" Nim merely looked puzzled and looked around as though he was trying to help her find the bowl. It was only when Laura threatened to hit him that Nim finally took her hand and led her to the sink beside the changing table. In the bottom of it was the half-finished bowl of cereal.

He also behaved in an amusingly childish way when Susan Quinby, another of his teachers, brought her cat in. He offered a spoonful of yogurt to the cat and was amazed when the cat licked the spoon clean. The next time he deliberately offered the cat an empty spoon. After that, he filled the spoon up with yogurt and fed himself.

Nim believed in joining in most of the household chores and other activities going on around him. He was particularly eager to help in the preparation of his own meals and showed great patience and care in mixing and stirring ingredients. Another chore which he relished was doing the dishes; he had a very intense look on his face as he dabbed with a sponge. If for some reason he was excluded from kitchen activities, he would retaliate by opening drawers and cupboards and throwing out their contents, or he would turn on the taps or knock over the garbage pail.

One hundred years ago Charles Darwin suggested that a chimpanzee's expressions of emotions such as joy, anger, affection, and curiosity all possess a distinctly human-like character. Nim's behavior cer-

"Oh, I do like to be beside the sinkside." Nim was a keen washer-upper. Photo: H. S. Terrace, Columbia University.

tainly confirmed Darwin's observations, except perhaps that Nim's emotions were expressed more directly and intensely than those of a human. If he had not seen someone he liked for a long time, he would greet that person with screeches of delight, smiling, pounding the ground with joy, hugging, kissing, and grooming.

A rather less attractive side of Nim's character was that he would try to establish dominance over people if at all possible. When a new teacher met Nim for the first time, Nim would put him or her to a severe test in order to gain the ascendancy. His unprovoked outbursts of aggression in these first meetings occurred with such speed and ferocity that new teachers often ended up scratched and bitten and with their clothes torn.

More surprising than Nim's ability to express emotional experiences was his great ability to see through people's attempts to disguise their emotions. Laura, perhaps the best of Nim's teachers, summed it up when she described the important aspects of a successful relationship with Nim: "It was more than just being relaxed. Nim had an uncanny ability to read one's feelings. I always felt that I had to be honest because he understood me . . . he made me feel as if I was 'naked.' "

Language training

Psychologists who have attempted to teach language to members of other species have focused primarily on chimpanzees. This is mainly because the personality of a chimpanzee resembles that of a human, which presumably makes communication easier. The importance of this became clear during Terrace's experiment, with Nim using sign language most freely with those he knew and liked best. The other major reason, of course, is that, among the primates, the chimpanzee's brain is closest in complexity and relative weight to that of man.

Teaching American Sign Language to Nim turned out to be much more difficult than Terrace had expected. (A constant shortage of funds to pay for the large number of people needed to look after Nim 24 hours a day, 365 days a year, meant that there was a rapid turnover in volunteer helpers to supplement the professionals. Nim was taught by sixty different teachers in only forty-six months; obviously such inconsistent relationships did not help.) This, for example, is how he learned the sign for "tea." Laura, his teacher, got Nim to pay attention as she poured hot water into a cup containing a tea bag. Then she molded his hands into the sign for "tea" and encouraged him to take a sip. After this, Nim offered his hands to Laura so that she could form his fingers into the appropriate sign. Next Nim tried to mold Laura's hands to make the sign for "tea." When he had achieved this, Laura responded by giving him the cup of tea that he wanted.

After this training, Nim gradually started making the sign for "tea" when his teacher made the sign in conversation; finally, he would make the sign upon seeing the teacup. Learning was still not quite complete, however. Just as a young child will often say "doggie" to a wide range

Nim offering a spoonful of yogurt to Susan Quinby's cat. Photo: H. S. Terrace, Columbia University.

of animals and objects, so Nim would sometimes overgeneralize (e.g., signing "play me tea" while playing a game of chase).

In at least one respect, Nim managed to show greater linguistic versatility than his human teachers. Terrace tickled Nim when he was holding on to the branch of a tree with both hands. Nim immediately thought of an easy way to indicate that he wanted the tickling to continue: he signed both "more" and "tickle" with his bare feet.

One very human skill that Nim acquired as his language powers developed was the ability to lie. He had obviously noticed that his teachers were very responsive when he signed either "dirty" (meaning he needed to go to the toilet) or "sleep" (meaning he was tired). He gradually started using these signs when they were obviously inappropriate, presumably because he was bored and wanted a change.

Nim mastered his first sign ("drink") at four months, and this was quickly followed by four more signs ("up," "sweet," "give," and "more"). It is interesting to note that there are several reports of deaf children learning their first sign by the age of four months. Words can be signed much earlier than they can be vocalized, probably because the muscular coordination required for sounds is much subtler.

In all, Nim learned to express 125 signs during his first 44 months, and he could probably understand more than 200 signs. His progress was very erratic and depended greatly on the skills of individual teachers and the rapport they had with him. Under Laura Petitto's expert guidance Nim managed to learn five signs a month, more than twice as many as before her arrival.

In the summer of 1975, under Laura's supervision, Nim started to produce several two-sign combinations, including "more eat," "tickle me," and "give apple." By the summer of 1976 he was signing combinations of three or more signs (e.g., "me more eat," "you tickle me," and "me brush baby"). As time went by, he started using the words available to him more and more. Between June 1, 1975, and February 13, 1977, Nim's teachers observed him signing over 19,000 utterances consisting of two or more signs. This huge total was not achieved by mere repetition of a handful of combinations: Nim produced 5,235 distinctly different combinations. The sheer variety of his sign combinations suggests very strongly that Nim was not simply memorizing them in rote fashion. Unfortunately it was not possible to see how far Nim's learning might have gone. Because of financial and other problems Terrace was forced to return Nim to the Institute for Primate Studies in Norman, Oklahoma, toward the end of 1977.

It could be argued that Nim was combining the signs which he knew in a more or less haphazard fashion. However, that was not the case. Consider a two-sign combination consisting of a transitive verb and "me" or "Nim." Was Nim just as likely to sign "tickle me" as "me tickle," or "tickle Nim" as "Nim tickle"? Not at all: he signed with "tickle" first on 107 occasions and with "me" or "Nim" first on 16 occasions. In other words, he chose the verb-first order 87 percent of the time. Overall, the verb was placed first 83 percent of the time by Nim when combining a transitive verb and "me" or "Nim." Several other analyses confirmed that there was a definite structure to Nim's utterances, just as there is with human utterances.

There was another important similarity between Nim's utterances and those of children. When children are at the stage of starting to produce two-word combinations, some 80 percent of these utterances can be interpreted as belonging to eight semantic categories. Two of these categories are object + beneficiary (e.g., "food Nim") and action + object (e.g., "eat grape"). When Terrace performed the same analysis on Nim's utterances, he discovered that 84 percent of his two-sign combinations fitted these semantic categories.

The evidence discussed so far suggests that Nim developed language in much the same way as a human child. However, there were some important differences. Videotapes of communications between Nim and his teachers were played in slow motion, so that it was possible to see exactly when Nim began an utterance in relation to the utterance of his teacher. Although his teachers had not been fully aware of it, Nim interrupted them much more frequently than a normal child interrupts its parents. It appeared that Nim was much more interested in telling his teachers what he wanted them to do than he was in what they were saying to him.

It has been found that less than 20 percent of a normal child's utterances consist of imitations of its parents' utterances, and about 30 percent of what a child says is spontaneous and not merely a response to an adult. Even after several years of language learning, 40 percent of Nim's utterances were fairly exact imitations of what had been said to him, and only 10 percent of his signings were spontaneous. Thus Nim used language in a less creative and innovative way than a child.

The most important of Terrace's findings casts still greater doubt on the comparability of the language skills of Nim and of a child. Children with normal hearing start by producing utterances containing an average of about 1½ words, but rapidly escalate to an average of 4 words or more per utterance (sometimes by the age of 26 months). Deaf children show the same escalation in the number of signs per utterance, but usually a little later than normal children. In striking contrast, the average length of Nim's utterances remained remarkably constant at about 1½ signs between the ages of 26 and 46 months.

Another major difference between Nim and children is that children's longer utterances usually communicate much more meaning than their shorter ones. Nim's did not, as can be seen in his longest utterance of all: "Give orange me give eat orange me eat orange give me eat orange give me you." A comparison of Nim's two- and three-sign combinations revealed that his three-sign combinations added practically nothing (other than emphasis) to his two-sign combinations; his most frequent three-sign utterances included "play me Nim," "hug Nim hug," "play me play," and "eat me eat."

If one compares learning a language to climbing a ladder, it looks as if chimpanzees are quite adept at climbing the first few rungs. After that, though, they seem to come to an almost complete stop. They may learn more words, but they do not improve their ability to combine these words into longer, more sentence-like forms. It is tempting to regard the chimpanzee's lack of a language acquisition device or something similar as the insuperable barrier to climbing further up the linguistic ladder. If so, Nim Chimpsky may have been well named, since he seems to have confirmed the views of his namesake, Noam Chomsky. On the other hand, chimpanzees have certainly been taught more about language than seemed remotely possible fifteen years ago, so perhaps any dogmatic conclusions are premature.

Conclusions

The social and emotional development of Nim Chimpsky was remarkably similar in many ways to that of a human child. Indeed, his emotional reactions were often simply stronger and more extreme versions of human emotions. He behaved in the mischievous and boisterous way familiar to untold generations of human parents.

Nim Chimpsky was very proficient at learning signs and expressing himself in a limited way, and there is a natural inclination to regard his very real achievements as revealing a mastery of language skills. However, more careful analysis suggests that there is perhaps less here than meets the eye.

8

All you need is love

Love is not an easy field of research. Poets, philosophers, and most ordinary men and women regard love as the most interesting and important of all the emotions, but psychologists have tended to give it a fairly wide berth. It is difficult to induce instant feelings of love in the sterile surroundings of the typical psychological research laboratory, but feelings of fear are quite easy to generate if one straps electrodes to people and threatens them with electric shocks. The paucity of psychological research on the nature of love led the American psychologist Harry Harlow to the following pessimistic conclusion: "The little we know about love does not transcend simple observations, and the little we write about it has been written better by poets and novelists."

In our view Harlow was being too modest about his own important discoveries concerning the nature of love. Indeed, his researches on love among rhesus monkeys appear to have major implications for the development of love in humans.

Key experiment   Love between mothers and babies (Harry Harlow)

Harry Harlow of the University of Wisconsin spent several years looking at the ways in which monkeys learn to solve various difficult problems. During the course of this work, he noticed that many of the baby monkeys reared in the laboratory showed great attachment to the cloth pads used to cover the floors of their cages. The infants clung to these pads, and displayed violent temper tantrums when the pads were removed for sanitary reasons. Now, human infants display much the same devotion toward cuddly toys and other soft objects.

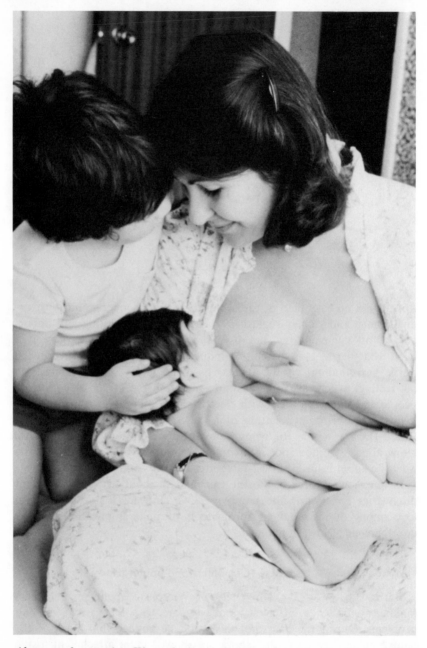

Above and opposite: Warmth, comfort, nourishment—the best possible start in life and the foundation of all future attachments. Photos: Multimedia Publications Inc. (Miki Koren).

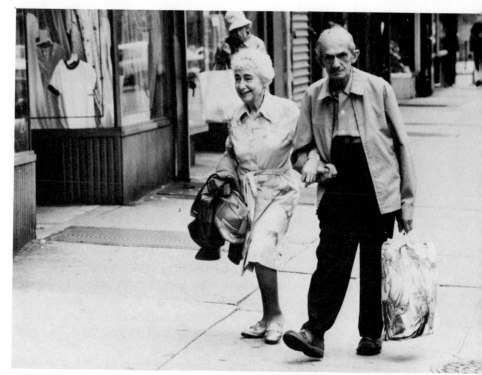

Harlow began to suspect that the obvious pleasure his baby monkeys derived from clinging to cloth pads might explain a major part of a baby's love for its mother: the mother, after all, usually spends many hours a day clutching her baby tightly.[1]

All kinds of reasons have been put forward to explain a baby's love for its mother. Some of the early American behavorists argued that a baby's attachment to its mother is due to the fact that she satisfies its need for food. Psychoanalysts from Freud onward have stressed the overwhelming importance of the breast.

Accordingly, Harlow devised an ingenious way of testing the ideas of the breast fanciers against his own notion that infant monkeys derive more comfort from contact with something soft (and warm). Two substitute monkey mothers were created. One, the "cloth mother," had a perfectly proportioned and streamlined monkey body made of wood, but she was covered with rubber and sheathed in tan cotton toweling, which made her soft to touch; a light bulb behind her radiated heat, which made her warm. The other "mother" was similar but was made of wire mesh and lacked "contact comfort." Both "mothers" had "breasts."

Infant monkeys were separated from their natural mothers shortly after birth and put in a room with the cloth mother and the wire mother. For some of the monkeys, only the cloth mother's breast provided milk; the rest could get their milk only from the wire mother. Which substitute mother did they prefer? Overwhelmingly, the softer cloth mother, which offered them contact comfort. On average they spent 18 hours a day cuddling against her compared with less than 2 hours a day against the wire mother. But the real surprise was that the results were almost exactly the same even for the group which could get milk only from the wire mother: these monkeys also spent most of the day against the cloth mother. In other words, infant monkeys do not love from hunger, rather they hunger for love.

Early critics of Harlow's work raised various objections to the validity of this experiment. Some argued that monkeys dislike wire. Others claimed that different substances might have proved more comforting than toweling. Harlow refuted the first set of critics by pointing out that baby monkeys spend a lot of time climbing up the sides of their wire cages and exploring the wire with their mouths and hands. The preference which small monkeys have for toweling was further demonstrated by showing that they chose to spend much more time on a cloth-covered mother than on mothers covered with rayon, vinyl, or rough-grade sandpaper.

Other critics wondered whether Harlow's observations had any real implications for love at the human level.[2] Harlow certainly set out to shed light on human needs for contact and affection. As he pointed out, "The only reason for using monkeys rather than rats is that the data will generalize better to man." Even so, monkeys are not human beings.

The most serious objection to Harlow's early work in this area was that it seemed to suggest that infant monkeys love their mothers only because of the contact comfort they provide. Harlow responded to this charge of oversimplification by constructing still more substitute mothers. He found that a very important factor, especially during the first two weeks of the monkey's life, was the warmth of the mother: infants really were "turned off" by substitute mothers with icy water in their veins. They also preferred mothers that rocked backward and forward to mothers that remained stationary.

In later studies, Harlow set out to investigate just how strongly his monkey infants became attached to their substitute mothers. He did this by creating four "monster mothers," all covered with toweling. One gave the infants occasional blasts of compressed air; the second shook so violently that the infants were often shaken off; the third contained a catapult that frequently flung the infants away from it; and the fourth was an "iron maiden" which had a set of metal spikes which poked through the fabric from time to time.

Naturally enough, the baby monkeys showed signs of emotional disturbance on first experiencing the unpleasant characteristics of each "monster mother." But as soon as the mothers returned to normal, the infants speedily went back to them and acted as if all were forgiven. Indeed, Harlow claims that it was only the people carrying out the experiment who experienced stress.

Harlow subsequently discovered other ways in which cloth mothers appear to be a substitute for the real mother. When baby monkeys were placed in strange surroundings littered with numerous objects (boxes, cups) known to be of interest to monkeys, they used their cloth mother as a base of operations, exploring their environment a little and then returning to her for security. When the cloth mother was absent, the infants would often freeze in a crouched position; some of them would run toward the middle of the room, where the mother was usually placed, and then rush quickly from object to object, crying and screeching.

Do infant monkeys really display the same kind of love for cloth mothers as they do for their real mothers? Here is Harlow's considered answer to that question after twenty years' study and observation: "Love for the real mother and love for the surrogate mother appear to be very similar. . . . As far as we can observe, the infant monkey's affection for the real mother is strong, but no stronger than that of the experimental monkey for the surrogate cloth mother, and the security that the infant gains from the presence of the real mother is no greater than the security it gains from a cloth surrogate."

One of the first things a human mother notices about her baby is that it often stares intently at her face. Harlow decided to find out how important facial characteristics were to baby monkeys. One infant was given a substitute cloth mother which had a featureless round wooden ball for a head. The baby reacted enthusiastically to this mother substitute—which suggests that even a face that would stop a clock doesn't stop a baby from loving its mother.

By the time the baby monkey, a female, had reached three months of age, the researchers had prepared a more monkey-like cloth-mother face. They proudly put it in place, but the baby took one look and screamed. She remained terrified for the next few days, then she had a brainstorm: she simply revolved the head through 180 degrees, so that she could once again look at a featureless face. When the experimenters put the head back in its proper position, the infant once again rotated the head so that the face was not visible. Shortly after that she lifted the head from the body, rolled it into a corner, and abandoned it.

To paraphrase Harlow's interpretation of this incident, a baby is capable of loving a faceless mother, but not a two-faced one.

Harlow's work with cloth and wire monkeys became very well known and was frequently discussed during the 1960s. While Harlow welcomed the publicity, he was not entirely happy at the way things were developing. His doubts were strengthened when an eminent psychologist and a leading psychiatrist independently made the same comment to him within a single month. What they both said was: "You know, Harry, you are going to go down in the history of psychology as the father of the cloth mother!" Not relishing that fate, Harlow began to consider other facets of love, starting with maternal deprivation and its implications.

Maternal deprivation

It may seem paradoxical, but the easiest way to study love is to look at what happens when love is missing. Prove that lack of love has serious consequences and you have proved that love is important. The vital importance of a mother's love is only too obvious in cases of "maternal deprivation," in which the baby is separated from its mother during some or all of the early stages of its development.

The effects of maternal deprivation were studied some thirty years ago by the British psychologist John Bowlby, who was asked by the World Health Organization to prepare a report on the mental health of homeless children. This was part of a study carried out by the Social Commission of the United Nations on the special needs of children separated from their families and placed in foster homes or institutions. Bowlby concluded that maternal deprivation is liable to have unfortunate consequences, including juvenile delinquency and psychopathy.

Unfortunately for Bowlby, other workers have not been able to replicate his findings, and he has been obliged to modify his views. There is now general agreement that it is not a mother that is needed so much as personal contact of a positive kind with a caretaker or peer group.

Among the primates, Harry Harlow was able to show that there are far-reaching consequences when baby monkeys are not allowed to see or interact with other monkeys for the first few months of life. When a number of monkeys isolated in this way were brought together, they reacted very aggressively. Many of them acted somewhat like patients in a mental hospital. For example, they would freeze into bizarre postures, make apparently purposeless repetitive movements, or simply stare into space for hours on end.

Harlow discovered that another major consequence of early isolation

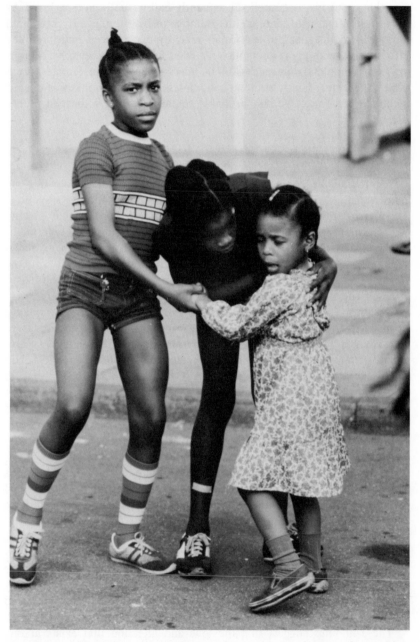

Comfort and attention from siblings: for some a substitute for mother love, for others just a lucky bonus. Photo: Multimedia Publications Inc. (Israel Sun).

was that monkeys so treated subsequently had virtually no sex lives. As part of an attempt to increase the number of his monkeys by breeding, he and his colleagues put a normal, sexually experienced male monkey into an area with some previously isolated female monkeys. This monkey was completely unsuccessful in making any of the females pregnant. As Harlow neatly summarized: unless a female monkey is chased when she is young, she will probably remain chaste for the rest of her life.

Socializing isolates

What could be done to help monkeys reared in isolation to become more sociable? The fact that normally reared young monkeys spend a lot of time playing with one another suggested to Harlow that placing isolated monkeys with normally reared monkeys of the same age might be beneficial. In the event, the results were disastrous. The isolated monkeys simply froze with fear and scarcely interacted at all with the normal monkeys. They spent most of their time engaged in self-clasping, self-chewing, and huddling in a corner.

Obviously, a major problem was the fear which the normal monkeys aroused in the isolates. One way of getting around the problem is to put isolates into the company of normally reared monkeys several months younger than they are. It appears that isolated monkeys can only learn adequate social behavior if they are initially exposed to monkeys possessing simpler social abilities, i.e., younger monkeys. In other words, the difference between the social skills of the isolates and those they are required to mix with must not be too great.

Melinda Novak, one of Harlow's research associates, has recently been able to demonstrate almost complete social rehabilitation in monkeys isolated for the first twelve months of life. This is a tremendous achievement. Until quite recently it was believed that the substantial social disadvantages produced by long-term isolation in infancy were irreversible.

Novak used monkey "therapists" who were less than one-third the age of the isolated monkeys, and was rewarded by the gradual disappearance of undesirable, maladaptive behavior on the part of the previously isolated monkeys, combined with a slow increase in play and social contact. But almost two years of hard work was needed to complete the transformation.

These findings suggest that the love and affection that exists among monkeys (or people) of similar age may be a more potent force for good than has been generally realized. While mother love may be the ideal, love between age-mates may be a reasonable substitute.

Many theorists from Freud onward have argued that appropriate stimulation in early life is essential for normal development; this is the "critical period hypothesis." Novak's data seem to disprove this hypothesis, at least for monkeys. Optimistically, it may suggest that human beings are also more resilient than Freud and his successors allow.

The maternal instinct

The spontaneous delight which most human mothers take in caring for the needs of their offspring has suggested to many psychologists the existence of an innate "maternal instinct." On the face of it this would seem to explain the months and years of selfless devotion which mothers give to their children, but there are various difficulties with the notion that all women possess a maternal instinct.

In the first place, it has been fairly conclusively demonstrated that humans have much weaker instincts of all kinds than other species. More tellingly, the worryingly high incidence of child abuse is difficult to reconcile with the concept of maternal instinct. Serapio Zalba, writing in the journal *Trans-action* in 1971, estimated that every year in the United States alone approximately 250,000 children suffer some form of physical abuse from their parents. Of these, something like 40,000 receive serious injuries. Zalba stated that most physically aggressive parents had themselves been neglected and abused as children, as a result of either "bad environment," "bad heredity," or a combination of the two.

Here, too, Harlow's work sheds interesting light. His plan was to observe mothering behavior in female monkeys brought up for the first few months of life in isolation. The difficulty was that these monkeys were sexually unaware, and it proved virtually impossible to turn them into mothers by simply letting nature take its course. In desperation, Harlow and his team of researchers created a device, affectionately known as the "rape rack," in which they could be strapped down. This had the desired effect.

What happened when these isolated females gave birth to their first baby? Typically they ignored it. Only if the infant was very persistent would they occasionally provide it with some of the contact comfort it demanded. Indeed, from the fourth month onward, some of the firstborn infants of these "motherless mothers" were actually punished less than the babies of normal mothers and allowed more contact with the mother's nipples. When such mothers had a second baby, they tended to look after it fairly adequately.

But things did not always work out so smoothly. A few of the motherless mothers trod on their babies, or crushed their infant's face into the floor of the cage. On one or two occasions, the experimenters did not react fast enough to prevent a mother from chewing off her baby's foot or fingers. The most terrible mother of all popped her baby's head into her mouth and crunched it up like a potato chip.

Indeed, Harlow's observations seem to suggest that the notion of a universal maternal instinct may be erroneous. Many monkey mothers (and probably human mothers too) who have not been brought up in a normal loving relationship with their own mothers give every appearance of lacking any maternal instinct.

The paternal instinct

Harlow has also looked at the role of the father. In all of the monkey families he studied, the father was unquestionably the dominant individual, maintaining his status without using physical force, unless one counts pseudo-slaps and nips, chasing, and the occasional threatening gesture.

In humans, fathers tend to be preferred to mothers as playmates by babies as young as eight months of age, and this preference is maintained through the second year of life. Exactly the same is true of rhesus monkeys brought up in captivity. Adult male monkeys indicate their readiness to play with their own or other monkeys' children by making a special signal: a dazed and glazed mesmerizing stare accompanied by a casual flip of the ear. Among the infants, little boy monkeys are content to play with any adult male, but daughters are more particular and prefer to play with daddy.

A recent study of free-ranging rhesus monkeys in the Katmandu Valley, Nepal, revealed that wild male monkeys are less inclined than captive male monkeys to help in the care of infants. During an exhausting 1,500 hours of field observations, there were only a miserly eighteen cases of pleasant interactions between an adult male and an infant. Eleven of these were brief play or grooming encounters, and only seven were more extended cases of male parental care. There were three times as many aggressive enounters, most of them involving mild slaps and swipes.

The most dramatic incident observed concerned a dominant adult male called Spock and the day-old infant of a mother who had died. At first, Spock cared for the infant in a remarkably gentle way, but he became irritated when the infant began to squirm and cry. On a number of occasions, the poor infant was held upside down or carried in the crook of Spock's arm while he ran to watch a fight. Unfortunately for the infant, Spock did not seem to realize that it needed food, and it died of starvation. The ineptitude of this large adult male was further shown by his apparent failure to grasp the fact that the baby had died. For many hours after its death he continued to groom it and carry it around with him.

Harlow found that there are important sex differences among monkeys in reactions to baby monkeys even before adulthood is reached. When pre-adolescent female monkeys were introduced to baby monkeys, they immediately behaved in a loving manner; by contrast, pre-adolescent males were either indifferent to the babies or even mildly abusive.

Does the general inattention and indifference of the adult male monkey to his own offspring equate with the "natural" reaction of the human father to his children? While there are great dangers in pushing the analogy too far, it is obviously true that many fathers chose to devote much of their leisure time to activities not connected with their families.

Many feminists have attacked Harlow's work because it seems to imply that human infants only thrive if they are looked after by full-time mothers. Harlow remains impervious to their accusations. In an interview with Carol Tavris in *Psychology Today,* he reacted to these attacks by saying, "Man is the only animal capable of speaking, and woman is the only animal incapable of not speaking."

Conclusions

Harry Harlow has spent more than twenty years investigating the importance of the phenomenon we call love in rhesus monkeys. His main strategy has been to look at the effects of removing different aspects of the normal loving environment in which baby monkeys develop. The first great success of this strategy was in identifying contact comfort as the most important contribution of the mother to the baby's well-being.

Harlow later found that maternal deprivation seriously affected the ability of young monkeys to mate or socialize successfully, and the same is true of humans. But he also discovered that love and attention from younger age-mates may eventually overcome the bad effects of the maternal deprivation.

The love of a mother for her child is something we take for granted, but is this "maternal instinct" universal, and is it quite as innate as we assume? Apparently it isn't, as Harlow very effectively demonstrated in his work with monkeys. Nevertheless, it appears that female adults usually make better mothers than male adults.

SECTION C

Brains, behavior, and biology

Psychologists are usually interested primarily in the way people behave, and they often use behavioral data to make informed guesses about what goes on inside people.

Let us consider an extremely simple example of such guesswork. Take someone who manages to remember word lists or nonsense syllables over a long period of time. It is tempting to assume that somewhere in that person's brain there are actual traces corresponding to the remembered information. Such an assumption is plausible, but it is inferred from behavior, not from direct observation of the memory traces themselves.

In that case, you may well feel inclined to ask, why not use some of the fruits of the technological revolution to probe inside the brain for better evidence? This is a reasonable question, and many physiologists have embarked on brain exploration in the hope of unraveling some of the mysteries of memory. Since there are an almost incalculable number of cells in the brain and many millions of pieces of information stored in them, the task of locating the particular memory trace one is looking for is rather more daunting than looking for a needle in a haystack. Even the notion that each item of remembered information is stored in a particular part of the brain seems far from certain; it is possible to receive severe damage to large areas of the brain yet suffer little impairment of memory.

The differences between the psychological and physiological approaches to man can be clarified by an analogy. Suppose a psychologist and physiologist who have never seen a car before are asked to try to

Video games are one way of measuring visual and motor coordination. Photo: Multimedia Publications Inc. (Miki Koren).

understand how it functions. The psychologist focuses on the speed of the car, its road handling, its reliability, its fuel consumption, and so on. He then uses this information to speculate on the processes and mechanisms inside it (i.e., engine, battery, gears, steering, etc.).

The physiologist, however, concentrates on the inside of the car, perhaps discovering a large black box (the battery) and paying minute attention to the lettering on the side of it. He has the difficult task of trying to decide which parts of the car do what and how they are interrelated.

This analogy shows that the psychologist looks at things from the outside and makes guesses about what is happening inside; the physiologist is more concerned with probing inside and trying to make mechanical sense of the things he sees.

Ideally, the approach of the psychologist and the physiologist should be complementary, and this is increasingly the case. Indeed, there is a new breed of scientists called "psychophysiologists" who attempt to use physiology to clarify psychological findings and vice versa.

In this section we consider research that has successfully integrated information from both physiological and psychological sources. Recent work on intelligence (Chapter 9) is a prime example of this multidisciplinary approach. Ever since Alfred Binet (at the request of the French Ministry of Education), devised the first standardized test of intelligence in the early years of this century, psychologists have been interested in the marked differences that exist between human beings when it comes to intellectual ability.

As a result of their endeavors, psychologists have learned a lot about the major factors which determine intelligence, the importance of heredity in determining intellectual potential, and so on. Despite these findings, the question "Is intelligence a meaningful concept?" continues to be asked. We contend that it is and that most of the savage criticism directed at intelligence tests is either misplaced, ill-informed, or prompted by prejudice. Having said that, one is forced to admit that we still have a lot to learn about the workings of intelligence. Until quite recently, for instance, we knew practically nothing about the marked differences in brain activity between people of varying intelligence. This gap in our knowledge is now being filled by the extremely exciting work of Allan and Elaine Hendrickson at the Institute of Psychiatry in London.

The Hendricksons discovered that people of varying levels of intelligence show very different patterns of brain-wave activity in response to simple sounds. There is the exciting prospect that we may be on the threshold of locating the physiological basis of intelligence. Furthermore, the physiological measurement of intelligence has one overwhelming advantage over conventional intelligence tests: it cannot be accused of being culturally biased (i.e., of favoring white middle-class groups).

Chapter 10 explores the roots of personality. There are two main ways of examining the biological basis of personality. The first is to examine personality similarities in identical and non-identical twins, the basic assumption being that the more similar identical twins are, as compared with non-identical twins, the greater the influence of heredity. Broadly speaking, the evidence suggests that individual differences in personality have more to do with heredity than is generally realized.

The alternative method of investigating personality is the physiological one. There are various recording techniques (measuring brain-wave activity, galvanic skin response, and heart rate, for example) which can be used to demonstrate that there are wide variations in physiological activity between one individual and another. H. J. Eysenck has used information obtained from twin research and physiological studies to propose a theory of the biological basis of personality.

There are, of course, much more drastic and dramatic ways of exploring the inner workings of the body. Parts of the brain can be

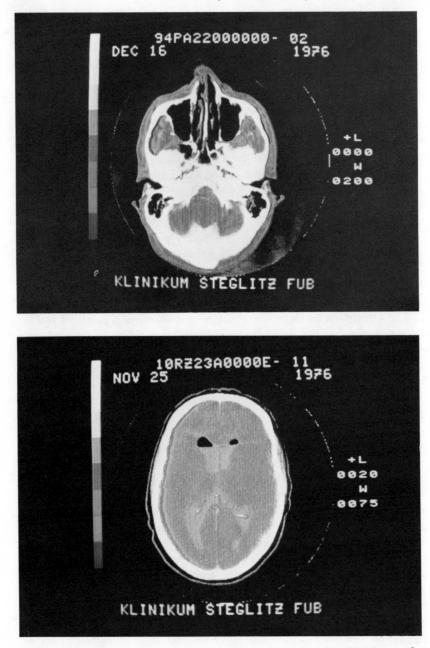

Sections through the brain mapped by laser scanner. As scanning techniques improve, more and more of the physiological secrets of the brain are revealed.

severed, isolated, or removed, for example. Not surprisingly, this usually has a considerable effect on behavior. Nor is it surprising, in view of the great complexity of the brain, that "psychosurgery," as it is called, often fails to work as intended.

Three main categories of psychosurgery are discussed in Chapter 11. Thousands of prefrontal lobotomies (in which the fibers running between the frontal lobes and other parts of the brain are severed) have been performed to alleviate the misery of obsessive and melancholic patients. Sometimes they achieve their goal, but the risk of reducing the patient to a mere vegetable is extremely high.

More recently, interest has switched to the use of amygdalotomy, in which part of the lower brain, the amygdala, is severed or burned out. The intention of the operation is to reduce fear and anger, but again there are many unfortunate side effects.

But the history of psychosurgery is not entirely a catalogue of mistakes and misfortunes—there is at least one major success story. In an attempt to reduce the effects of severe epileptic attacks, surgeons developed the procedure of cutting through the corpus callosum (the bridge connecting the two halves of the brain). This had two important consequences: first, epileptic attacks became fewer and more manageable; second, Roger Sperry of the California Institute of Technology discovered fascinating differences in the workings of the two halves of the brain by following up a number of patients who had had the "split brain" operation.

In Chapter 12 we explore emotion, again through the eyes of psychologists and physiologists working in tandem. Emotional states obviously depend on people and things in our immediate environment, but they usually involve distinctive physiological changes as well. These changes include increased heart rate, sweating, and other manifestations of heightened physiological activity. The classic theory of emotion put forward by Stanley Schachter and Jerome Singer places equal emphasis on psychological and physiological causes. Their method of manipulating physiological functioning was not surgical—they achieved increases or decreases in physiological activity by means of drugs.

In sum, this section reveals the wide range of valuable overlaps between the work of psychologists and physiologists specifically in the areas of intelligence, personality, emotion, and abnormal behavior. There is also great variety in the techniques that have been used to affect the physiological systems of the body, including direct intervention by surgery, physiological recordings taken from the skin or scalp, and the administration of drugs.

9

Brain waves do happen

Until recently, there was fairly general agreement among experts on the concept of intelligence. Intelligence was a kind of general, all-pervasive cognitive ability which enabled you to do well at anything resembling a mental problem. This highly prized ability was largely a genetic endowment; while the environment might influence the way in which intelligence showed itself, and might act as a handicap if very disadvantageous, it did not contribute more than perhaps 20 percent to the total amount of variability in intelligence found in the population studied. There were also several special abilities—verbal, numerical, rote memory, perceptual—but as far as intellectual capacity was concerned these did not account for anything resembling general intelligence. The consensus view was that intelligence was of great importance educationally, and also socially; your income and your job depended quite significantly on your intelligence, as did your social status. Luck, personality, and family connections of course also played a part, but a less important one than innate endowment.

In recent years these views have received a lot of criticism. Many critics have denied that intelligence is a meaningful concept. They do not accept that heredity determines differences in this nonexistent ability. They argue that social class and other environmental influences are all-powerful in deciding educational and work success and social status.

Most of these criticisms have come from people not fully conversant with the rather technical fields of genetics, psychometry, and mental test construction, and the majority of them have appeared in popular magazines, daily newspapers, and political tracts rather than in the scientific journals. Nevertheless, because these criticisms were so widely disseminated, they influenced political decisions of far-reaching importance. The rejection of selection in schools and the abandonment of tracking and other devices were largely influenced by these arguments. The sad affair of Sir Cyril Burt, who is now known to have fudged some of his data, gave a lot of ammunition to the critics. However, Burt's faulty data constituted a very small part of the empirical material on which the orthodox view of intelligence was based, and much recently gathered evidence has strongly supported the traditional view (the arguments are put forward in H. J. Eysenck's book *The Inequality of Man*).

Meanwhile, physiologists have been coming up with novel approaches to the whole question which bid fair to revolutionize the measurement of intelligence. These new ideas also suggest new answers to such difficult questions as the possible causes of decline in mental ability with age, the existence of racial differences in intelligence, the determination of social class differences in intelligence by nature or nurture, and so forth.

Briefly, these new approaches enable us to measure intelligence by means of psychophysiological methods, i.e., by using the electroencephalograph or "brain-wave machine." More than that, by being based on far-reaching theories of the nature of intelligence and its physical substructure, these new approaches give us much deeper insight into the nature of intelligence than was possible before. The work referred to has been published by two American psychologists at the Institute of Psychiatry in London, Allan and Elaine Hendrickson, who joined the department there some twenty years ago and who specialize in computer technology (the relevance of computers will soon become apparent).

Correlating physiological data with IQ

Head size and brain size and weight have some correlation with measured IQ, but the relationship is so slight as to be of no practical importance. Electrical conductivity of the skin, which is often regarded as a sign of mental alertness and motivation, has been found to be greater in bright than in dull children, but while the relationship between skin conductivity and IQ is closer than that between brain size and IQ, it is still not close enough to be of really practical importance.

Much the same would once have been said of attempts to measure reaction times as an indication of intelligence. In this type of measurement the subject is confronted with a light and a press key; when the light goes on, an electric timer is started, whereupon the subject presses the key as quickly as he can to stop the timer; his reaction time can be measured very accurately. It was thought at first that perhaps the speed of conduction through the neurone pathways inside the brain might be measured by this device, and that conduction speed might be related to intelligence; but the relationship has never been found to be at all close.

However, by using the same experimental idea but making certain changes, much closer correlation between reaction time and intelligence can be obtained. The subject sits in front of a console with his index finger resting on the "home" button—when one of the lights lights up he immediately moves his finger to depress the push button associated with that light. It is possible to mask all the lights except one or to present the subject with a choice of two, four, or eight lights. When only one light shows, it is "simple reaction time" which is being investigated; when more than one light shows, it is "choice reaction time." Obviously, the more choices there are, the longer the reaction time. Usually we count the increase in the number of choices offered not just by the number of lights but by "bits" which are counted as the logarithms of the numbers, so that a choice of two lights constitutes one bit of information, of four lights two bits, and eight lights three bits. Reaction times increase linearly with each additional bit.

Psychologists who have compared mean simple and choice reaction times for high middle, and low thirds of a sample of schoolgirls scoring high, average, and low respectively on a typical test of intelligence have discovered that the three groups are quite well separated, except perhaps at the simple reaction time level (zero bits of information), with the dull girls always having the longer reaction times and the bright girls the shorter reaction times.

There are other ways of using the reaction time experiment. One of them is the so-called Posner paradigm, a type of experiment in which subjects are shown stimuli which may be either identical or different; the subject has to press a button to indicate as quickly as possible whether the stimuli are identical or different. It was found that the decision "different" takes a longer time to reach than "identical" for both bright students (i.e. high scorers on a verbal test) and dull students (low scorers on a verbal test), but that dull students take longer for both types of stimuli and particularly long for the more difficult of the two tasks.

A third method, again different, is the so-called Sternberg paradigm, where the subject is presented with a small set of digits, or letters, followed immediately by a single "probe" digit or letter to which the subject responds "yes" or "no," depending on whether the probe was or was not included in the set originally shown. The subject's reaction time or decision time in pressing the "yes" or "no" key is the time measured. It was seen that as set size increases, so reaction times increase; that "no" answers take longer than "yes" answers; and that bright subjects are much quicker in their reactions than dull subjects, as becomes more and more evident as the set size increases.

We may conclude on all these grounds that, whatever the paradigm, there is a fairly close relationship between reaction time and intelligence and that this relationship becomes closer the more complex the task. None of the tasks set in reaction time experiments have any cultural determinants, so the results obtained may be considered almost

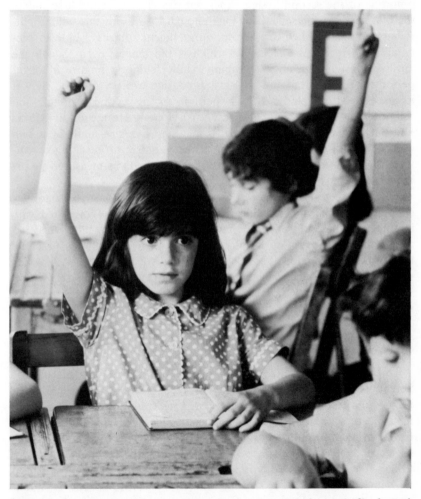

First to put their hands up to answer questions in class. A display of brightness or self-confidence? Photo: Multimedia Publications Inc. (Israel Sun).

entirely free of the environmental influences that are often said to be so important in determining success in ordinary IQ tests. Here, then, we have an objective, culturally fair way of measuring intelligence.

One other measure, in some ways also indicative of mental speed, has been used: the speed with which subjects can identify correctly the difference in length between two lines. The technique is rather complex; it involves exposing the two lines in a special apparatus for a very brief period of time (something like one-fifth of a second); thereafter the two lines are whipped away and another design is presented to the subject. This technique is called "backward masking" because the presentation of the second design wipes out recognition of the first, unless the first has been presented for long enough to prevent this wiping out. It has been established that the more intelligent subject is able to recognize the two lines and decide which is the longer, even though the masking design appears very rapidly; duller subjects require a longer period for recognition, and the masking design can be tolerated only if it appears after relatively long periods of inspection ("long" and "short" are of course comparative terms; "long" here means something like one-fifth of a second, "short" something like one-tenth of a second). The test is again a very simple one, requires no teaching or cultural knowledge, and correlates very highly with IQ as measured by ordinary tests.

While these tests are interesting, in that they demonstrate that very simple perceptual and reaction time behavior is highly correlated with intelligence, they do not throw much light either on the theoretical nature of intelligence or on its physical basis. However, this is precisely the sort of information that can be supplied by the so-called "evoked potential" on the electroencephalograph (EEG) and it may be worthwhile to discuss the most recent developments of this technique in some detail.

Brain waves and IQ: a new correlation

Through electrodes placed upon the scalp, the EEG records electric potentials generated by the brain. Until recently these waves had never been found to be at all closely correlated with intelligence. Evoked potentials are series of waves that appear suddenly when the subject of the experiment has a bright light flashed into his eyes or hears a sudden click delivered over earphones. Figure 4 shows the resulting waves for three subjects, each of whom had had an IQ test (the Otis group test) on which they scored 137, 100, and 73 respectively. The first four waves, lettered E_1, E_2, E_3, and E_4, are most tightly spaced in the case of subject B.A. (Otis 137) and most widely spaced in the case of subject R.L. (Otis 73). This particular recording of evoked potentials was published by J. P. Ertl, the Canadian psychologist who pioneered research into the relationship between IQ and evoked potentials. Ertl measured the latency of these waves, in other words how quickly they came after the stimulus (a visual one) had been presented to his subjects, who were children. What he found was that for the brighter children the latencies were shorter. That is to say, the waves arose more quickly in brighter children than in duller ones. As Figure 1 shows, the

Figure 1

Subject B.A.
Otis 137

Subject G.H.
Otis 100

Subject R.L.
Otis 73

Time (Milliseconds)

waves for the dullest child are the most elongated and drawn out. This was interesting news, but not sensational; when much larger groups were tested the relationships between intelligence and latency potentials were not so close. Furthermore, other workers found it difficult to duplicate Ertl's work at first; when finally it was shown that his results did stand up to repetition, there were still disappointingly low correlations between IQ and potential latency.

Measuring brain-wave activity in response to auditory stimulation may lead psychologists to an understanding of the physiological basis of intelligence. Photo: Multimedia Publication Inc. (Miki Koren).

Key experiment   (Elaine and Allan Hendrickson)

At this point work began at the Institute of Psychiatry in London. It was inspired by the thought that perhaps if we looked in detail at the theoretical foundations underlying the measurement of evoked potentials, and if we improved the actual methods of measurement used, we might be able to get the observed correlations up to more significant levels. Dr. Elaine Hendrickson changed the stimulus from visual to auditory (partly because visual stimuli produce many artifacts in the recording of EEGs) and also began to measure the amplitudes of waves as well as their latencies. She soon found that bright people had bigger waves, as well as faster ones, and by combining these two indices she achieved a much more respectable level of correlation— something, indeed, that made one sit up and take notice. But the major step still lay ahead; the elaboration of a theoretical rationale for the whole procedure and the working out of a proper measure based on this rationale. It is this that has recently been accomplished.

The theory, which was elaborated by Allan Hendrickson, was first applied to the concept of memory and then to that of intelligence. It is well known that information reaching the brain's cortex through the sense channels is encoded and then sent from one part of the brain to the other through neurons connected to each other by way of synapses. The passage of information through the cortex was the part of the whole process which the evoked potential was thought to tap, but there were many queries concerning the way the information was encoded, passed across the synaptic gap, and finally related through the evoked potential to IQ. Hendrickson, by virtue of his expertise in computer technology, was able to produce a theory which explains how information can be encoded in neuronic pulse trains, and he also furnished a theoretical account of the biochemical events which take place when information is passed across synapses; these mechanisms are too complex and technical to be discussed in detail here. What is important is the additional hypothesis that in the processing of information errors are likely to occur. Now, individuals have a consistent and characteristic mean probability of such errors occurring, and it is this which the Hendricksons believe is the biological basis of differences in intelligence. It stands to reason that a person can act quickly and appropriately on information received only to the extent that the incoming information is transmitted correctly. The Hendricksons symbolize the probability of an incoming message being correct enough to be recognized by the individual by the letter "R" and consider individual differences in "R" to be the biological foundation of intelligence. They have shown, by means of computer simulation, the effects on message transmission of introducing errors of varying degree and have shown that the picture so obtained fits the known facts very well.

How is all this related to evoked potentials? There is evidence, from studies of single neuron recordings, that there is some relationship between the EEG and the pulse train which transmits a given message and hence the possibility that records of the evoked potential might reveal details of the pulse train and possible errors in transmission. Such errors should have the effect of "smearing" the peaks and troughs, in other words making them less distinct; transmission errors would change the shape of the wave forms. Furthermore, errors in transmission which would make recognition difficult or impossible would give a different pulse train from that which was error-free; this is important because several evoked potentials are usually averaged to produce the published diagrams. This averaging is necessary because of the low signal-to-noise ratio in recording; wave forms become clear only when several waves are averaged. Averaging correct and incorrect pulse trains would eliminate finer details and make the resulting curve more regular.

Figure 2

High IQ subjects [1]

Low IQ subjects

Time (Milliseconds)

This is indeed a feature of the three curves in Figure 1. The most intelligent subject has a curve which shows far more squiggles; the least intelligent has a very bland, smooth curve. If it is these squiggles which represent aspects of the message being transmitted, then clearly the message is relayed much more efficiently in the cortex of subject B.A. than in that of subject R.L., with subject G.H. coming somewhere in between. Nor are these squiggle features accidental correlates of IQ in just these three subjects. Figure 2 shows the wave forms of ten bright and ten dull subjects in a study by Ertl and Schafer; the numbers on the left of the vertical lines give the Wechsler IQ recorded for each child. Even on very cursory inspection one can see that the two sets of curves differ very profoundly in complexity, just as predicted by the Hendricksons' theory, as well as in amplitude and latency.

How can we measure this intuitively obvious characteristic of "complexity"? As a very rough and ready measure, the Hendricksons used what they called the "string measure." They projected an enlarged version of the observed curves onto sheets of paper, put large numbers of pins along the contour, and then threaded a piece of string in and out of the pins; having done this, they unthreaded the string and measured its length. The result was very impressive; the correlation between "string measure" and IQ was as high as that between one good IQ test and another. Nothing so convincing had ever been achieved before, suggesting that perhaps theory and measurement were along the right lines. Now, of course, the string measure has been abandoned—the computer measures the length of the curved line with much greater accuracy.

Implications of the evoked potential technique

Elaine Hendrickson has by now tested hundreds of children and adults, using both recognized intelligence tests and the evoked potential technique, scored in the manner described above; replications have given pretty much the same results. There seems to be no doubt that we can now measure intelligence physiologically with an accuracy that compares favorably with the best IQ tests currently available. The implications of this advance are immense, both from the theoretical and the practical point of view. Nor is this the end; it seems likely that considerable refinement can still be made in the measurement. We can use more complex signals, in the hope that by making the messages more detailed, more errors will occur during transmission–after all, a simple auditory click does not give much room for misunderstanding. We can analyze separately the different portions of the curves (contrast the first 250 milliseconds with the second 250 milliseconds, for example).

Electrodes being applied to specific areas of the scalp to record brain activity. Photo: Rex Features.

There are other possibilities which require investigation, but the results so far obtained are quite enough to indicate that something truly important and novel has been achieved in the measurement of intelligence.

What of the future? We can now claim to have a measure of intelligence that is free of the cultural determinants that in some degree still adhere to even the best IQ tests (i.e., the 20 percent due to environment). We should be able to make predictions, undertake selection, and give advice to people on the basis of a pure measure of their general mental ability, no matter what their education, family, or life history. We should be able to investigate aspects of intelligence that have always raised almost insuperable barriers to research in the past, with better hope of success, for example the growth of intelligence in babies and young children below the age of 6. There are baby tests, but they are not really good measures of intelligence; they tend to test physical rather than mental development and do not correlate at all well with adult intelligence. At the other end of the scale, we should be able to investigate the decline of mental powers with age; this has proved difficult in the past because previous learning interferes with the measurement of intelligence, so that tests give different results depending on whether they measure mainly "fluid intelligence" or "crystallized intelligence." And finally, we should be able to say something about racial and class differences without the possibility of cultural factors interfering and causing endless argument.

Understanding how the brain works

There is one additional theoretical problem which it may now be possible to solve. We have mentioned the existence of special abilities in addition to general intelligence. These in turn group themselves into two major classes, one comprising verbal abilities of all kinds and the other perceptual and mechanical abilities. Now there appears to be a relationship between these two types of abilities and the two cerebral hemispheres. Verbal performance seems to be mostly controlled by the left hemisphere of the brain (certainly in right-handed people), while perceptual-mechanical ability seems to be controlled much more by the right hemisphere. Split-brain studies have been particularly instructive in this respect. The two halves of the brain are joined by the corpus callosum, a bundle of fibers going across from right to left. For medical reasons (to control epileptic seizures, for example), this bundle of fibers may have to be cut, leaving the two halves of the brain more or less isolated from each other. Material can be presented to one half, but not to the other, and we can study in detail how each half functions on its own (see Chapter 11 for a detailed discussion of the "split brain").

It will be fascinating to see, in normal and split-brain people, how performance on verbal and non-verbal tests relates to the patterns of evoked potentials taken from the two hemispheres separately. In theory, we should find that among people who show discrepancy between verbal and non-verbal IQ, those with a high verbal IQ should show more complex wave forms on the left half of the brain, while those with a high perceptual-mechanical IQ should show more complex wave forms on the right half of the cortex. This is only the most obvious of the many experiments that will now be possible. We are, it seems, on the threshold of a revolution in the study of mental ability.

10

Can we inherit personality?

Over two thousand years ago the Greek philosopher Theophrastus, then 99 years of age, wrote a book entitled *Characters,* in which he asked a question which is central to a large body of modern psychological research: "Why is it that while all Greece lies under the same sky, and all the Greeks are educated alike, it has befallen us to have characters variously constituted?" In other words, Theophrastus, like many people since, wondered why different people behave so differently, have different abilities, and different personalities. He did not succeed in finding an answer; his book simply described various people who show in an exaggerated form traits normally found in many people, such as miserliness, or courage, or persistence.

The "four humors" brought up to date

However, the Greeks did elaborate a descriptive system of personality which has lasted a long time, so that even now we use the terms they used to characterize the four main "types" they recognized: the melancholic, the choleric, the phlegmatic, and the sanguine. They also posited a biological cause to explain why a particular individual might be choleric or phelgmatic; this cause had to do with bodily secretions, but they knew so little about the inner workings of the body that we may dismiss this pseudo-biochemical theory as quite useless.

Modern psychologists have found the Greek theory of personality useful in parts, but it is much too narrow and schematic to enable us to say very much about the majority of people, who are not melancholic, choleric, phlegmatic, or sanguine. Wilhelm Wundt, the founder of the first psychological laboratory in Leipzig, a hundred years ago, drew attention to the fact that melancholics and cholerics are alike in having strong and volatile emotions, whereas phlegmatics and sanguinics have rather stable emotions. He therefore postulated a dimension of "emotionality," going from extreme instability to extreme stability. He also drew attention to the fact that cholerics and sanguinics are alike in being somewhat changeable in their behavior, whereas melancholics and phlegmatics are rather unchangeable. Substituting the more modern terms "extrovert" and "introvert" for changeable and unchangeable, we can say that Wundt foreshadowed the second major dimension of personality which is now widely recognized. The picture painted by the ancient Greeks, and made more widely applicable by Wundt consists of two major dimensions of personality: emotionality or neuroticism as opposed to stability, and extroversion as opposed to introversion.[1] Though each person has a position on these two axes, it would not necessarily fall in one of the four quadrants; indeed, most people will center around the point of intersection, showing personalities that are neither extremely stable nor extremely unstable, neither extremely extroverted nor extremely introverted, but "ambivert"— halfway between the two. The validity of this picture is supported by a vast body of evidence from different sources. The words around the inside of the circle indicate the traits which together cause a person to be designated an introvert or an extrovert, stable or unstable.

How can we measure these traits, and how can we measure "personality"? At first sight it seems almost a contradiction in terms to speak of the "measurement" of personality; how can we measure something so protean, complex, and non-physical? In a sense this objection is sensible; we cannot measure personality as such. But we can measure different *aspects* of personality. (Similarly we cannot measure the universe, but we can measure different aspects of it, such as stellar distances or the physical composition of the planets.)

Measuring personality

There are in fact many different measures of personality. All have their strengths and weaknesses, but all derive from one overriding fact: that personality is a concept which is derived from behavior, and behavior is by definition observable and measurable.

Consider a personality trait such as persistence. We call a person persistent if we have seen him exerting himself, perhaps over long periods, against pain, fatigue, boredom, and other influences which would tend to make him give up. We can measure the length of time from the beginning of his exertions to the moment when he gives up; and we can measure most of the forces which he has to overcome in order to continue. Thus the concept of "persistence" is based on observable, measurable behavior, and much the same is true of other personality traits. Measurement is not always easy, but in principle it is usually possible to design an experiment which will be relevant to the particular trait one is looking at. In fact, it is usually quite easy to design measures of personality; the difficulty lies in ensuring that they actually measure what we want to measure. There are ways and means of getting around these difficulties.

Questionnaires and casual observation

The oldest and most widely used methods of personality measurement are by means of observation and questionnaires. Questionnaire measurement itself is derived from a much older technique, namely self-observation; all that we are doing, in fact, is asking people to tell us the results of their own observations of their behavior over the past few years. Let us assume we are interested in the trait of "sociability." We could observe the person, see how frequently he goes to parties, how many people he talks to at parties, how much time he spends alone by himself in his room, etc. This would be casual or uncontrolled observation; we are doing nothing here to constrain our subject, and we cannot, obviously, observe all his relevant behavior—we cannot shadow him for twenty-four hours a day, and even if we could, our presence would undoubtedly modify his behavior. So his own account of his habitual behavior, either given verbally or given in the form of answers to a questionnaire, might be much more reliable than mere observation—after all, he is always with himself. We would, of course, have to trust him; if he had any good reason for deceiving us, then no reliance could be placed on his answers. But for most purposes there is good agreement between outside observation and rating of a person's conduct, and self-ratings as given in response to a questionnaire or during an interview.

Controlled observation

We can refine our observation by making it a controlled observation. Suppose that as part of our interest in sociability we wanted to find out exactly how sociable and unsociable people behave during discussions with strangers. Casual observation would not enable us to be very precise in our rating, chiefly because of the random nature of the strangers our various subjects would be meeting; we would not be able to tell to

One type of interview that might be used to measure personality. Photo:
Multimedia Publications Inc. (Miki Koren).

what extent their reactions were determined by their own personality or
by the personality of the strangers. We could get over this by arranging
an experimental confrontation between our subjects and a trained
stooge who always behaved in a predetermined manner regardless of
whom he met. For example, the stooge might be instructed to make no
spontaneous remarks during the first five minutes, to become voluble
during the next five minutes, and then revert to taciturnity. The confrontation could be staged in a laboratory, and the conversation could
be tape-recorded. The experimenter could also watch it through a one-
way screen; he might even film the behavior of the subject, to make it
possible to count the number of times he smiled, blinked, looked at the
stooge, etc. In this way we would get a very accurate record of exactly

what took place, and could compare one subject's behavior in this standardized situation with that of others. Controlled observation can be a very good method of personality measurement.

Another way of improving casual observation is to introduce a time sampling system. Suppose that we are interested in the aggressiveness shown by children and try to rate a group of children for this quality. We could go to the playground a number of times and observe their behavior. But this would not be very accurate; we might pay more attention to some children than to others. The correct method would be to get a list of the names of all the children and spend exactly sixty seconds observing child one, sixty seconds observing child two, going on down the list and watching each child for an identical period; when we got to the end of the list, we would start again at the top. We would also have a list detailing precisely what behaviors we should watch out for, and a stopwatch to tell us for how long each type of behavior went on. If we continued our observations repeatedly over a period of months, we could then analyze our results and see how consistently each child behaved—in other words, is it always the same children who are aggressive, or is aggressiveness just a random type of behavior? This type of observation would still be naturalistic, but it would be much better controlled and therefore more reliable than casual observation.

These improvements in observational technique bring us very close to an experimental technique which has been found to have many advantages for the measurement of personality, the "miniature situation technique." This is based on a very simple idea: since it is often difficult or impossible to observe people in a natural setting, and in any case the types of situation encountered by them are not usually identical, why not set up a simple situation in the laboratory, taking care that in all essentials it duplicates the sort of life situation we are interested in. This would obviate all our difficulties, and would enable proper measurement to be undertaken.

Let us go back to our example of persistence. It is easy to set up laboratory tasks which call for persistent behavior; we can then measure each person's reaction to the tasks involved and see whether statistical analysis of the data supports the notion that it is indeed persistence that we have measured. How would we set about it? We might go into a school[2] and arrange for the teachers to give their pupils a series of tests, making sure, of course, that the children did not realize that tests were being carried out. The teacher might, for instance, take them to the gymnasium and announce a competition to see who can pull the hardest on a dynamometer (an instrument which registers strength of pull). Having found out each child's maximum pull, the teacher then announces that he wants to see how long each child can hold the dynamometer at two-thirds his maximum pull (thus ruling out differences in strength between the children). The more persistent children would, according to theory, keep going longer than the less persistent, overcoming the pain and fatigue that sets in after a very short while.

In another quite different test the teacher might give the class an intelligence test, timing each item for each child. Among the easy and the moderately difficult items there are some items too difficult for any of the children to solve. We are interested in finding out how long each child continues to grapple with these problems before giving up. This time is then a measure of his persistence.

If we devised, say, twenty persistence tests, all of this miniature situation type, and tested all the children on each test, could we show that the sum of all the scores on the twenty tests actually measured persistence?

Our first duty would, of course, be to demonstrate that the children who are persistent in one test are also persistent in the others. If this were not so, then the tests would not all be measuring the same trait, and it would be meaningless to add their scores together. But if all the tests do correlate together, we must next see whether perhaps this is because they all measure some other factor, such as intelligence. No, they don't; dull children do not have higher or lower persistence scores than bright children. Next we would have all our children rated for persistence by their teachers, on the assumption that teachers know their children pretty well; we would find that these correlations are positive and pretty high. Children who are rated as persistent by their teachers also perform persistently on our tests. We would then argue that persistent children probably do better in school than non-persistent ones, and indeed, when the necessary corrections are made for intelligence, we find that this too is true. Last, when we construct a questionnaire asking questions about persistence, the persistent children in the experiment are also the persistent children on the questionnaire. Taking all this together makes it pretty clear that our miniature situations do indeed measure what they are supposed to measure.

Experimental methods

Going one more step away from the common-sense approach characteristic of the techniques of observation and questionnaires, we come to experimental measures based on specific theories. These are difficult to discuss because to do so sensibly requires a detailed statement of the theories involved, which can be a lengthy and complex business. Let us take a rather oversimplified example. The theory has been advanced that introverts are more sensitive to external stimulation than extroverts; how can we test this? What follows is an example of just one experimental approach. First we measure the rate at which the subject salivates by putting some cotton in his mouth for twenty seconds; we weigh this before and after, and thus determine the amount of saliva which has been absorbed. After a short rest we perform the same experiment again, but this time we put four drops of lemon juice on the subject's tongue. It is known that this increases the rate of salivation for most people; the hypothesis states that if introverts are more sensitive, then we would expect their rate to increase more than that of extroverts. If we know our subjects' degree of extroversion or introversion from questionnaire answers, then we can correlate their extroversion scores with the increase in salivary flow, and show that this is in fact negative; introverts who score low for extroversion show a greater increase in salivary flow than extroverts. That is the result we would expect, and it bears out our theory.

Experimental tests of this kind are particularly interesting and important for two reasons. The first is that they cannot be faked; in fact, the subject has no idea that we are testing his personality, and even if we told him he would not know what the meaning of his scores was. And the second is that by putting forward theories of this kind we hope to gain a better understanding of the mechanisms underlying our personality dimensions.

But there is also a disadvantage in using tests of this kind for practical purposes. They lack "face validity"—in other words, they are not obviously relevant to whatever purpose they are being used for. A candidate for a job which requires introverted traits would be very surprised if he found his rate of salivation measured after four drops of lemon juice had been dropped on his tongue. It would be very difficult to persuade him that this was a useful test, relevant to a decision regarding his employment.

Physiological tests

Much the same is true about another category of tests, namely personality tests based on physiological measures. It is well known that emotional reactions are closely connected with physiological changes; thus fear and anger are accompanied by an increase in heart rate. If we had to select candidates for a job which required them to remain very calm and stable under conditions of considerable danger, we might expose them to stress in the laboratory (threat of electric shock, say) and measure the increase in heartbeat caused by either the threat or the actual administration of an electric shock. Subjects whose heart rate increased rapidly, and died down again very slowly, might not be the best choice for a job requiring a lot of low-key "cool."

There are many such physiological indicators which can be and have been used as measures of personality; they usually require elaborate laboratory equipment and are therefore not very useful for ordinary personality assessment. In special cases, however, and when the number of subjects involved is not too large, physiological tests can be extremely useful.

Projective tests: the least reliable of all

We now come to a quite different sort of test, collectively known as "projective devices."[3] These are based on the hypothesis that we tend to project our ideas and fears, our ambitions and thoughts, onto material which is poorly structured, and that the expert can then study our imaginative products and argue back from these to the ideas and thoughts which gave rise to them.

The best-known example is the Rorschach inkblot test. The subject is shown a series of inkblots, which are symmetrical but fundamentally meaningless in shape and either colored or black and white. He is asked to say what he thinks each inkblot looks like. The sort of answers one usually gets are: "a couple of witches," "a butterfly," "two old women," and so on. There are various rules which are supposed to tell the experimenter how to argue back from these answers to the personality of the subject; usually the experimenter tries to obtain an all-around picture of the temperamental characteristics of the subject. In this sense one might say that projective tests are the only real personality tests—all the others attempt to measure only very limited aspects of personality.

Another very widely known test is the T.A.T. (Thematic Apperception Test). In this the subject is shown a series of drawings or pictures, the content of which is purposely vague. He then has to make up a story about each picture, and these stories are then scored and interpreted. The hypothesis in this case is that an aggressive person will write stories which contain a lot of fighting; an oversexed person will write stories full of sexual activity; and an ambitious person will write stories in which the hero of the story succeeds in various endeavors. There are a vast number of different types of projective test, but the inkblot test and the T.A.T. have remained the most widely used and the best known. The question must now be asked: do they actually work?

After many years of great enthusiasm, the answer from literally hun-

Hermann Rorschach's famous inkblots. What do you make of them?

dreds of experimental studies is quite unequivocal: projective tests do not work very well. They do not agree with findings obtained on other tests of personality; and even projective information about the same person may result in quite different interpretations of his character if scored by different "experts."

One typical experiment will suffice to give the reader an idea of the sort of investigation which has been done on the claims of the experts themselves. During the war a large number of candidates for the U. S. Air Force were put through a whole battery of projective tests; these were not scored at the time but put aside until the end of the war. When the war was over an experimenter unearthed the tests of fifty candidates who had done exceptionally well in the Air Force and had come through all their trials and tribulations with flying colors; he also took out the records of fifty failures, people who had crumpled up under the stress and never got anywhere. A large number of experts in these various projective techniques were then approached and asked to sort out the old records into potential "successes" and potential "failures"; all of them had worked in the Air Force, knew what was involved, and considered the experiment a fair one. To cut a long story short, only one of the experts gave answers outside the limits of chance, and he got his predictions significantly wrong. So much for the projective experts.

Many other similar experiments have come to similar conclusions. In one of them, fifty severe neurotics and fifty perfectly normal controls were tested with the Rorschach cards, and the results were then assessed by several experts; not one could tell with above-chance accuracy which were the neurotic and which were the normal subjects. There is little doubt that as tests of personality these projective devices are not reliable and therefore not to be recommended.

However, such wholesale condemnation should not necessarily include the T.A.T. When the T.A.T. is used to test specific traits rather than assess all-around personality, and when pictures are specially chosen to probe one particular facet of a person's temperament (need for achievement, fear of failure, etc.), then the scores are likely to be fairly trustworthy. In one study an attempt was made to measure the aggressiveness of Communists. But apart from such specific uses, even the T.A.T. does not emerge unscathed from experimental evaluations of its usefulness.

Why then do people believe in projective testing? The answer is very simple: the psychologist prepares a "characterization" for his client which has universal validity; nearly everybody would recognize themselves as "having a good sense of humor" or "being anxious occasionally." In one study, the experimenter obtained Rorschach records from a large group of students and said he would submit them to an expert. The next week he handed out a sheet of paper to each student with a personality reading on it. He then asked how many of them thought this was an accurate reading of their temperament and character, and practically everyone put his hand up. He then got one of the students to read out his sheet, and all realized that they had been given identical readings. So much for the value of projective test successes. There is probably a modicum of truth in the belief that a person's perceptions as expressed in his interpretations of vague blots and pictures are characteristic of some aspect of his personality; but the sad truth is that no one has yet succeeded in tracing the chain back from the interpretation to the personality.

Projective tests are just one example of a wide group of "tests" which all share this lack of experimental proof that they are of any practical use. Astrology is another. People like to believe in the supernatural, and attempts to link "the stars" with personality, however fraudulent, have been successful with the credulous since the beginning of time.

Handwriting

Yet some methods usually grouped with astrology and projective techniques do have some validity, in that they correlate better with more reliable methods of personality assessment: graphology (handwriting analysis) is one.[4] In one study, fifty subjects filled in personality inventories, and a graphologist attempted to predict their answers from separate samples of their handwriting. She was correct in 62 percent of the cases, where chance or expectation would have predicted 50 percent; on judgments of which she was particularly sure she was correct 68 percent of the time. Subjects tended to differ in consistent ways with regard to the ease with which their handwriting could be diagnosed, and personality traits differed according to the ease with which their presence or absence could be detected in each subject's handwriting. The graphologist also succeeded in matching character sketches of the subjects, and other material, with their writing. Psychiatrists and psychologists who tried to judge personality from handwriting failed abysmally. In sum, it is possible for a skilled graphologist to diagnose personality traits from handwriting with better than chance success.

The genetic basis of personality

The very notion of "personality" implies consistency. We assume that a person who is sociable, or talkative, or anxious shows these traits consistently over many years, rather than at odd intervals. This suggests that genetic factors may be involved in the determination of personality.[5] This is certainly what the physicians of ancient Greece thought.

What, then, is the evidence regarding heredity? Does it influence personality? The best evidence here comes from studies of twins. Nature occasionally provides us with exciting ready-made experiments in the form of identical twins and fraternal twins (see introduction to Section A).

Studying twins gives us the opportunity of investigating the influence of heredity along two rather different routes. We can examine identical twins who have been separated at birth or shortly after and who have been brought up in quite different environments (by foster parents, in orphanages, or in some other way). Any similarities between separated identical twins can only be the effect of heredity, not environment—they ceased to share the same environment shortly after they left the womb.

The other route makes use of comparisons between identical twins on the one hand and fraternal twins on the other. Let us suppose that a given trait, say sociability, is due entirely to environmental causes. Now the only difference between identical and fraternal twins is, of course, that the former have more heredity in common; this is irrelevant to our hypothetical trait, and consequently identical twins would be no more alike with respect to sociability than would fraternal twins. But let us now suppose that heredity does play an important part in producing differences in sociability; in that case we would expect identical twins to be much more alike than fraternal twins, simply because they share more heredity. The general rule might be stated as follows: the more similar identical twins are with respect to the trait one is studying, the greater the influence of heredity; conversely, the more similar fraternal twins are with respect to a certain trait, the greater the influence of environment. This relation can be expressed numerically, and may be used to estimate the relative contribution of nature and nurture, heredity and environment.

Such formulas make certain assumptions, which can be checked. For instance, they assume that there is no "assortative mating" (that is, men and women marry in a random manner as far as personality traits are concerned—i.e., introverted men do not necessarily marry introverted women, or extroverted ones for that matter). Is this assumption true? When personality questionnaires are given to large samples of married people, and their personality scores are correlated, it is found that there is no correlation at all for extroversion-introversion; mating is quite random as far as this major dimension of personality is concerned.

The position is slightly different for neuroticism (emotionality versus stability). Here there is some evidence for assortative mating, the more emotional tending to marry the more emotional, and the more stable tending to marry the more stable. But this tendency is very weak. Altogether, assortative mating for personality is weak or absent in our society, which is rather curious, as one might have expected a marked tendency either for like to marry like or for like to marry unlike. As it happens, like *does* marry like with respect to intelligence—quite high correlations are found between spouses—but not with respect to personality.

What is the outcome of the many personality studies on twins which have been carried out in Britain and the United States, where most such work has been done? Let us take first the experiments using identical twins brought up separately. Here the outcome is rather unexpected; it has been found that identical twins brought up apart are, if anything, slightly more alike than identical twins brought up together. Both groups, in fact, are very similar with respect to extroversion and neuroticism; knowing one twin, one can make a very good guess about the personality of the other.

But how is it possible that environment not only fails to make twins who grow up together more alike, but may actually make them somewhat less like each other than twins who grow up separately? The answer may lie precisely in the great similarity that exists between them; often identical twins resent the fact that they are not regarded as separate persons and tend to magnify any small and accidental differences in behavior, simply in order to appear different. Thus one twin may take over negotiations with the outer world, while the other takes over internal management of their affairs. This parceling out of roles is often facilitated by the fact that identical twins interfere with each other in the womb more than fraternal twins do, because in most cases they share a common placenta; thus one twin may deprive the other of part of its share of their joint blood supply, leading to differences in birth weight which are often correlated with intelligence, dominance, etc. Thus, contrary to expectation, identical twins share a prenatal environment but may not share it as equally as fraternal twins. Slight differences of experience in the womb may then lead identical twins to emphasize and exaggerate these differences subsequently.

Whatever the truth about these complex matters, there is no doubt that the evidence from identical twins brought up separately demonstrates very clearly that heredity plays a very important part in producing differences in personality. The hereditary effect is particularly strong in people with more extreme scores on either extroversion/introversion or neuroticism/stability; the effect is least strong in the middle of both axes, i.e., among run-of-the-mill people who are not particularly extroverted or introverted, emotional or stable.

Experiments comparing identical and fraternal twins bear out this conclusion. Out of some twenty studies, there is not one in which the correlations for identical twins have not been larger, and usually much larger, than those for fraternal twins. This applies not only to the major personality variables, such as extroversion/introversion and neuroticism/stability, but to a large number of other measurable traits as well.

The only personality measures which have on the whole failed to show much difference between identical and fraternal twins have been projective tests, such as the Rorschach and the T.A.T., and expressive tests like graphology. But here the reason seems to be not so much that there are no differences between the different kinds of twins, but rather that such tests possess low reliability and little validity; in other words, they fail to measure personality with any precision and consequently cannot be used to prove anything regarding the importance of heredity or environment.

When proper personality tests are used, whether questionnaires or objective experimental testing procedures, the results always support the proposition that heredity plays a most important part in producing differences in personality.[6] It is not easy to give a numerical value to the propositional importance of nature and nurture. The results of tests depend in part on the actual instruments used for making the measurements; also the numbers of twins studied have often been too small to give very accurate results. But the minimum value for the contribution of heredity is something like 50 percent, with the maximum being in the region of 80 percent. Probably something like 70–75 percent would be the best guess one can make at the moment; this would apply to the heritability of major personality characteristics (i.e., extroversion/introversion, neuroticism/stability). Simpler traits, like sociability, or impulsiveness, give lower values, but still up to the 50–60 percent mark. Thus there can be no doubt that personality has a hard core of innately determined behavior patterns; this hard core (the "genotype," as geneticists call it) interacts with the environment to produce the actually observed behavior (the "phenotype").

The physiological basis of personality

These findings raise some interesting problems. It is, of course, quite impossible to inherit conduct; we can only inherit physical structures that can be identified by the physiologist or the anatomist. Yet what we measure when we talk about personality is conduct, or behavior. This suggests that there must be physical structures in our nervous system which give rise to behavior of the kind which causes us to diagnose a person as extroverted or introverted, neurotic or stable. We now have some idea what structures are involved. Consider Figure 2, which is a very simple diagram of the cortex and the spinal cord. At the base of the brain is the so-called visceral brain. This coordinates the activities of the more primitive part of our nervous system, which governs the expression of the emotions through two subsystems, the sympathetic and the parasympathetic systems. Emotions like fear and anger are always accompanied by physical symptoms (increased heartbeat, more rapid breathing, sweating, the cessation of digestion, dilation of the pupils, etc.) which are mediated by the sympathetic system and coordinated by the visceral brain. Once the occasion for the emotional outburst is over, the parasympathetic system calms things down again (brings heartbeat and breathing back to normal, restarts digestion, and generally relaxes the organism). The visceral brain and the structures of the autonomic system are the physical base for individual differences in neuroticism and stability. In interaction with the environment, they produce the phenotypic behavior which we measure with our questionnaires.

Extroversion/introversion, on the other hand, is closely connected with the habitual arousal level of the cortex. We are all familiar with different arousal levels; we get tense and wound up, highly aroused, before an important examination; we are relaxed and drowsy late in the evening in front of the television. The higher the arousal level, the better the brain is able to function.

Introverts have higher habitual levels of arousal, which is why they tend to be better at learning, conditioning, and remembering. The cortex also has the function of keeping the lower levels of the brain in check, which is why the behavior of introverts is more inhibited than that of extroverts. An illustration may make things clearer here. Alcohol makes people more extroverted, whereas the amphetamines, which are stimulant drugs, have the opposite effect; because they increase the level of cortical arousal they make people more introverted. So do nicotine and caffeine, which is why students studying hard for an examination tend to smoke and drink coffee to keep awake and learn better. Therefore, by giving people depressant or stimulant drugs, we can alter the physical basis of their personality and thus alter their behavior. The effect of such drugs can be tested by psychophysiological tests which fairly directly measure the activity of the cortex. Many such studies (of electroencephalographic brain waves, now measurable with such accuracy, of heart rate, of the electric conductivity of the skin, of breathing rate, of changes in pupil diameter, etc.) have now been carried out, and in general support the theory that extroversion/introversion is linked to levels of arousal.

Such studies are not only of academic interest. They have important

Figure 2

VB = Visceral brain
AAP = Ascending afferent pathways
ARAS = Ascending reticular activating system

practical applications and throw light on behavior we often find difficult to understand, such as neurosis, vandalism, and criminality. Extroverts, as we have seen, have a low level of arousal, whereas introverts have a high level. In fact, most people seek intermediate levels of arousal. Too high or too low a level of arousal is unpleasant, and people will try to avoid them. This suggests that extroverts will on the whole be "sensation seekers," that is, they will seek to increase their arousal level by indulging in behavior that brings them in contact with bright lights, loud music, sexual excitement, and so on. This sensation seeking also accounts for the sociability of the extrovert; associating with other people increases his or her arousal level. Conversely, introverts avoid contact with too many people because it increases their arousal level to an unpleasant degree.

Or consider another consequence of an individual's arousal level. Neurotic symptoms and disorders are now believed to be acquired through a process of conditioning, that is, through associating a painful stimulus with a neutral stimulus which, through force of circumstance, accidentally becomes linked with the painful stimulus. For example, one woman acquired a lifelong phobia for cats because her sadistic father drowned her favorite cat in front of her eyes when she was a child. But the ease of conditioning is determined to a large extent by the arousal level of the cortex. This means that introverts, having a higher arousal level, condition much more readily and are therefore more susceptible to neurotic disorders. This association between neurosis and conditioning has been powerfully demonstrated in many studies (as we have already seen in Chapter 1).

Since personality has such a strong biological basis, it follows that people in general are much more different from one another than might at first be supposed. We tend to believe that most people are like ourselves, perhaps differing slightly due to events in their past. We also believe that they could quite easily be converted to our way of thinking and change their behavior to be more like us. But this belief is quite wrong (see Chapter 22). The long history of our failure to rehabilitate criminals, make vandals behave like ordinary human beings, cure neurotics, and so on, is eloquent testimony to the fact that people differ profoundly from each other. Given that fact, the search for utopia is ultimately a foolish exercise. What is heaven for one may be hell for another, and the best we can hope for is some form of compromise that does not offend or injure too many people.

This may be a very tame and unacceptable conclusion for eager idealists seeking a heaven on earth but, unfortunately or perhaps fortunately, it is an accurate statement of the facts of the case. Our differences make living together extremely difficult, whether in a family, state, or international context. Understanding that people are incorrigibly different from each other is the beginning of wisdom for the budding psychologist.

11

Brain surgery:
the unkindest cut of all?

The human brain has long been regarded as the repository of the mind, hence its great symbolic significance. The brain has been held responsible for many of the positive achievements of mankind, including great works of art and major scientific discoveries. But when the brain malfunctions, tragic and debilitating effects follow, including, of course, the bizarre patterns of behavior found in madness and mental illness; someone who is mentally ill is, in common parlance, "out of his mind" or "off his head."

The notion that the brain is the seat of mental illness has led many people over the centuries to advocate direct action on the brain to effect a cure. This has involved a variety of horrifying methods of treatment, one of the best known being trepanning, which appears to have been used even in the Stone Age. The patient, unanesthetized, had a hole drilled in his skull in order to release the imagined accumulation of unwanted vapors in his head. Skulls found in Peru show evidence of healing around the hole in the skull, which means that some of our ancestors actually survived the operation.

Another crude method still in use today is electroconvulsive therapy. This involves administering electric shocks of between 70 and 130 volts to the patient. These shocks induce convulsions similar to grand mal epileptic seizures. This technique, which is sometimes useful in the treatment of depression, was first discovered in the late 1930s. It is not clear exactly why it works. However, it is instructive to consider the story of the new ECT machine, installed in a hospital in England, which was used with the normal success rate for over six months—un-

The human brain contains between 8,000 and 10,000 million nerve cells, any one of which may be connected to 25,000 others. But brain size is not consistently related to IQ. It is quite possible for very intelligent people to have lighter and smaller brains than "half-wits."

til the mechanic called and found it wasn't connected up properly. Obviously the power of suggestion can be a key factor in producing improvement.

In spite of the relative newness of electroconvulsive therapy, it has its roots in the eighteenth-century opinion that maniacs were best treated by exposing them to a very severe physical stress. There is also a popular, though entirely fallacious, view that epileptics are protected from schizophrenia by their natural convulsions. Even as far back as Roman times, there was interest in techniques that foreshadowed electroconvulsive therapy. The physician Scribonius Largus described the application of an electric fish to a patient's head as a cure for headache, and Pliny the Elder recommended the stunning shock from such a fish as an excellent remedy for the pain of childbirth.

The lobotomy story

The most significant landmark in the history of brain surgery was a conference of neurologists held in London in 1935. Jacobsen and Fulton discussed their work, in which they had significantly moderated the behavior of two chimpanzees by surgically removing their frontal lobes. At the end of the talk, the Portuguese neurologist Antonio Egas Moniz

rose to his feet and asked the following question: "If frontal lobe removal prevents the development of experimental neuroses in animals
and eliminates frustration behavior, why would it not be feasible to
relieve anxiety states in man by surgical means?"

Moniz and his colleague Almeida Lima enthusiastically set to work
to provide an answer to that question. They used the surgical method
of prefrontal lobotomy in an attempt to modify the mental lives of
obsessed and melancholic patients. What they did was to cut certain
fibers running from the frontal lobes to other parts of the brain. The
instrument used was a special knife called a leucotome, which they in-
serted through a small opening drilled in the skull. Film buffs will be
reminded of Ken Kesey's *One Flew over the Cuckoo's Nest.* In that
film, it is a lobotomy operation that puts a permanent halt to Randle
Patrick McMurphy's heroic struggle against Big Nurse.

Moniz performed twenty lobotomies during a ten-week period at the
end of 1935. He claimed that seven of his patients were "cured" by the
operation and that a further eight became much less violent and agitated and generally easier to manage. However, he seems to have been
fairly uncritical of the deficiencies of these operations. He was full of
self-praise and hailed the advent of lobotomy as "a great step forward
. . . in the study of psychic functions on an organic basis."

The publicity which Moniz attracted for his new form of brain surgery led to a tremendous upsurge of interest in prefrontal lobotomy. In
the twenty years between 1935 and 1955 approximately 70,000 lobotomies were performed in the United States and Britain. Walter Freeman, the acknowledged doyen of American lobotomists, personally
performed more than 3,500 lobotomies. The fame and prestige of
Moniz was such that he received a Nobel Prize in 1949.

As the years went by, however, there were increasing indications that
prefrontal lobotomy was not the panacea which Moniz claimed. There
were frequent reports of a variety of unfortunate side effects that
tended to follow the operation; these included apathy, irresponsibility,
diminished intellectual powers, impaired judgment, reduced creativity,
and even coma and eventual death. As the disadvantages of this form
of brain surgery became more obvious, so the number of patients receiving lobotomies dropped, until very few were being done at all.
Moniz got what some might regard as his just deserts when he was shot
in the spine by one of his own lobotomized patients.

But the irony of the whole saga of prefrontal lobotomy was this: it
eventually came to light that one of Jacobsen and Fulton's lobotomized
chimpanzees had suffered a brain abscess as a result of poor surgical
technique and that the other had not actually shown the reported good
effects of lobotomy.

Amygdalotomy

With the abandonment of the lobotomy operation, the major focus of attention among "psychosurgeons" shifted from the frontal lobes of the brain to the limbic system. Loosely speaking, the limbic system occupies an intermediate position between the lower and higher parts of the brain. There are indications that part of the limbic system, the amygdala, is involved in rage and aggression.

Arthur Kling and his colleagues performed amygdalotomies (lesions or cutting of the amygdala) on monkeys that had been living in a free-ranging colony. The good news was that they became less aggressive and friendlier toward their human handlers. The bad news, which has failed to deter some psychosurgeons, was that these animals appeared to be confused and fearful when they rejoined their old colony in the wild. They were quite incapable of coping with the complexities of social life and rapidly became social isolates.

Psychosurgeons usually get at the amygdala by directing fine wire electrodes toward the intended target through a small hole drilled in the skull. By passing strong currents through the implanted electrode, the surgeon then destroys the tissue around the electrode tip.

The casualties of psychosurgery

The most notorious application of the amygdalotomy technique was in the United States, where it was used on criminals serving jail sentences. The then attorney general of the state of California was reported to have called publicly for amygdalotomies on all violent criminals housed in the state's prisons in order to remove "the brain centers responsible for fear and anger."

One case that made banner headlines involved L.S., a psychopath convicted of first-degree murder and rape who had spent eighteen years in a Michigan mental hospital. When a lawyer named Gabe Kaimowitz heard of the plan to make L.S. the first recipient of psychosurgery at the Lafayette Clinic, he told the Detroit *Free Press* of his concern and initiated court proceedings. According to L.S.'s testimony at the hearing, he had given written consent to psychosurgery only because he thought he might be released after the operation. He also claimed that he had been misled into thinking that he was agreeing only to electrode implantation, and not to destructive surgery.

The three-man panel ruled that people who are involuntarily confined cannot give legally adequate consent to dangerous brain operations. They also decided that in this case psychosurgery violated the

First Amendment (guaranteeing the right to free expression), in that it could have the effect of impairing memory and intellectual powers.

Another well-known case involved a 34-year-old engineer named Thomas R., who received an amygdalotomy at the hands of Vernon Mark and Frank Ervin. After surgery he was confused and delusional and unable to work. When he was rehospitalized because of his bizarre and dangerous behavior, he was discovered on one occasion walking about the wards with his head covered by bags, newspapers, and rags. He said he did this because he was frightened other bits of his brain might be destroyed. His mother described his behavior after psychosurgery in the following words: "The poor guy has been almost a vegetable. . . . We know he was destroyed by that operation."

Legal constraints on the use of psychosurgery have increased in recent years as a result of public outrage at some of its unsavory consequences. One example is California State Assembly Bill 4481, restricting the use of electroconvulsive therapy and psychosurgery in California, which was signed into law in late 1974 by the then Governor Ronald Reagan (it was later replaced by Assembly Bill 1032, operative from January 1, 1977).

It is undeniably true that the complexities of the human brain make it very difficult for surgeons to operate on it without producing a number of unpleasant and disturbing side effects. However, there are some success stories, and this chapter is mainly concerned with one such story, based on the impressive work of Roger Sperry[1] of the California Institute of Technology and his colleagues. This work has not only alleviated human suffering but has also produced exciting new insights into the physiological and psychological workings of the brain.

Key experiment   The split-brain operation (Roger Sperry)

The work of Roger Sperry and his associates was done with a small number of advanced epileptics whose severe convulsions could not be controlled by medication. The first patient, for example, was a 48-year-old war veteran who had been having seizures for more than ten years, averaging two major attacks a week, each of which left him debilitated for at least a day.

The radical form of treatment decided upon for these epileptic patients was based on the fact that the human brain is a double organ, consisting of a right and a left hemisphere connected by a bridge of nerve tissue called the corpus callosum. This bridge of nerve tissue was severed surgically, the surgeons in this case being Philip Vogel and Joseph Bogen. Though this procedure is popularly referred to as the split-brain operation, this is slightly inaccurate, because the deeper parts of the brain remain connected.

An experiment in which feedback during a spatial task is delayed in order to study performance by each half of the brain. Photo: Multimedia Publications Inc. (Miki Koren).

Was such drastic surgical interference justified? The basic idea was that cutting the corpus callosum would confine the epileptic seizures to one hemisphere, thus providing a measure of relief for the patients. There was also some evidence that possible unpleasant side effects would be few (Ronald Myers and Roger Sperry had previously found that cutting the corpus callosum in cats and monkeys did not seriously impair their mental faculties).

Generally the effects of this operation were very beneficial. In the case of the 48-year-old war veteran not a single large-scale convulsion occurred in the several years following surgery. The second patient, a housewife and mother in her thirties, also remained free of seizures after recovering from surgery. A minority of the patients did continue to have seizures, but their convulsions were much less severe and less frequent than before and were usually confined to one side.

All the patients showed some short-term memory loss, problems of orientation, and mental fatigue immediately after the operation. Some of them were unable to speak until two months after the operation. But in all cases there was gradual recovery. Within a few months none of them felt any different from the way they had felt before the operation.

All in all, a substantial reduction in epileptic attacks was achieved, and at very low cost in terms of long-lasting side effects.

Sperry's work has achieved considerable publicity. Naturally the media sensationalized the difficulties the patients had in coping with their two half-brains. Considered objectively, however, the most remarkable result of the split-brain operation is its apparent lack of effect on ordinary behavior. Indeed, Sperry had to devise a special test to demonstrate the drawbacks of split functioning.

This test was based on the fact that information presented visually to the left half of each eye is projected to the right hemisphere of the brain, whereas information presented to the right half of each eye goes to the left hemisphere. Provided that the patient's direction of gaze was controlled and that information was presented for a tenth of a second or less to prevent eye movements, Sperry could ensure that only one hemisphere of the brain received the information.

One of Sperry's first discoveries was that the patients had two separate visual inner worlds. If the picture of an object was presented to one hemisphere, the patient recognized it when it was presented again to the same hemisphere. However, if the picture was then presented in the other half of the visual field, so that it was projected to the opposite hemisphere, the patient responded as if he had no recollection of having seen the picture before.

More striking evidence of the existence of two quite separate visual worlds in these patients was obtained when the word "heart" was flashed across the center of the visual field, with "he" to the left of center and "art" to the right of center. Since language and speech are very largely left hemisphere functions, the patients said they could see the word "art" when it was presented to the right and projected to the left hemisphere. However, when they were asked to point with the left hand to one of two cards ("art" or "he") to identify the word they had seen, they invariably pointed to "he." The reason is that the right hemisphere controls the movement of the left hand and "he" had been presented to the right hemisphere.

It has been known for a long time that language is associated to a far greater extent with the left hemisphere than with the right, although the opposite is found among some left-handed people. The original evidence for this came from studying patients who had received head injuries or suffered strokes. A gunshot wound to the left side of the head, for example, or a stroke in the left hemisphere, is much more likely to affect speech or writing ability than is a similar injury to the right side.

Sperry was able to confirm this very convincingly. He found that visual material projected to the left hemisphere could be described by the patients in speech and writing in an essentially normal manner. But when the same material was presented to the right hemisphere, the patient would insist that he had not seen anything, or that there had been only a flash of light. Yet if the patient was then asked to use his left hand to point to a matching picture or object, he had no trouble in indicating the very item which he had just insisted he had not seen.

In an amusing variation of this experiment, a female patient was presented with a series of neutral geometrical figures. A photograph of a nude woman was then flashed to the right hemisphere. The patient said that she had not seen anything, but a sly smile spread over her face and she began to laugh. When she was asked what she was laughing at, she replied: "I don't know . . . nothing . . . oh, that funny machine."

We have already mentioned that the right hemisphere is not usually the one which controls speech. However, other observations made by Sperry and his co-workers indicated that the right hemisphere is able to understand both written and spoken words to some extent. If the name of an object (e.g., "eraser") was flashed to the right hemisphere, the pa-

Diagram showing an anterior-posterior section through the midline of the brain. The stalk is the medulla oblongata, the offshoot on the right is the cerebellum, the darker shaded areas represent the corpus callosum, with the hypothalamus beneath and the little knob of the pituitary to the left.

tient was able to select an eraser from among other objects by touch alone using the left hand (controlled by the right hemisphere). The right hemisphere was even able to respond appropriately to a command such as "Retrieve the fruit monkeys like best"—patients were quite capable of pulling a banana from a bag of plastic fruit with their left hand. The patients varied in terms of the linguistic powers of the right hemisphere. The most adept patient was able to spell simple words by placing plastic letters on a table with his left hand; but after he had spelled a word as directed, he could not name the word he had just spelled.

So far, we have focused mainly on the problems Sperry's patients encountered in dealing with visual information. Similar difficulties were experienced when objects were placed unseen in either the left or the right hand. Information from the left hand goes to the right hemisphere, and information from the right hand to the left hemisphere. Objects placed in the right hand for identification by touch were easily described or named in speech or writing. If the same objects were placed in the left hand, the patients could only make wild guesses and often seemed unaware that anything at all was in their hand. However, if one of the objects which the patient said he did not recognize was taken from his left hand and placed among a dozen other items, he was then able to feel it out and retrieve it, again with the left hand, even after a time lapse of several minutes. The major limitation on performance here was that the patients could retrieve the object only if they used the same hand throughout—they could not recognize with one hand something identified only moments before with the other.

The superiority of the left hemisphere over the right across a wide range of tasks has led many people to refer to the left side of the brain as the "major hemisphere" and to the right side as the "minor hemisphere." This is a profoundly mistaken view. If we move away from verbal abilities and consider other kinds of skills (e.g., spatial), the position is quite different. Tests by Sperry and Bogen showed that the right hand, which is under left hemisphere control, was unable either to arrange blocks to match a pictured design or to draw a cube in three dimensions, whereas the left hand could perform both tasks quite satisfactorily.

There is interesting recent evidence to suggest that the right hemisphere may also be more intimately involved in emotional experiences. Lesions in most areas of the left hemisphere are accompanied by the feelings of loss that might be expected as the result of any serious injury, whereas damage in much of the right hemisphere sometimes leaves the patient unconcerned about his injuries and their possible consequences.

After Sperry's patients had been tested a number of times, they started using various strategies to cope with the tasks they were asked to perform. When a red or green light was flashed to the right hemisphere, the patient would at first simply guess at the color. With practice, however, if the right hemisphere saw the red light and heard the left hemisphere guess "green," it produced a frown and a shake of the head. This cued the left hemisphere to the fact that the answer was wrong.

Although the media have emphasized the problems that split-brain patients experience in performing relatively simple activities, Sperry found that it was sometimes a positive advantage to have two half-brains. He asked his patients to perform two different visual discrimination tasks simultaneously, with one task being presented to each hemisphere, and this they did just as well as if they were performing each task on its own. In contrast, normal people find that the two tasks definitely interfere with each other if they attempt to perform them simultaneously.

The functions of the two hemispheres

One of the most challenging issues that arise from Sperry's pioneering research is whether he has conclusively demonstrated the existence of two minds, each with its own consciousness. Sperry himself believed that he had. He announced: "Everything we have seen so far indicates that the surgery has left these people with two separate minds, that is, two separate spheres of consciousness. What is experienced in the right hemisphere seems to be entirely outside the realm of awareness of the left." A very categorical statement indeed.

Experts have been of two minds, as it were, about whether or not to accept Sperry's bold assertion. Part of the difficulty revolves around what we mean by "conscious experiences"; it has been defined semi-facetiously as "the dimension that makes you more like a dog than a computer," but various other definitions are possible.

The best attempt so far to come to grips with the question of double consciousness was undertaken recently by LeDoux, Wilson, and Gazzaniga.[2] They pointed out that it is relatively easy to assess the nature and limits of consciousness in the "talking" left hemisphere, but much more difficult to do the same with respect to the mute right hemisphere. They partially overcame this problem by carrying out tests on Paul S., a boy who had greater language representation in the right hemisphere than had been observed in any other split-brain patient.

On one occasion, words were presented to one hemisphere of Paul S.'s brain, and he evaluated them on a good-bad scale. Many of the words elicited quite different evaluations from the two hemispheres,

Spatial tasks like painting appear to involve more activity in the right side of the brain than in the left. The reverse is true of verbal tasks. Photos: Multimedia Publications Inc. (Israel Sun).

with the right hemisphere rating being consistently closer to the bad end of the scale than the left hemisphere rating. Words such as "Paul," "mother," and "sex" were rated very good by the left hemisphere and very bad by the right hemisphere. These differences suggest that each hemisphere may possess its own unique system for assigning subjective values to people and events.

It is especially intriguing that Paul was difficult to cope with on the day that these differences in hemisphere evaluations were obtained; it is almost as if he were literally at odds with himself. When he evaluated the same words on a second occasion he was calm and tractable. His improved mood on this occasion was mainly reflected in more positive right hemisphere evaluations, supporting the idea that the right hemisphere is more "emotional" in some sense. On this second occasion, too, the good-bad ratings were very similar in each half-brain.

Further evidence in favor of the notion that each hemisphere has a mind of its own was obtained when Paul was asked what job he would like; the left half-brain spelled out "draftsman," whereas the right half-brain spelled out "automobile race." It thus looks as if Sperry may not have been far wide of the mark in suggesting that two minds can coexist in one body, but this may only happen when some language skills are present in each hemisphere.

Many popular writers have drawn sweeping conclusions about normal people, and even the inadequacies of entire human societies, on the basis of Sperry's work with a handful of severely epileptic patients. We have been told that the verbal, logical culture of the Western world is managed by the left hemispheres of its population, whereas the mystical, artistic, and religious cultures of the East are based on right hemisphere domination.

This analysis has suggested to the psychologist Robert Ornstein that there ought to be a revolution in Western education, with much greater emphasis being placed on non-verbal skills. Just as there are people who are politically left-wing and others who are right-wing, so also there are left and right hemisphere supporters. Hugh Sykes Davies, a scholar of English, has recently attacked the "rightist" movement to which Ornstein belongs, and complained that crucial left hemisphere verbal skills are rapidly degenerating in our society. Unfortunately most of the contributors to this controversy seem to have made the bizarre assumption that the two hemispheres of a normal man or woman are as divided as those of Sperry's patients. Presumably what actually needs to be done is not to pamper one hemisphere at the expense of the other, but rather to harmonize and integrate their joint functioning.

A very important question that has almost been lost sight of by popular writers is whether or not we can safely assume that the differences between the two hemispheres in normal individuals are the same as those found by Sperry in split-brain patients. It could well be that frequent epileptic seizures in the brain, combined with all the problems of adjustment after surgery, make such patients' brains quite different from normal brains.

How can we look at the way each hemisphere performs in normal people? One useful method is to record the brain waves evoked by some stimulus or other via small metal electrodes pasted onto the scalp, and to amplify these responses electronically, using special computer techniques to distinguish them from continuous brain-wave activity. This technique measures what are known as "evoked potentials" (see Chapter 9), and depending on where we choose to place the electrodes we can measure brain-wave activity in either the left or the right hemisphere.

In one typical experiment, subjects were asked to carry out a number of verbal tasks (e.g., vocabulary test, finding synonyms) and spatial tasks (e.g., constructing a cross out of six plastic pieces, drawing a human figure). There was more pronounced brain-wave activity in the left than in the right hemisphere when a verbal task was being performed; the opposite occurred when a spatial task was being carried out. These observations fit in well with Sperry's notion that the left hemisphere is dominant for language skills and the right for spatial abilities.

There have been attempts recently to apply brain-wave techniques to a well-known sex-related difference, namely that women tend to be better than men at verbal tasks, while men are better at spatial tasks. Do women have better verbal skills because they have greater language representation in the right hemisphere than men, and does the organization of their right hemisphere for language interfere with the right hemisphere's attempts to handle spatial tasks? The answer to both questions seems to be yes. Women show relatively more brain-wave activity in the right hemisphere than men when engaged in verbal activities.

However, cross-cultural studies have somewhat dented the view that the right and left hemispheres have fairly specialized functions. Tsunoda Tadanobu of the Tokyo Medical-Dental College has found interesting differences between the brains of Japanese people and those of other groups. He discovered that the sounds of insects, animals, rain, wind, and waves activated the left hemispheres of Japanese-speaking people and the right hemispheres of other groups. He also found that the sounds of traditional Japanese musical instruments like the *shakuhachi* produced the same pattern.

What is the reason for this unusual response to sounds? According to Tadanobu, the peculiarities of the Japanese language play a major role. In Japanese, all vowel sounds and their derivatives are meaningful words. This means that many naturally occurring sounds resemble Japanese words and so activate the language-processing systems of the left hemisphere.

All the evidence indicates that our hemispheres typically operate in an asymmetrical fashion, that is to say, many activities depend much more heavily on one hemisphere than the other. In other species, symmetrical functioning of the two parts of the brain is often found. What are the advantages and disadvantages of asymmetrical brain functioning?

One advantage can be illustrated by means of a tale related by the fourteenth-century monk Jean Buridan: an ass was faced with the dilemma of choosing between two equally appetizing and equidistant bales of hay, but it perished because it had no logical reason for moving toward one bale rather than the other. In real life, nature has provided for this eventuality by equipping animals and humans with a response bias that would usually lead them to select the bale on their right.

In general terms, asymmetry can be an advantage if you are trying to do two very different activities at once; if each activity can be dealt with by a different hemisphere, interference between the two activities is reduced. On the other hand, if you are attempting to cope with a single, complex task, it may be more difficult to coordinate behavior if each hemisphere is doing part of the necessary processing on its own.

Marcel Kinsbourne tested some of these ideas with a very simple task that you can easily try yourself. This involves balancing a rod on either the right or the left index finger for as long as possible. If right-handed people do this while remaining silent, they can balance the rod longer on the right than on the left, because the right hand is more generally skilled. However, if people are speaking while they attempt to balance the rod, then the opposite result is obtained: they can now balance the rod longer on the left than on the right. When the right hand is used, it is as if speaking knocks the rod off the finger.

What on earth is happening here? Speech and the right hand are both controlled by the left hemisphere, and so interfere with each other. In contrast, speech and the left hand are controlled by different hemispheres, and so only interfere with each other to a modest extent. This simple but ingenious experiment shows the potential advantages of asymmetry; if each hemisphere concentrates on a single task, two different activities can be successfully performed at the same time.

Conclusions

The history of attempts to modify human behavior by direct action on the brain shows that it is all too easy to produce radical behavioral changes. The problem is that many unforeseen and unfortunate changes usually accompany the desired ones. This has led to increasing legal constraints on the use of various psychosurgical techniques.

However, there are some brain operations that have proved to be worthwhile under certain circumstances. The work of Sperry is especially important in this context, because it has provided major benefits in terms both of the welfare of epileptic patients and of the accumulation of knowledge about the mysterious workings of the brain.

12

Where do emotions come from?

There is an endless fascination about emotional experiences that has kept generations of novelists and poets in gainful employment. One of the reasons for this fascination is the lack of agreement about the proper significance of major kinds of emotional feeling. Consider as an example the intense emotion of love. To the poet Shelley it was "the universal thirst for a communion not merely of the sense, but of our whole nature." George Bernard Shaw referred to it as "a gross exaggeration of the difference between one person and everybody else."

We shall not attempt to settle such differences of opinion. However, we shall consider the interesting matter of exactly what it is that leads people to have emotional experiences. In other words, where do our emotions come from?

Key experiment   Emotion $=$ arousal $\times$ emotionality of thought (Stanley Schachter and Jerome Singer)

The classic study on emotion was carried out some twenty years ago by Stanley Schachter of Columbia University and Jerome Singer[1] of Pennsylvania State University. They started by asking themselves what ingredients were vital before someone can experience an emotional state and decided that there were two. One ingredient is a state of physiological arousal, which can include pounding of the heart, sweating, trembling hands, and a warm, flushed face. The second ingredient is the way in which the person interprets this state of arousal; he must explain the arousal in emotional terms in order to feel in an emotional state. If he accounts for the arousal in non-emotional terms, he will not experience emotion.

Normally, of course, arousal is interpreted as an emotional experience; a man who becomes aroused at the sight of a pretty girl normally attributes his arousal to feelings of sexual attraction. However, according to Schachter and Singer, it is entirely possible for us to feel aroused or "stirred up" without experiencing any emotion at all. Some work done by a medical doctor named Maranon in the 1920s suggested the reason why. He injected 210 of his patients with Adrenalin, which is a drug whose effects mimic almost perfectly a naturally occurring state of arousal. When he asked his aroused patients to say how they felt under this drug, 71 percent simply reported their physical symptoms, attaching no emotional overtones to them whatsoever. But the remaining 29 percent did respond in an apparently emotional fashion. The really interesting thing here was that the great majority of patients described their feelings in a way that Maranon labeled "cold" or "as if" emotions.

Why did virtually all of Maranon's patients fail to experience any true emotions in spite of their aroused state? Schachter and Singer put forward the plausible suggestion that these patients sought to explain why they felt stirred up; the most obvious cause was the drug they had been injected with; because they could neatly account for their high level of arousal in non-emotional terms, they felt no emotional state.

Schachter and Singer also argued that the same state of physiological arousal was associated with all kinds of emotional experience: "Precisely the same state of physiological arousal could be labeled 'joy' or 'fury' or 'jealousy' or any of a great diversity of emotional labels depending on the cognitive aspects of the situation." That is, the great variety of emotions we experience are the result of changes in the way we interpret our aroused state.

If it is true that there is very great flexibility in the way in which we apply emotional labels to aroused states, then we are likely to make mistakes—in other words, apply them incorrectly—from time to time. For example, some women become tense shortly after their period starts each month; often they attribute this tension to external causes, to other people being awkward or irritating, rather than to their monthly cycle.

The Romeo and Juliet effect is another example of misattribution of emotions; the more parental interference young people in love are confronted with, the greater the amount of romantic love they tend to experience. It may be that the attitudes of the parents create a state of unpleasant arousal which is then relabeled romantic attraction, or, to put it another way, adrenaline makes the heart grow fonder.

Schachter and Singer carried out a quite complicated experiment to investigate some of these ideas. Their basic prediction was fairly simple and straightforward: for genuine emotion to be experienced, there must be a state of arousal, and it must be interpreted in emotional terms; if either ingredient is lacking, no emotion will be experienced.

They decided to test their prediction by varying both the amount of arousal that was experienced and the way in which the arousal was interpreted. All the participants were told that the experiment was designed to find out how the vitamin compound Suproxin affects vision. Although they were told that they had been injected with this vitamin compound, they actually received either Adrenalin (which increases physiological arousal) or a saline-solution placebo (which, of course, has no effect on arousal).

The various groups of participants were told different stories about the side effects of the drug. Those receiving Adrenalin were either correctly informed about the effects of the drug, misinformed ("Your feet will feel numb, you will have an itching sensation over parts of your body, and you may get a slight headache"), or kept in ignorance, being told merely that the injection was mild and harmless and would have no side effects. Those given the placebo were also told that the drug would have no side effects.

After they had received the injection, all the participants were told that the vision tests would begin in twenty minutes, so as to allow time for the Suproxin to get into the bloodstream. During that time, each individual was placed in a situation designed to produce either euphoria or anger.

In the euphoria situation, the participant and a confederate of the experimenter waited together. The confederate doodled on a note pad, threw crumpled pieces of paper at the wastepaper basket in a mock basketball game, made and flew a paper plane, made a catapult out of a rubber band and used it to shoot bits of paper at a tower of manila folders, and played with a hula hoop. The general idea was that the participant would respond to the boisterous enthusiasm of the confederate by becoming happy or euphoric (it has since been pointed out that other emotions might be aroused by such behavior, including curiosity, disgust, and irritation).

In the anger condition, the participant and the confederate spent the twenty minutes filling in questionnaires that became increasingly personal and insulting, finishing up with the question: "With how many men (other than your father) has your mother had extramarital relationships?" The confederate became progressively more annoyed and agitated, and eventually tore up his questionnaire, screwed up the pieces and flung them on the floor, saying, "I'm not wasting any more time. I'm getting my books and leaving."

How much emotion should the various groups have shown in both these conditions? According to Schachter and Singer, those given Adrenalin and told about its arousing effects should not have experienced much emotion; they would interpret the arousal they felt as stemming from the drug rather than from their reaction to the behavior of the confederate ("I feel this way because I have just received an injection of Adrenalin").

Those given the innocuous placebo should also have experienced relatively little emotion: they would not be in an aroused state, because they had not received an arousing drug. In contrast, those given Adrenalin and misinformed about its effects should be highly aroused, and would be unlikely to interpret their arousal as due to the drug; they would presumably tend to attribute their aroused state (anger or euphoria) to the behavior of the confederate. A similar prediction followed for those given Adrenalin and told it would have no side effects: they should be aroused and would account for their arousal in emotional terms.

In view of the fact that Schachter and Singer's experiment constitutes one of the most celebrated investigations of emotion, the striking thing about their findings was that some of them did not accord too well with their predictions. The basic problem was that those who had been given the placebo, and were therefore supposed to be relatively unaroused and unemotional, actually experienced quite a lot of emotion. A further experiment designed to probe this particular problem will be considered in a moment. However, there was reasonable evidence that states of high arousal are labeled in different ways in different circumstances. Of the people injected with Adrenalin, it was only those who were told precisely what they would feel, and why, who remained relatively unmoved by the anger- and euphoria-provoking situations, presumably because they believed that the drug rather than the situation was producing the arousal.

It is possible that those given the placebo rather than Adrenalin did, in fact, become aroused as a result of being exposed to the confederate, in which case, of course, the assumption that they would be relatively unaroused was false. Schachter and Singer argued that the way to prevent people from becoming aroused was to give them a drug that actually *reduces* arousal rather than a placebo. The drug they chose for this purpose was the depressant chlorpromazine. All participants were told that they would receive Suproxin, a highly concentrated vitamin C derivative with no side effects, but they were actually injected with either chlorpromazine, the placebo, or the arousing drug Adrenalin. They then watched a fifteen-minute excerpt from a Jack Carson film called *The Good Humor Man* involving a slapstick chase scene.

Since everyone was expected to attribute any feelings of arousal to the same source, namely the film, the prediction was that the amount of emotion experienced would depend mainly on the amount of arousal caused by the injections given. Thus, the Adrenalin-injected people should have been most aroused and most amused, and the chlorpromazine-injected people least aroused and least amused.

Reactions to the film were assessed by asking the participants how enjoyable and funny they had found the film and by observing the number of smiles, grins, laughs, and belly laughs during the showing of the film. Exactly as predicted, those injected with Adrenalin found the film funniest and showed most signs of overt amusement, and those injected with chlorpromazine were the least amused by the film. The placebo-injected participants tended to react to the film with quiet amusement, whereas several of the Adrenalin-injected participants reacted with belly laughs. Interestingly, some of those injected with Adrenalin were aware of a discrepancy between their actual behavior and their impressions of the film; for example, one participant said, "I just couldn't understand why I was laughing during the movie. Usually, I hate Jack Carson and this kind of nonsense."

In the twenty years or so since this seminal work, much has been said both for and against Schachter and Singer's viewpoint. Some of the most critical points were made by Gary Marshall and Philip Zimbardo[2] of Stanford University, who did a follow-up study in 1979. They noted that, despite the obvious importance of the Schachter and Singer study and the unclear nature of some of their results, no one had attempted to replicate it in the intervening twenty years. In their study, Marshall and Zimbardo used only the euphoria situation, because the Stanford University Medical School Human Subjects Committee argued that it was unethical to induce anger in unsuspecting people.

In essence, Marshall and Zimbardo found that the injection of Adrenalin failed to make the participants more happy or euphoric than those receiving the placebo. They were disappointed by these results, and tried larger doses of Adrenalin. People injected with these larger doses and then exposed to the euphoric confederate actually reported that they were unhappier than the other groups, which is precisely the opposite of what Schachter and Singer would have predicted.

Why didn't the high level of arousal produced by Adrenalin make the participants more receptive to a pleasant state of emotion? It may be that unexplained arousal is normally regarded as unpleasant. After all, substantial levels of physiological arousal are far more often associated with negative emotional experiences than with positive ones; the universal exception is sexual excitement.

Even when the Adrenalin-injected participants behaved in a mildly euphoric way, it was still something of a pretense. As one participant said, "It's like being at a party when everyone is clearly having a good time and you have a headache or feel depressed for some unknown reason. You don't want to rain on their parade; you might even laugh and try to join in, but you don't really feel happy."

Schachter and Singer hypothesized that all emotional states involve the same churned-up physiological state. Other psychologists, however, have wondered whether things are really that simple. For example, Daniel Funkenstein found some support for the idea that anxiety is associated with the production of adrenaline within the body, with noradrenalin release being associated with anger or aggression. Some fairly fanciful support for this notion comes in the finding that predatory species of animals such as lions and tigers produce more noradrenalin than non-predatory species such as deer and sheep. But how does this relate to human emotional states?

Lennart Levi tested Funkenstein's idea in a study in which he asked people to watch four films designed to elicit different emotional reactions: *Paths of Glory* (an early Stanley Kubrick film about a World War I episode in which several French enlisted men were accused of cowardice, court-martialed, and shot, in order to cover up the bungling of an incompetent general); *Charley's Aunt* (a comedy in which the main male character capers about in woman's clothing to avoid the consequences of some supposed breach of family propriety); *Mask of Satan* (a horror film in which there are several gruesome killings); and a neutral film of nature scenes.

Those watching the films experienced anger while watching *Paths of Glory,* amusement during *Charley's Aunt,* and fear during *Mask of Satan*—different emotional reactions in each case. It was found that adrenaline flow increased to a similar extent during all three of these films, but not during the neutral film. This, of course, agrees with Schachter and Singer's notion that all emotional experiences have a common underlying physiological basis. (Unfortunately for Funkenstein's own theory, noradrenalin flow did not significantly increase during *Paths of Glory,* but it did increase during *Mask of Satan.*)

A final important way of assessing the value of Schachter and Singer's contribution to the study of emotion is to consider the emotional life of paraplegics and quadriplegics, whose spinal cord injuries are so severe that they have little or no direct experience of physiological arousal. If Schachter and Singer's theory is right, they should lead relatively unemotional lives, and this does indeed seem to be the case. Although they sometimes behave in an apparently emotional way, they tend not to feel very emotional: "Sometimes I act angry when I see some injustice. I yell and cuss and raise hell . . . but it just doesn't have the heat to it that it used to. It's a mental kind of anger," or "Seems like I get thinking mad, not shaking mad, and that's a lot different."

Romantic love

On the face of it, romantic love is an odd topic to try to study within the gray walls of the psychology laboratory. However, some bold researchers have done just that. The usual idea has been that romantic love, or at least sexual attraction, can be produced in the laboratory, provided those taking part in the experiment are aroused and the situation enables them to interpret their state in sexual terms.

Stuart Valins took this argument one step further. He wondered whether it was really necessary for people to be physiologically aroused; perhaps if they mistakenly believed themselves to be aroused, that would prove sufficient for them to experience pleasant feelings of a sexual nature.

Valins persuaded (little persuasion was needed!) young men to look at slides of semi-nude women taken from the pages of *Playboy* magazine. While they were performing this arduous task, they listened to what they were told was an amplified version of their heartbeat. In fact, the heartbeat was completely faked; it remained steady for some of the slides, but speeded up or slowed down for others at random. The semi-nudes associated with the apparent increase in heart rate were rated as the most attractive and appealing, followed by those associated with the decreased heart rate, and then those for whom the heart rate had remained steady.

When the men were looking at a slide that apparently caused their heartbeat to speed up, they tended to look at the slide more closely, obviously in an attempt to justify their fast heartbeat by magnifying the girl's positive characteristics.

Valins apparently demonstrated that sexual attraction can be enhanced by an imaginary increase or change in arousal. However, it has subsequently been found that fake changes in heart rate when watching female nudes trigger off genuine changes in heart rate, so that actual changes in arousal may be necessary to increase sexual attraction. It has also been found that men watching slides of male nudes were not affected emotionally by fake heart rate increases; they merely found the whole experiment distasteful and offensive.

Joanne Cantor showed excerpts from an erotic film called *Naked Under Leather* to young men either immediately after or five minutes after they had performed vigorous physical exercise (bicycle pedaling). She found that those who viewed the film five minutes after exercise, rather than immediately afterward, were more sexually aroused by it. Immediately after exercise, people are physically aroused but attribute arousal to the aftereffects of exercise. A few minutes later, however, people are still aroused but do not realize that they are. In Cantor's experiment this residual arousal combined with the arousal produced by watching the film led to an augmented erotic response to the film. Thus, if you take up jogging, you may find yourself giving your partner the glad eye after your daily run!

This research showed that arousal produced by one aspect of the environment (in this case, exercise) can sometimes be misattributed to a completely different aspect of the environment (in this case, an erotic film). The notion that sexual attraction can be increased by arousal from an irrelevant source has a long history. In classical times, a Roman expert on love recommended that would-be lovers should take their ladies to gladiatorial contests, presumably on the principle that the ladies would misattribute the arousal and excitement generated by the events in the arena to their male companions and fall in love with them.

Many authorities have even suggested that the arousal produced by unpleasant emotions such as fear, anger, and frustration can often fuel the flames of desire. In the words of Sigmund Freud, "Some obstacle is necessary to swell the tide of libido (sexual energy) to its height." The same thought was expressed less bluntly by the Greek writer Vassilikos: "Once upon a time there was a little fish who was a bird from the waist up and who was madly in love with a little bird who was a

Though mankind has developed hundreds of thousands of languages and dialects for conveying information, non-verbal signals remain a very reliable guide to our feelings. Photo: Yael Braun.

fish from the waist up. So the Fish-Bird kept saying to the Bird-Fish: 'Oh, why were we created so that we can never live together? You in the wind and I in the wave. What a pity for both of us.' And the Bird-Fish would answer: 'No, what luck for both of us. This way we'll always be in love because we'll always be separated.' "

Donald Dutton and Arthur Aron wondered whether the emotion of fear could be used to enhance sexual responsiveness. Men on their own were approached either by an attractive female interviewer or by a male interviewer. The interview took place either on a sturdy bridge overlooking a 10-foot drop or on a 5-foot-wide, 450-foot-long suspension bridge which tilted, swayed, and wobbled rather alarmingly, creating the impression that one might easily fall 230 feet to the rocks and shallow rapids below. It was assumed, with some justification, that the suspension bridge would create more fear than the other bridge. The interviewer asked each man to invent a story based on a picture, and found the greatest number of sexually toned responses when the interviewer was female and the interview took place on the fear-provoking suspension bridge. The female interviewer also gave each participant her phone number and the men on the suspension bridge showed more sexual interest in her than the men on the sturdy bridge, because more of them telephoned her afterward.

Dutton and Aron may have succeeded in showing that arousal associated with fear can be misperceived as sexual attraction, but it seems a little far-fetched to suggest that the men on the swaying bridge really interpreted their sweaty palms and trembling legs as due to the irresistible charms of the female interviewer. It is more likely that she helped to reduce their fear by distracting them from their dangerous situation, and that this is why they responded to her so positively. Alternatively, she may have been perceived as more daring or thrill-seeking in the more fear-inducing situation, and the male participants assumed or hoped that this would also be true of her sexual behavior.

Clinical implications

Most, if not all, forms of mental illness involve a considerable amount of emotional disturbance. If there is any validity to the theoretical approach to emotion pioneered by Schachter and Singer, then it ought to have some implications for clinical treatment. Some preliminary work has already been carried out, and some intriguing results have been obtained.

Imagine that you are faced with the problem of treating people suffering from chronic insomnia, who report taking almost an hour to get to sleep every night. You have in your possession some sugar-pill placebos, which are entirely innocuous. Should you tell the insomniacs that these pills will increase their level of arousal or that they will decrease arousal and help to relax them? One's initial reaction would be to tell the insomniacs that the "drug" will relax them.

However, let us assume that the insomniac's problem is that he tends to go to bed in a state of arousal and that he associates that arousal with emotionally toned thoughts. If he then takes a "drug" that allegedly reduces arousal but is actually a placebo, he is likely to start thinking: "If I feel as I do now, when a drug is operating to lower my arousal, then I must be very aroused indeed." In contrast, if he takes a placebo which he believes to be capable of producing arousal symptoms, he may very well attribute most of his arousal to the drug and only a small proportion of his arousal to his worries and problems.

Paradoxically, then, insomniacs might worry more and take longer to get to sleep when given a "relaxing" drug than when given an "arousing" drug, and this is what the researchers found. Insomniacs given the "arousing" placebo got to sleep at least 20 percent faster than previously, whereas those taking the "relaxing" placebo took over 40 percent longer than usual to get to sleep.

Why were the results exactly the opposite of those usually achieved with placebos? Part of the answer may be that insomniacs are all too familiar with their own symptoms, and therefore know that their overall state of arousal at bedtime is neither much greater nor much less than usual. If they believe that the "drug" lowers or raises arousal level, as the case may be, they can only suppose that the amount of emotion-generated arousal must be more, or less, than usual in order to achieve the same result.

The same technique has been applied to pain tolerance. People who were led to believe that their experience of pain was due to a placebo (because they were told it would cause heart pounding, increased rate of breathing, and hand trembling) were able on average to tolerate 1,450 microamperes of electric shock, whereas those who had no reason to attribute pain to the placebo could tolerate only 350 microamperes. The former group also reported less experience of pain. Strange though it may sound, a visit to the dentist might be less unpleasant if the dentist gave you a "drug" which you thought would cause sweating, hand clenching, and a feeling of blind panic. You would blame the "drug," not his treatment.

Rather than allowing people to become aroused and then trying to persuade them to give a non-emotional label to their arousal, it might be easier to prevent the arousal from occurring in the first place. A. Lazarus has adopted the latter approach. The stimuli he uses are anxiety-provoking films: in one film, adolescent boys have their penises deeply cut in a Stone Age ritual; in another, a board is caught in a circular saw and rammed with tremendous force through the body of a worker, who dies writhing on the floor.

Most people respond to these films with considerable arousal and anxiety. However, if they are asked to consider the Stone Age ritual from the perspective of an anthropologist watching strange customs, and to remember that the people shown in the factory accident are actors, there is a marked reduction in arousal and anxiety. Similarly, one might be frightened by strange noises in the night, until one discovers that the neighbor's cat is the culprit. Whenever possible, it seems, we try to cope with unpleasant situations by giving them a non-emotional interpretation.

Conclusions

In broad terms, Schachter and Singer are correct in assuming that the most important ingredients in producing an emotional experience are a state of physiological arousal and an emotional interpretation of the reasons why the arousal has occurred. They are also right in saying that a similar state of physiological arousal seems to be involved in several quite different subjective and emotional states.

The theory implies that people frequently misperceive the cause of their stirred-up physical state, and this may help in the treatment of some clinical patients. The theory also suggests explanations for some of the puzzling aspects of romantic love, particularly the way in which unpleasant emotions such as fear and anger can act as a spur to romantic ardor.

However, it would be fair to say Schachter and Singer have adopted an oversimplified view, a view which requires certain modifications and extensions. They focused on the notion that a state of arousal triggers off an interpretation of that state; but it is equally true to say, as Lazarus does, that the way in which a situation is interpreted affects the level of arousal.

SECTION D

Making sense of our world

The most obvious fact about the way in which human beings interact with the environment is the skill and success with which they manage to manipulate it. This is, of course, the major reason why *Homo sapiens* has become the dominant species on this planet. Even the most unintelligent human beings can control their environment to a degree that cannot be matched by any other species. This capacity to impose our will on our surroundings is taken so much for granted that we are puzzled and concerned when someone lacks the ability to control his or her own immediate situation. We assume they are suffering from some kind of physical or mental disorder and put them in a hospital in an attempt to restore their capabilities.

Psychologists attempting to understand how people process information and cope with situations often resort to the use of analogies. Some of Sigmund Freud's theories, for example, imply that human "drives," including the sexual drive, operate on a simple hydraulic principle. Using the analogy of a water tank, if one lowers the water level, the pressure on the sides of the tank is reduced; similarly by indulging in sexual activity (or some other energy-releasing activity) the strength of the sexual forces (or other pent-up forces) of the id can be reduced to a tolerable level.

Another favorite analogy in recent years has been between man's natural "data-processing" system and that of computers. Computers can store information for long periods of time, a capacity which mirrors man's long-term memory. Computers sometimes hold information only briefly while they perform various operations on it, which is similar to man's short-term memory. Computers also have executive programs which direct the sequencing of processing operations, and it has been argued that in man conscious attention serves the same function.

In spite of the popularity of this analogy, there is no very good reason for supposing that a human being operates at all like a computer. An alternative approach, much beloved of academic psychologists and used by generations of textbook writers, is to divide information processing into a series of stages, starting with attention and perception, going on to short-term and long-term memory, and finishing with retrieval. But this, too, has little to recommend it. The reason is that each of these processes affects all of the others in a number of very complex ways, and the idea of a rigid sequence of processing stages oversimplifies a complex reality.

The approach we propose to adopt is more flexible. Our basic assumption is that the best way of trying to understand man's flexible information-processing system is to consider some of the major situations in which the system seems unable to cope with the demands placed on it.

Under normal circumstances, human beings are quite proficient at attending to important information in their environment while ignoring the trivial and the non-essential. This is not always the case, however; if a very important event occurs suddenly and unexpectedly, we do not always manage to notice vital details about that event.

Such failures of observation are especially unfortunate when they occur while a crime is being committed. Chapter 13 is about eyewitness testimony and deals with the difficulty witnesses have in reconstructing the details of crimes. The inaccuracies of eyewitness reports have been well documented in the media; here we consider why these errors occur and what can be done to prevent them.

As overworked housewives and harassed business executives are well aware, it is often impossible to do two or more things at once. Why should this be so? In Chapter 14, we argue that it is because our powers of attention are limited; it is frequently extremely difficult to attend to more than one thing at a time. But there are ways in which we can overcome the narrowness of our attention, several of which are discussed in Chapter 15; frequent practice over a long period appears to offer the most promising line of approach.

One of the most obvious weaknesses of our information-processing system is our inability to remember some of the things we want to remember. Students taking examinations, housewives shopping in supermarkets, and college professors trying to track down an elusive reference have all wished that they had been blessed with a better memory system. The whole question of forgetting (and what to do about it) is dealt with in Chapter 15. It may come as a relief to know that being blessed with perfect and total recall is no blessing at all. Fortunately our memory system has provided itself with devices to minimize the disadvantages of its tendency to forget things.

In Chapter 16, we deal with the mysteries of non-verbal communication (eye contact, smiling, frowning, personal space). We tend to use non-verbal rather than verbal communication to express our feelings of liking or disliking for others. The most surprising aspect of non-verbal communication is that often neither the initiator nor the recipient is consciously aware of what is happening. Yet despite this limited awareness, non-verbal signals seem to be used in an amazingly sensitive and well-orchestrated way.

Most people like to behave in ways that are consistent with their attitudes (people who are religious go to church; whites who are racially prejudiced do not have black friends). However, there is often strong conflict between what people do and what they think (smokers continue smoking although they know that smoking can endanger health). Such conflicts can be upsetting and difficult to resolve, producing what Leon Festinger calls "cognitive dissonance." He has shown very clearly that people in a state of cognitive dissonance often experience bizarre and unpredictable attitude changes. His work in this field is discussed in Chapter 17.

The message implicit in all the chapters in this section is that although we are generally successful at coping with our environment, we are fallible and in some circumstances find it extremely difficult to make sense of our world. However, gaining an understanding of our cognitive limitations is the first step toward overcoming them.

13

Can we remember
what we see?

The psychologist has been compared to a man searching under the
light of a streetlamp for his wallet although he has already seen the
thief throw it into some thick bushes in a dark garden; he searches near
the light simply "because he can see what he is doing." Do psychologists really retreat into their ivory towers to carry out simple but
meaningless experiments which yield nothing of any practical
significance?

One of the earliest attempts to step outside the narrow confines of
the laboratory in the pursuit of psychological knowledge was made
shortly before the turn of the century by a leading German psychologist, Hugo Münsterberg. He was interested in the relevance of psychology to the presentation of evidence in court, and it was his studies
which first revealed that eyewitness testimony is often very unreliable.
Münsterberg was worried that innocent people might be being imprisoned solely on the basis of what one or more witnesses said they
remembered but might have remembered wrong.

There are some famous examples of mistaken identity. A recent one
was that of Peter Hain, the well-known opponent of apartheid in South
Africa, who was charged with robbing a bank in South London on the
basis of eyewitness accounts. Fortunately he was acquitted.

Somewhat surprisingly in view of the valuable work that has been
done, the fruits of psychologists' endeavors to unravel the complexities
of eyewitness testimony and its reliability have had very little impact
on the admissibility of evidence. We may be biased, but we believe
(and hope to demonstrate) that psychologists have a valuable contribu-

tion to make. That the current state of debate resembles a dialogue between the deaf, however, is clear from the 1976 Devlin Report on Evidence of Identification in Criminal Cases, which considered whether studies in psychology threw any light on such problems. The Report said: "It has been represented to us that a gap exists between academic research into the powers of the human mind and the practical requirements of courts of law and the stage seems not yet to have been reached at which the conclusions of psychological research are sufficiently widely accepted or tailored to the needs of the judicial process to become the basis for procedural change." Is this pessimistic view of psychology's contribution to the legal system justified?

In order to answer this question, we need to consider the nature of the processes of perception and memory, which are the basis for eyewitness testimony.[1] One common view is that perception and memory both involve a copying process. In other words, the human brain handles the wealth of sensory information available in the external world in the manner of tape recorders and movie cameras, which provide semi-permanent records of sounds and visual events. So failure on the part of a witness to remember what happened can be put down either to a lack of sufficient effort or to unwillingness. It is probably not an exaggeration to say that that is the view of many, if not most, of those involved in the law.

However, most psychologists nowadays feel that it is very misleading to regard perception and memory as being straightforward copies of the world outside. They prefer to regard perception as an active and constructive process, depending not only on information arriving from the external world but also on personal attitudes, beliefs, and motives.

A London bus line. How long have they been waiting? Their answers probably depend on how bored and irritated they feel. Photo: Multimedia Publications Inc. (Miki Koren).

A speeding car or a passing car? Bystanders' memories for incidents which lead to accidents are notoriously fragile. Photo: Multimedia Publications Inc. (Miki Koren).

The most obvious implication of this theory is that there will often be systematic, though unconscious, distortions in perception. At an informal level, the notion that people see what they want to see rather than what actually happens can be confirmed any Sunday afternoon at a football game. The award of a penalty to one team is seen as fair and reasonable by that team's supporters, but as disgraceful by the other team's supporters; the referee is seen either as an excellent judge of the game or as someone of dubious parentage in urgent need of a white stick.

Key experiment   Distorting the evidence (Elizabeth Loftus and John Palmer)

Elizabeth Loftus and John Palmer[2] of the University of Washington wondered whether the memory of an eyewitness might be similarly susceptible to distortion by information encountered after an accident or crime. To explore whether this was in fact the case, they carried out two experiments, both in the early 1970s. In the first experiment, participants were shown seven different films, each showing a traffic accident, and were then asked to answer a series of questions about each accident. Those who were asked the question "About how fast were the cars going when they smashed into each other?" consistently gave higher estimates of their speed than those asked to answer the same question, but with the word "smashed" replaced by "collided," "bumped," "contacted," or "hit." Indeed, the average estimated speed was almost ten miles an hour higher when "smashed" was used than when "contacted" was used. The *actual* speed at which the cars were traveling was almost irrelevant to estimates of speed: the average estimate was 38 mph when the cars collided at 40 mph, and 38 mph when they collided at 20 mph.

These findings clearly suggest that our memory for events is relatively fragile and fairly susceptible to distortion. Even stronger evidence was obtained in the second experiment, in which participants watched a short film depicting a multiple-car accident. In this film, the first car made a left turn to enter the main stream of traffic, causing cars in the oncoming lane to stop suddenly, with the result that five cars were involved in a bumper-to-bumper collision. At the end of the film, the participants answered a series of questions about the accident. One of the questions was either "About how fast were the cars going when they smashed into each other?" or "About how fast were the cars going when they hit each other?" As in the previous experiment, the average estimate of speed was greater for those interrogated with "smashed" than for those questioned with "hit."

One week later, all the participants returned and answered a series of questions about the same accident, but without viewing the film again. One of the questions asked was "Did you see any broken glass?" Of those who had answered the question about cars "smashing" into each other the week before, 32 percent said they had seen broken glass; only 14 percent of those who had answered the question about cars merely "hitting" each other said they had seen broken glass. Since there was, in fact, no broken glass in the accident, it appears that fairly subtle wording of questions can lead eyewitnesses to "remember" details that did not actually occur.

Information overlay

How did Loftus and Palmer account for their findings? Basically, they argued, two kinds of information go into one's memory when one is witnessing a complex event like an accident or a crime. The first is information obtained from perception of the original event, and the second is external information supplied subsequently. As time passes, information from these two sources is integrated in such a way that it is not possible to say from which source any specific detail is recalled: all we have is one "memory."

Of course, those involved in the legal process are aware of some of the difficulties inherent in the way in which questions to eyewitnesses are worded. Questions which either by their form or by their content suggest to the witness what answer is desired, or "lead" him to that desired answer, are called "leading questions" in the courtroom. Most countries have rules designed to exclude such questions; in the United States, for example, these are enshrined in the *Supreme Court Reporter* of 1973.

In spite of such precautions, there is still an obvious danger that a witness's fragile memories of an event will be systematically distorted either by conversations with other witnesses or by police interrogation. long before the start of court proceedings. Apparently trivial changes in the wording of questions can exert considerable influence. Take, for example, another memory experiment conducted by Elizabeth Loftus and Guido Zanni. This time the film showed a minor collision between a man backing out of a narrow space in a supermarket parking area and a woman pedestrian carrying a large bag of groceries. The observers were then asked questions about items that were not in the film. Those who were asked questions which included the definite article ("Did you see the bottle?") were more than three times as likely to say they saw the item as observers asked the same questions with the indefinite article ("Did you see a bottle?").

Transferring one memory to another

In further research, Elizabeth Loftus studied what is known as "unconscious transference." This occurs when a person seen committing one act is confused with a person seen committing another act. In one

The results of a recall experiment. At the top is an incomplete triangle accurately drawn from memory shortly after being presented, and below the same incomplete triangle as recalled one month and two months later. Note how the later triangles more and more closely approach the conventional notion of a triangle.

real-life case, a ticket agent at a railway station was robbed at gunpoint. He subsequently identified a sailor in a lineup as the criminal, but the sailor had a watertight alibi. It turned out later that the sailor had bought tickets from the agent on three separate occasions prior to the robbery. In other words, the ticket agent mistakenly assumed that the familiarity of the sailor's face related back to the robbery when in fact it related back to the three ticket-purchasing occasions.

In one experiment on unconscious transference, Loftus presented a tape-recorded narrative concerning six college students, each student being introduced by a slide at the appropriate point in the story, which went like this: Steve Kent picked up a heavy paperweight and threw it at Fisher, hitting him on the back of the head; one of the onlookers was Robert Dirks, who was shown wearing a small brown hat. Approximately one hour later, the participants in the experiment were asked either, "After the guy with the hat threw the paperweight at Fisher, did he run away?" or the same question with the words "with the hat" omitted.

Three days later, the participants tried to pick out the culprit from among the slides of the six students. Fifty-eight percent of those who had been asked the leading question (implying that the person with the hat committed the deed) chose the actual culprit; 24 percent chose the man with the hat. Eighty percent of those who had been asked the straightforward question made a correct identification, and only 6 percent chose the man with the hat. The implication of this experiment is alarming: suggestive questions can quite easily induce a witness to accuse an innocent person of something he didn't do.

Remembering criminal events

The fact that perception of a complex event such as a crime can be affected by the past knowledge and experience of the witness, as well as his attitudes, needs, beliefs, and expectations, was clearly demonstrated in the 1920s by Gordon Allport of Harvard University. All he did was to ask a number of people to take a brief look at a drawing of several people on a train. The drawing included a black man and a white man standing close to each other. In spite of the fact that it was the white man who was holding the cutthroat razor, almost 50 percent of Allport's observers said they saw the black man holding the razor. At the time the razor was regarded by many white Americans as a stereotyped symbol of black violence. Presumably it was this common prejudice which caused the distorted recollection of the event shown in the picture.

The clear message from the Allport study was that people tend to see

No prizes for guessing who this is. But take away any two of the four clues, and would you be so sure? Photo: Rex Features.

what they expect to see. This has now been demonstrated many times. Two prominent American researchers, Jerome S. Bruner and Leo Postman of Harvard University, showed observers a display of playing cards for a few seconds, and then asked them to report the number of aces of spades they thought they had seen. Most people said they saw three aces of spades; in fact, there were five, but two of them were colored red. Once again, past experience distorts the process of perception: we are misled by our knowledge that aces of spades are usually black.

Apart from the biasing effects of past knowledge and prejudice, are there any other reasons for assuming that eyewitnesses often misperceive events? At first glance, it would appear not. After all, people with amazingly good memories for visual information often turn up in laboratory studies. In one American study, it was found that observers were subsequently able to recognize correctly 90 percent of a huge set of 2,500 photographs of unfamiliar paintings, scenes, and events presented for a few seconds each. Even when 10,000 photographs were presented, there was still correct identification 86 percent of the time.

But in contrast to these laboratory studies, recollection of staged events in which actors pretend to steal purses, attack each other, and so on, is sometimes extremely poor. Why is there such a large difference in the two sets of findings? The answer is that the circumstances are entirely different. Observers in a laboratory know what to look for, they know where the visual information will be presented, and they know when it will be presented. Eyewitnesses to a crime are taken by surprise, are exposed to a complicated series of events, and are often quite naturally more concerned about their own safety than about memorizing the license plate of the robbers' getaway vehicle.

A point that is often overlooked is that people tend to pay more attention to those aspects of an event or another person which they find interesting. In everyday life, women always notice if another woman is wearing clothes which do not match or if she is wearing false eyelashes, whereas men notice that Mr. Smith down the road has bought himself a new car or a lawn mower. Peter Powers of the University of Washington investigated this phenomenon. Observers watched slides showing a man and a woman walking through a parking lot and spotting two people who are apparently fighting each other. The man rushes in to stop the fight while the woman goes off to phone for help. Female observers were more accurate than male observers in recalling the description and actions of the main female character, whereas male observers were more accurate in recalling information about the main male character and about a nearby car.

The effect of fear on memory has been researched by examining eye-

witness reports taken down by policemen within minutes of their arrival on the scene. The typical report conveys a general impression of
the assailant, but lacks specific features such as color of hair or eyes. In
general terms, less complete descriptions are obtained in connection
with the more fear-provoking crimes (e.g., rape or assault) than with
other crimes (e.g., robbery). Irrespective of the type of crime, unin-
jured victims give more complete descriptions of their assailant(s) than
injured victims.

It is often said that the members of a different race "all look the
same," and there is partial support for this assertion. White witnesses
show much greater accuracy in identifying white faces than black faces;
however, black witnesses show equal accuracy whether identifying
black faces or white faces.

It is also true, of course, that some faces are easy to remember because they are distinctive. Indeed, it is the unusual features of a face
that we remember best. Thus, it is Charlie Chaplin's mustache, Brezh-
nev's eyebrows, and Mick Jagger's lips which we remember.

It is plausible to assume that witnesses will pay less attention to trivial
crimes than to those which are more serious. In one experiment
witnesses saw an object being stolen; some believed it was worth about
£1, others that it was worth about £25. Fifty-six percent of the
witnesses who believed the object was worth £25 picked out the correct person from a six-person photo spread, compared with only 19
percent of those who believed the object to be relatively cheap. However, witnesses who saw an expensive item being stolen showed worse
recall of the various physical characteristics of the thief than people
who thought they were witnessing the theft of the cheap item. When
eyewitnesses believe that a serious crime is being committed, they pay
attention to just one crucial visual aspect of the scene (i.e., the facial
features of the criminal). Thus, an attempt to devalue all the testimony
of a witness during cross-examination by demonstrating the fallibility
of some of his recollections may be unfair.

Picking out the culprit from mug shots and lineups

A crucial stage in the process of using eyewitness testimony comes
when the witness is confronted with the suspect, either "live" in a
lineup or among a set of photographs or mug shots. It is important that
the other people included in the lineup or set of photos be broadly similar in appearance to the suspect. If it is generally agreed that the person who committed a crime was very tall and black, there is little point
in having a lineup comprising a huge black man and several short
white men.

There are some real-life examples of such bias. In the case of the militant black activist Angela Davis, one set of nine photographs used to check identification included three pictures of the defendant taken at an outdoor rally, two police mug shots of other women with their names displayed, a picture of a 55-year-old woman, and so on. Any witness could immediately rule out five of the nine pictures as ridiculous choices. The chances of selecting one of the pictures of Angela Davis was therefore at least 75 percent.

Robert Buckhout has claimed that one kind of bias in the use of mug shots is the implicit assumption that the witness ought to be able to pick out the suspect; in other words, there is social pressure to "cooperate" with the police. Buckhout staged an assault on a California state university campus in which a distraught student "attacked" a professor in front of 141 witnesses. Another person of the same age as the distraught student was present as a bystander. After the incident, the witnesses were asked to pick out the assailant from a set of six photographs; the unbiased photo spread used equivalent photos of all the suspects, whereas the biased photo spread had the assailant's photo at an angle to the others and with a different expression. The instructions to the witnesses were either unbiased ("Do you recognize any of the people in these photos?") or biased ("The actual culprit is among this set of photos").

Identification performance was affected by both kinds of bias. More witnesses picked out the culprit under biased than under unbiased conditions, and they were also more confident that they had selected the right person. The combination of biased photo spread and biased instructions led to over 60 percent of the witnesses selecting the perpetrator; only 40 percent were correct in their identification under unbiased conditions.

It is obviously worrying that the way in which suspect identification is carried out can produce such large effects on the apparent accuracy with which eyewitnesses remember events. It is also worrying that 25 percent of all the witnesses (including the attacked professor) mistakenly identified the innocent bystander, whose picture was also included in the photo spread, as the attacker.

In further research, Buckhout has shown very clearly that witnesses are usually prepared to identify someone, perhaps because they feel they would be wasting everyone's time unless they do. Fifty-two students witnessed a live purse-snatching incident in a classroom and were then exposed to two different lineups with five people in each. One lineup included the actual purse snatcher and the other lineup included someone who looked like the purse snatcher. Eighty percent of the witnesses picked out a suspect, even though most of them were mistaken. Fourteen witnesses correctly identified the culprit in one lineup, but half of them then rather spoiled things by going on to iden-

Three photographs of the same man: Ilich Ramirez Sanchez, alias "Carlos," leader of the terrorist attack on OPEC ministers in Vienna in December 1975. If the same photographs were mixed in with two dozen others, would you confidently identify them as photographs of the same man? Photos: Rex Features.

tify the person who merely resembled the culprit in the other lineup. Seven more witnesses picked only the look-alike, eighteen selected an innocent person who didn't even look like the culprit, and three went so far as to pick out two innocent people, neither of whom resembled the culprit.

One of the difficulties with mug-shot identification is that we tend to remember some kinds of information better than others. For example, we have probably all had the experience of recognizing someone's face without being able to "place" him. This typically happens when we normally see someone in just one setting, and then see him in a different setting. The TV star buying groceries and the company chairman prowling the red-light district of town provide examples of this phenomenon. In one experiment, students were presented with twenty-five photos of faces in one room, and with twenty-five more two hours later in another room radically different from the first. In a subsequent test, the faces were correctly recognized 96 percent of the time, but most observers could not remember at better than chance level in which room they had seen the faces. This inability to remember the circumstances in which a face has been seen can be especially troublesome if the eyewitnesses to a crime have encountered any of the suspects in other circumstances.

The accuracy of mug-shot identification is also affected if suspects look the way they looked at the time of the crime. In one British study, 91 percent of faces were correctly recognized when there was no alteration between initial viewing and the identification test. However, correct recognitions dropped to 82 percent when the pose and facial expression were changed, and there was a drastic decline to only 45 percent correct when the faces were disguised by adding or removing beards or glasses or changing the hairstyle. Those criminals who invest in false beards and dark glasses obviously have an intuitive appreciation of some of the principles of psychology.

The police often use a lineup in addition to mug shots to try to secure an identification. Very confusing things can happen when this is done. In one study, a staged crime was followed by the witnesses being shown a number of mug shots and then a "live" lineup of suspects. The key finding was that anyone seen in a mug shot was more likely to be picked out at the lineup as the guilty party. The actual "criminals" were selected by 65 percent of the witnesses when seen in mug shots, but by only 51 percent when seen only at the lineup; innocent people previously seen in mug shots were unjustly picked out 20 percent of the time at the lineup, compared to 8 percent of the time when not previously seen in mug shots. Obviously, a false identification rate of 20 percent is far greater than ought to be allowed by any reasonable system of criminal justice.

A final potential problem is that of unintentional (or even intentional) bias caused by the actions of the police officer organizing the lineup or mug-shot identification procedure. If the policeman knows which person is the prime suspect, then he may communicate this knowledge by subtle changes in facial expression when the witness is looking at that person. This kind of bias has even been found to influence the behavior of rats. Students who are told they have been given clever rats find their rats running mazes more rapidly than students who are told they have been given dull rats, even though the rats are allocated on an entirely random basis. It may well be that people are even more sensitive than rats to the cues provided by a human experimenter.

Eyewitness testimony: fragile, handle with care

Many psychologists who have investigated eyewitness testimony and discovered its fallibility have said how dangerous it is for the courts to place much reliance on the recollections of witnesses. However, if we were to discount all eyewitness testimony, it would be impossible for an innocent defendant to prove an alibi.

Psychologists also tend to think—without having provided much evidence—that judges and jurors believe witnesses to be more reliable than they actually are. But in fact there are some grounds for supposing that eyewitnesses are less fallible than psychologists believe them to be. In a number of ways, staged crimes differ importantly from real-life crimes. Participants in experiments nearly always know that the "crime" was staged by the time they are given an identification test, and so may well be relatively unconcerned about pointing the finger of suspicion at an innocent person. In real life, criminals often have distinctive characteristics; in experimental studies, researchers often go to great lengths to ensure that the "criminal" has no outstanding features. Finally, while the police usually focus their attention on those witnesses who indicate that they might be able to make a positive identification, researchers nearly always ask all the eyewitnesses to attempt identification. All of these differences may mean that real-life witnesses are not quite so prone to error as has sometimes been thought.

While there is probably no way of making eyewitnesses pay more attention to important details at the time of criminal events, it may be possible to improve their ability to recall vital information by means of hypnosis. In one case, California police used hypnosis on the 55-year-old driver of a school bus with twenty-six children on board which was hijacked. Interviewed by the police shortly after the crime, he remembered very little about the vans the three criminals had used to transport the children from the bus to an underground hideout. However, under hypnosis he managed to provide a vital clue in the form of the last five letters and digits of the license plate of one of the abduction vans.

Hypnosis has been used fairly extensively by the Israeli police; in one year they made seventeen arrests on evidence obtained under hypnosis. It is not yet entirely clear why hypnosis should be so successful. However, under normal conditions we always devote some attention (known as "spare processing capacity") to monitoring the environment for possible sources of important information. In contrast, under hypnosis people stop monitoring the environment, leaving their attention entirely free to concentrate on the task at hand (e.g., recollecting a criminal event).

The main focus of attempts to improve the value of eyewitness testimony ought to be to prevent recollections of the details of a crime from being systematically contaminated by subsequent occurrences. Police questioning should be entirely neutral, and should not suggest, directly or indirectly, that certain events actually occurred. When attempts are made at identification, whether by mug shots or by lineup, the person directing proceedings should have no knowledge at all of the case; this will help to eliminate any bias. Witnesses should be told emphatically that they are expected to identify someone only if they are confident that they have picked the right person; failure to identify anyone is entirely acceptable. Finally, either a videotape of the lineup or a set of the mug shots used should be made available to the defense lawyers so that checks for bias can be carried out.

Conclusions

The main reason for psychological investigation of eyewitness testimony is to clarify the conditions under which such testimony can be relied on. While many psychologists are inclined to discount the value of witnesses' recollections altogether, they may have overstated the case. Eyewitness testimony *can* provide extremely useful information, but it is vital to recognize the fragile nature of the memory of a criminal event. Simple questioning of a witness, unless handled with extreme care, can produce profound distortions of memory and thus render eyewitness testimony almost valueless. Similarly, identification procedures must be conducted in an entirely unbiased way if further distortions of memory are not to occur. If the judicial system would listen to psychologists, and if all reasonable attempts were made to prevent distortions of memory, then eyewitness testimony could become a much more reliable source of court evidence.

14

Doing two things at once

Everyday experience tells us that we are often surprisingly good at doing two things at once. For example, most people can hold a conversation while driving a car, or whistle a tune while they are working. On the other hand, there are some simple things which we find rather difficult to do simultaneously, such as tapping our head while rubbing our stomach. Unless one really concentrates, there is a tendency to start either rubbing the head or tapping the stomach, or both. And try asking a friend to multiply 24 by 17 while you are walking along together. Unless he is a mathematical wizard, he will probably have to stop walking so that he can devote all his attention to doing the mental arithmetic.

When we think about it, we may decide that we can attend to only one thing at a time, but thinking about it prompted the nineteenth-century philosopher and psychologist William James to adopt a more complicated position: "If, then, by the original question, how many ideas or things can we attend to at once, be meant how many entirely disconnected systems or processes of conception can go on simultaneously, the answer is not easily more than one, unless the processes are very habitual, but then two, or even three, without very much oscillation of the attention." As we shall see, William James was being his usual perspicacious self.

There are large differences between people in the extent to which they can pursue several activities at once. As a result of long practice, an individual can become a one-man band or a simultaneous translator, listening to a communication in one language while at the same

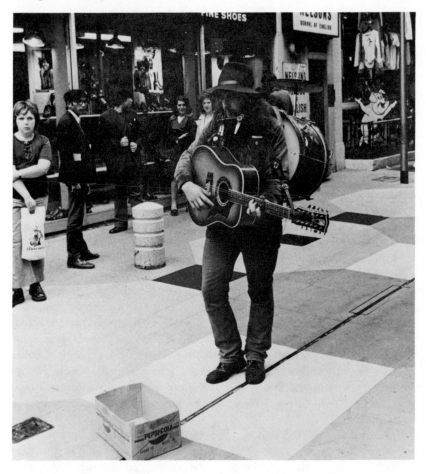

A one-man quartet. Natural ability to split attention varies, but it can be immensely improved with practice. Remember how you felt the first time you drove a car? Photo: Rex Features.

time translating the meaning and speaking it out loud in another language. In general terms, we would expect highly intelligent people to be most proficient at doing two things at once. This was presumably what Lyndon B. Johnson had in mind when he said of Gerald Ford that he couldn't fart and chew gum at the same time. This comment has often been toned down in the retelling with "walk" replacing "fart," but in either case it is an unflattering reflection on Ford's intelligence.

One of the first systematic attempts to evaluate man's powers of attention was made nearly thirty years ago by an English researcher, Colin Cherry. His pioneering work has served as the basis of much subsequent interest and research.

Key experiment   The cocktail party problem (E. Colin Cherry)

In the early 1950s, Colin Cherry was working in a laboratory at the Massachusetts Institute of Technology. Despite the fact that he was engaged in psychological research, he was working in an electronics research laboratory, and his exciting discoveries were later published in a physics journal, thus exemplifying the multidisciplinary nature of contemporary psychology.

Cherry was interested in what he referred to as the "cocktail party problem." Cocktail parties can pose a number of problems, but the one that concerned Cherry was how people manage to follow just one conversation when there are several different conversations going on within earshot.[1]

One obvious possibility is that we make use of the fact that each conversation concentrates on a different topic, and we simply "tune in" to one conversation on the basis of meaning. Of course, at an actual cocktail party the various conversations come from different directions, and people's voices tend to be distinctive, so there are other possible reasons for this ability to attend selectively to what one person is saying. Cherry eliminated these other factors by playing his subjects a tape recording of two different messages on the same tape spoken by the same person.

His subjects reported that it was extremely difficult to follow just one message while ignoring the other, and shut their eyes some of the time to assist concentration. While they always worked out what the message was in the end, some of the phrases had to be played up to twenty times. In other words, focusing on meaning is *not* the way in which people at a cocktail party cope with the information overload to which they are exposed.

If they do not use meaning to tune in to the right conversation, what do they use? Cherry argued that the direction from which the sought-for conversation was coming was probably vitally important. He tested this notion by equipping his listeners with headphones and feeding one spoken message into their left ear and a different message into their right. Although the two messages were spoken in the same voice, they experienced no difficulty in listening to either message at will while simply tuning out the other one. Thus the fact that the different speakers at a cocktail party are in different spatial locations may be of great importance in solving the cocktail party problem.

A party situation: the ear listens while the eye roves. Photo: Multimedia Publications Inc. (Miki Koren).

With one message coming in at each ear, listeners were then instructed to repeat back one of the messages while they were listening (this is known as "shadowing" the message). Their shadowing was slightly delayed behind the message, and they spoke in a very monotonous voice, although they were not aware of this.

Cherry's most important findings were obtained with this shadowing technique. Basically, he discovered that listeners showed an amazing degree of ignorance about the message that was not shadowed. When this message was in German, and they were asked about the language spoken on the unshadowed ear, they simply said that they had no idea what it was but assumed it was English. When the unshadowed message consisted of reversed speech, a few listeners reported that there was "something queer about it," but most claimed that it was in normal

English speech. Even when the unshadowed message was in English, the listeners could not recall *any* of the words or phrases in it immediately afterward. However, when there was a change from a male to a female voice on the unshadowed message, or a pure tone was played, these changes were obvious enough to be detected.

In later work, it was found that listeners shadowing one message showed absolutely no retention of English words presented thirty-five times in a different message played at the same time. This was true even if the listeners were told to try to remember as much as possible of the unshadowed message.

Divided attention

Cherry's findings were widely regarded as demonstrating that we can really attend to only one thing at a time, since extremely little of the information played to the unshadowed ear appeared to leave any impression. However, it would not be true to say that the ear receiving the unshadowed message hears nothing. This was shown rather ingeniously by Zelniker, using what is known as "delayed auditory feedback," in which one hears what one is saying with a delay of a fraction of a second. Many tape recorders allow you to examine the effects of delayed auditory feedback for yourself. Simply set the machine to record and speak into a microphone while wearing headphones. What usually happens is that speech is disrupted and there is very noticeable stuttering.

As the listeners repeated the message heard in one ear, Zelniker tape-recorded their voices and played them back, with a short delay, to the other ear. If that ear were doing nothing, then there should have been no disruption of the shadowing. However, his listeners showed a certain amount of stuttering, enough to suggest that some attention was being paid to the unshadowed message.

Most psychologists argued that Cherry's findings could best be accounted for by assuming that man has only limited attentional capacity, and that the shadowing task is so demanding that it uses up virtually all of this capacity. While this certainly explains why so little of the unshadowed message was registered, things are actually more complicated than this simple theory might suggest.

An important additional factor which must be considered can be demonstrated quite straightforwardly. Try to form an auditory image (e.g., of the sound of a train or a musical instrument) and then a visual image (e.g., of a person's face or an animal). The chances are that you found it useful to close your eyes while forming the visual image, but quite unnecessary to do so while forming the auditory image. Why is it easy to keep looking at our immediate surroundings while imagin-

Another sight versus sound situation. The wristbands the girl is wearing measure pulse rate and thus monitor switches of attention between auditory and visual stimuli. Photo: Multimedia Publications Inc. (Miki Koren).

ing a sound, but difficult to combine seeing with visual imagery? The answer seems to be that the more dissimilar two activities are, the easier it is to attend to them both at the same time, because it is more likely that different parts of the brain are involved.

Perhaps what Cherry has really shown is that listeners cannot attend to two extremely similar activities at the same time (i.e., listening to two auditorily presented messages). What would happen if shadowing an auditorily presented message were combined with the very different activity of looking at a series of pictures? Cherry tried this, and found that his subjects could remember some 90 percent of the pictures afterward. In other words, it *is* possible to attend to two activities at once, even when one of them is the complicated task of shadowing a message. Several of the participants in this experiment were surprised how easy it was to combine the two activities, although at first they felt a strong desire to look away or close their eyes while shadowing in order not to be distracted by the series of pictures.

It seems to be just as difficult to attend to two visual scenes at once as to two auditory messages. Paul Kolers of the University of Toronto devised and wore a headgear fitted with a half-silvered mirror, which brought both the view ahead of him and the view behind him into his field of vision together. He reported that it was quite easy to concentrate on the front or the rear view, with the other view simply disappearing.

You can achieve the same effect by looking at a window from a lighted room at dusk. If the intensities of illumination are adjusted appropriately, you can choose whether to watch the outdoor scene or the reflection of the room, and you will find it is virtually impossible to look at both at once.

Ulric Neisser and Robert Becklen had a more systematic look at this phenomenon. They used two videotapes, and either presented one videotape superimposed on the other to both eyes of their subjects, or presented one videotape to each eye. In either case, it was extremely easy to follow one videotape or the other. It was easier when a different videotape was presented to each eye—the unwanted videotape just disappeared. When both videotapes were presented to both eyes, the viewers were always aware that "something else was going on." When the viewers tried to follow both videotapes at the same time, however, they discovered it was virtually impossible. However, they did find it a little easier to cope when the videotapes were presented to both eyes.

Practicing doing two things at once

From the evidence that we have considered so far, it would seem improbable that someone could read a text and understand it while at the same time understanding words copied under dictation (if you doubt the difficulty, just try it). But Ulric Neisser and his co-workers Elizabeth Spelke and William Hirst decided to train two students, John and Diane, to perform those two activities together.

When John and Diane first attempted to read short stories by American, English, and translated European writers while taking dictation, their reading speed dropped dramatically and the quality of their handwriting during dictation was much worse than normal. However, after some thirty hours of practice, they were able to combine reading and taking dictation very efficiently. At this stage, they seemed to be taking down the words in an unthinking way, for they often copied a list of related words (e.g., trolley, skates, truck, horse, airplane, tractor, car) without realizing that the words all belonged to the same category.

With several more hours of training, John and Diane learned to spot sets of related words in the dictation list, and they could even write down the categories to which the words belonged rather than the words themselves—all the while reading a text as rapidly and with as great a degree of comprehension as if they were reading it on its own.

The main message of this study is that the ability to attend to two activities at once can be improved dramatically as a result of extended practice. Altogether, John and Diane had over eighty hours of training each before reaching their final level of performance. This is borne out by the familiar example of car drivers who talk while driving, a feat that can safely be performed only by those with considerable experience.

Practice also has a profound effect on the task of shadowing one of two messages presented together, as in Colin Cherry's experiment. Beginners managed to detect only 4 percent of the key items presented on the unshadowed message. But Neville Moray, who has spent hundreds if not thousands of hours taking part in shadowing experiments, was able to detect no less than 83 percent of them.

Extended practice also plays a major role in two recent striking demonstrations of the ability to perform two activities together. Highly skilled pianists were able to play unfamiliar music at sight while shadowing passages read aloud from a book, with both the piano playing and the shadowing being done as well as they would normally be done on their own. In the second study, a skilled typist was able to type at about 100 words a minute while shadowing an auditorily presented passage or reciting nursery rhymes continuously.

The reason why practice at one activity (such as typing or piano playing) allows us to combine that activity readily with another activity is that less attention is required to perform a well-learned skill. Indeed, experienced typists are often not consciously aware of the order of the letters on the keyboard; it is as if the fingers "know what to do" with only minimal guidance.

Spare attentional capacity in job performance

Suppose you were to go for a one-mile run with an Olympic long-distance runner, and that he was kind enough to slow down to your pace so that you both took exactly the same amount of time to complete the distance. Would that mean that you were equally good runners? Obviously not, because you would be red in the face, sweating profusely, and lying moaning on the ground afterward, while he would be quite unaffected by the run. In other words, although you would both have run at the same speed, you would have had to use more of your available resources than he would. If you were to attempt a repeat performance with both of you wearing very heavy army boots, the champion runner would be only modestly slowed down, whereas you would not be able to run at all.

It follows that it may be very misleading to assume that two people who do a task equally well have achieved that level of performance at equal "cost" to themselves.[2] In the case of activities that require attention, some people may need to use much more of their attentional capacity than others to perform them adequately.

Ivor Brown of the Applied Psychology Research Unit in Cambridge, England, applied these ideas to a very practical problem. A large number of men were taking a course of instruction in bus driving with a view to passing the test for public service vehicles. The problem was that several of them failed this test, thus wasting their own and the bus company's time and money. It was not possible to use driving performance during training as a basis for weeding out potential failures, because there were no obvious differences in performance between those who subsequently failed or passed the test for public service vehicles.

Brown's ingenious solution to the problem was to read out a set of eight digits every few seconds while the men were driving. Each set of digits was the same as the immediately preceding set except for one digit, and the task was to spot the digit that had changed. Those trainees who later passed the crucial test did this digit task almost twice as well as those who failed. In other words, the unsuccessful trainees had to put much more effort and attention into driving than the successful ones, and so they were unable to cope with additional demands made on them.

The same basic notion was applied to a comparison of two aircraft instrument display systems. The issue was whether it was preferable to have a conventional instrument panel or a pictorial display generated on a cathode-ray tube. It was difficult to decide because pilots doing flight simulations performed equally well with either display system. However, when they were also asked to read out digits appearing on a separate display, performance using the pictorial display remained high whereas errors increased with the conventional display. It being less attentionally demanding to read the pictorial display, this was the system that was chosen.

Another interesting example of using a second task to assess the attentional demands of the first occurred during test simulation of the

X-15 rocket aircraft. The pilot handled all the various phases of the simulated flight satisfactorily, but it was argued that a more automated system would be less tiring. This was tested by requiring the pilot to turn off a periodically appearing light as well as performing the flight simulation. Performance on this extra task indicated that the more automated system demanded less of the pilot's attention, especially during the highly critical release from the parent aircraft, after engine burnout, and at the time of reentry into the atmosphere. Findings such as these led to a number of improvements in the design of the X-15.

Attending to two activities at once may cause problems that have not yet been fully appreciated. One example is the increased number of radiophones fitted to road vehicles, or the numerous citizen's band radio transmitters. Ivor Brown wondered whether a driver's judgment might be adversely affected by using a phone at the same time. In simulated driving tests he arranged a series of gaps that were either just large enough to allow a car through or were just too small, and found that drivers who were on the phone were much more willing to try to drive through gaps which were smaller than their cars. Indeed, 47 percent of the time they attempted to get through a gap that was three inches less than the car's width.

At a more commonplace level, is it advisable even to listen to a car radio while driving? Most drivers feel that listening to a car radio has a beneficial effect on driving, in that it wards off monotony and drowsiness. However, it has been found that braking and gear changing are occasionally delayed when there is something particularly interesting on the radio.

The reason why these two activities can normally be performed together is that driving and listening involve different senses (vision and hearing). However, if you listen to a football game on your car radio, and try to follow the play by forming visual images, you may quickly find yourself in the ditch.

Anxiety and attention

We all know that anxiety often disrupts performance, especially under stressful conditions. This was convincingly shown by Mitchell Berkun of the U. S. Army Leadership Human Research Unit. New army recruits were taken up in a plane and led to believe that it was about to make a crash landing. The plane lurched, one of the engines stopped, and the recruits could see fire engines and ambulances down on the airfield. The pilot announced that the landing gear would not function properly, so they would have to ditch in the sea. Not surprisingly, his terror-stricken passengers showed very little ability to follow the details of the emergency procedures; their memory proved only half as good as that of recruits who were not exposed to the stress.

Berkun's work was done some twenty years ago, and no present-day ethics committee would let anyone get away with an experiment like that. However, everyday anxiety is typically less intense, and we can study its effects on attention and performance. Since people suffering from anxiety usually become self-conscious and start concentrating on their worries, the obvious prediction is that anxiety should impair performance. The actual effects are both more interesting and more complex than that.

Gershon Weltman of the University of California locked student volunteers into an altitude chamber and led them to believe that the chamber had descended through the water to a depth of sixty feet—with a little ingenuity (extraneous hissing noises, an artificially manipulated pressure gauge, and so on) it was not too difficult to be convincing. This produced a certain amount of anxiety induced by the claustrophobic feeling of being confined in a small space, fears of the dreaded "bends," and apprehensions about the life-support equipment failing. During the time they were apparently sixty feet down, the volunteers were given the task of detecting small gaps in rings. In addition, a light source was fixed in the lower right-hand corner of the oval diving mask and their subsidiary task was to detect the light when it came on.

Weltman found that anxiety had no effect at all on the accuracy with which the main task was done. This was unexpected. The probable answer is that, while anxiety has a natural tendency to worsen performance, the volunteers compensated for this by using more of their attentional capacity than they normally would when not anxious. Dr. Samuel Johnson may have had something similar in mind in 1777 when he observed: "Depend on it, Sir, when a man knows he is to be hanged in a fortnight, it concentrates his mind wonderfully."

Since these anxious people were maintaining reasonable performance on the main task only by employing most of their resources, they should have been at a disadvantage on the subsidiary task of detecting the light. This proved to be the case; the subsidiary task was done only half as well under the anxiety-inducing conditions.

What can be done to prevent anxiety from having undesirable effects on attention and disrupting performance? There is intriguing evidence that the body can learn to develop certain coping mechanisms. Novice parachutists are most reluctant to jump, and most "stirred up" physiologically just before they jump. This means that they are highly anxious during the crucial phases of the parachute jump. Experienced parachutists are somewhat anxious on the morning of the jump and on landing, but remain relatively calm at the moment of jumping. As a result of practice, people can apparently either inhibit anxiety or displace it before and after the main part of a task in order to prevent anxiety from disrupting performance.

Conclusions

There is no simple answer to the question whether we can attend to two things at once. If two activities are dissimilar, and they have been extensively practiced, then it is often surprisingly easy to combine them effectively. If they are similar and have not been practiced, then it is usually impossible to attend properly to both at the same time.

It is not always easy to tell how much attention a person is devoting to a task. However, we can obtain some idea by giving him a second task to do at the same time; the worse the second task is done, the more of his available attention and resources must have been applied to the first task. This approach has been used with some success to answer a number of practical problems and to shed light on the effects of anxiety on performance.

15

Why do we forget?

No one can deny the importance of memory;[1] without it everything would seem as novel and surprising to us as it does to a newborn infant. When you ask most people about their memory, the first thing they usually say is that they have the bad luck to have a very poor memory. There is an interesting contrast here with what happens when you ask people about their intelligence or sense of humor: only a very small percentage of people will admit to below-average intelligence or a poor sense of humor.

Is it really true that the human memory works fairly inefficiently? This is a difficult question to answer. Memory can certainly perform some impressive feats that we tend to take for granted. For example, if someone asked you whether "sextant" was a word in the English language, it would take you less than a second to decide it was, and you would decide just as quickly that "mantiness" wasn't.

Forgetting can, of course, be a fairly painful and embarrassing experience. The forgetting of wedding anniversaries, birthdays, people's names, or the punch line of a joke are commonplace failings. Several years ago, the British royal family visited several countries in South America. As they departed by plane from one airport, a member of the crowd waving them off realized with a sinking feeling that, as part of the royal family's entourage, he ought to have been on the plane!

Since the workings of memory are immensely complicated, it should come as no surprise to discover that forgetting can occur in several different ways. This chapter is devoted to a consideration of some of the reasons why our memories fail us.

Endel Tulving, an Estonian-born psychologist now working in Canada, has perhaps shed more light on forgetting than anyone else.[2] He has pointed out that at any one moment we think about or remember only one event, meaning that memory must work in an extremely selective way. How is this single event selected? The philosopher Henri Bergson supplied an answer with which Tulving finds himself in agreement: "We trail behind us, unawares, the whole of our past; but our memory pours into the present only the odd recollection or that which in some way completes our present situation."

Tulving takes this to mean that remembering an event depends on two things, both of which are essential: a memory trace containing information about that event and something in the immediate situation that reminds us of the event (he calls this a "retrieval cue"). Tulving has sometimes likened the way in which these two ingredients combine to form a memory or recollection to the way in which sperm and egg combine in the conception of a child.

Thus, there are two major reasons for forgetting: either the memory trace has deteriorated or decayed or there is no suitable retrieval cue to trigger off the memory. It seems natural to argue that we forget things because the memory trace in the brain has faded; however, this is often not the case. For example, most people find that their recollections of childhood become fainter as the years go by. Is this due to fading memory traces? But when they return to the streets and fields they played in as children, or visit their old school, they are often amazed at the number of childhood experiences which come flooding back. The fact that the appropriate environment can trigger off these memories proves that many of the memory traces laid down in childhood are not eliminated from the memory system. They are there waiting to be activated by the appropriate cue.

Endel Tulving and Joseph Psotka of the University of Toronto were interested in the question whether forgetting is due to a fading of memory traces or to a lack of appropriate triggers or retrieval cues. They asked the participants in their study to learn lists of twenty-four words, four words in each of six categories. A sample list was as follows: hut, cottage, tent, hotel; cliff, river, hill, volcano; captain, corporal, sergeant, colonel; ant, wasp, beetle, mosquito; zinc, copper, aluminum, bronze; drill, saw, chisel, nail. The words were presented by means of a closed-circuit television system.

Some groups of participants were presented with one list, some with two lists, and others with three, four, five, or six lists. Immediately after each list had been presented, the participants wrote down as many words as possible from that list. All of the groups did equally well on this immediate test.

After they had learned the appropriate number of lists, the participants were asked to write down as many words as they could remember from all of the lists which they had received. Tulving and Psotka were especially interested to see how well the different groups managed to recall the first list. They expected that those who had learned several lists after the first list would be somewhat confused by all the words they had seen, and therefore forget more of them, a phenomenon known as "retroactive interference."[3] Furthermore, the time interval between learning the first list and recall was greater for those who had learned several lists, and this might also lead to a greater tendency to forget.

Tulving and Psotka found that the more lists people learned after the first list, the more forgetting they showed for the words in that list. Indeed, recall fell from about 70 percent when only one list was learned to under 30 percent when five other lists had been learned. Does this mean that the memory traces for the words in the first list faded more for those learning many lists than for those learning only one or two?

Tulving and Psotka tried to show that this was not the case. The experiment continued with the participants spending ten minutes completing as much as possible of an intelligence test, and then they tried again to recall all the words; this produced very similar results to the previous recall. Finally, the participants were supplied with the names of all the categories of words they had learned (for the sample list: types of building; earth formations; military titles; insects; metals; and carpenter's tools), and were asked to use these retrieval cues to aid their recall of all the words.

This cued recall produced a dramatic change in the number of words remembered from the first list. On the average, about 40 percent more words were recalled than before, demonstrating that much of the previous forgetting was not due to decay of memory traces. Indeed, the retrieval cues were so powerful that they allowed the participants to recall virtually as many words as they had originally learned; in other words, the forgetting of the originally learned words was practically eliminated by the cues. The use of cues greatly reduced the differences in recall for participants learning various numbers of lists which had been so pronounced before; apparently, retroactive interference is much more a question of a lack of appropriate retrieval cues than of trace decay.

Tulving and Psotka interpreted their findings on the basis of a very simple logical argument. If observed forgetting is reversible when the retrieval cues are changed, then the original forgetting was not due to loss of information from the memory traces. That is precisely what they demonstrated in this experiment.

Mnemonic aids

Much everyday forgetting occurs because the environment does not supply the appropriate memory prompts. If someone has to remember to perform an unusual action like buying a book for a friend or flowers for someone in the hospital, they will quite frequently forget to do it. What can be done to avoid the kind of embarrassment that is caused by such omissions? Anecdotal evidence suggests that the humble knotted handkerchief will often do the trick; the reason for this is that it acts as a retrieval cue, reminding the individual of what has to be done.

Apart from that done by Tulving and Psotka, there are several other experiments which have shown that much forgetting can be reversed when more powerful or appropriate retrieval cues are used. It is tempting to argue that everything we have ever learned is still stored in the brain, although much of it is inaccessible, of course. This was exactly the conclusion which Wilder Penfield came to as a result of his work with epileptics.

Penfield performed over 1,000 craniotomies involving unilateral removal of a portion of the temporal lobes and adjacent areas in an attempt to relieve focal epilepsy. The patients were conscious during the operation, and in 520 cases Penfield used mild electrical stimulation to explore one or another of the temporal lobes.

About 8 percent of patients reported "flashbacks" during stimulation, in which they became suddenly aware of experiences from the past. Penfield's most interesting discovery was that electrical stimulation of the temporal lobes sometimes produced detailed reenactments of a single experience that had been unavailable to normal recall for many years. Many of the patients spontaneously remarked on the very vivid nature of these memories. These findings suggest that much more information about events and experiences is stored than we are able to recall under normal circumstances. However, Penfield interpreted his data in far more dramatic fashion, claiming that he had shown that storage of information was permanent.

There are some weaknesses in Penfield's data. It appears that several of the recollections produced by electrical stimulation could quite easily have been recalled without it. For example, patient J.T. could hear his two cousins Bessie and Ann laughing when he was electrically stimulated. A greater problem is that the small percentage of epileptic patients reporting these vivid recollections may merely have been very suggestible; and, unfortunately, Penfield had no evidence about the accuracy of these memories.

A practical way of using some of Tulving's ideas to reduce forgetting is to carry your own retrieval cues around with you. A popular way of doing this owes its origins to a tragic accident in ancient Greece 2,500 years ago. Simonides was chanting a lyric poem at a banquet when he was called away by a messenger. During his absence, the roof of the banqueting hall fell in, crushing and mangling the guests so that their bodies were unrecognizable. Simonides remembered the places at which they had been sitting, and so was able to point out the dead to their grieving relatives.

This led Simonides to propose a memory technique in which he stressed the importance of orderly arrangement as an aid to memory, and in which he showed how this could be achieved by linking images of places and of facts or objects. This developed into the "method of loci" technique, which involves starting with something very familiar, such as an individual's favorite walk. Several places along the walk are then associated, by the use of imagery, with facts which that person wants to remember. When recall is required, the person simply uses the places on the walk as self-generated retrieval cues that allow him to "read off" the needed facts in the correct order.

A similar technique was proposed in the 1930s by Dale Carnegie, author of *How to Win Friends and Influence People*. The first task is to learn a rhyme scheme for remembering twenty items; Carnegie suggested the following: one-run, two-zoo, three-tree, four-door, five-beehive, six-sick, seven-heaven, eight-gate, nine-wine, ten-den, eleven-a football eleven, twelve-shelve, thirteen-hurting, fourteen-courting, fifteen-lifting, sixteen-licking, seventeen-leavening, eighteen-waiting, nineteen-pining, and twenty-horn of plenty.

The next step is to learn images which correspond to the critical words (e.g., "run" might suggest a sprint race, and "zoo" a caged lion). Finally, a series of up to twenty objects or ideas are visualized in bizarre association with the critical words. Forgetting is quite rare with this system; the main reason is that the individual has equipped himself with powerful retrieval cues.

Some applications of Tulving's ideas

The general approach propounded by Tulving has been applied with some success to the clinical problem of understanding memory deficiencies in patients with severe amnesia, many of whom are chronic alcoholics who have developed Korsakoff's psychosis. On most memory tasks their performance is so much lower than that of normal adults that it is tempting to conclude that there must be either some sort of inability to learn or a substantial decay of memory traces.

Elizabeth Warrington and Larry Weiskrantz of the National Hospital in London compared the memory of amnesics with that of normal people. In one experiment, in which recall of a list of words was asked for, normals recalled three and a half times as many words as amnesics. A similar result was obtained in a second experiment. However, when fragments of the words or their initial letters were available as retrieval cues, there was no difference in recall between normal people and amnesics. So, perhaps surprisingly, at least part of the amnesic's tendency to forget is due simply to unusual difficulty in gaining access to stored information.

Other evidence indicates that amnesic patients are able to name only about one-sixth as many photographs of famous faces taken from different time periods as normal people. However, if they are supplied with one or two letters of the surname as cues, their performance resembles that of non-amnesics who are not given cues. The optimistic implication of recent work on the amnesic syndrome is that the chronic levels of forgetting typically shown by amnesic patients can be partially reversed.

State-dependent memory

A question which has much occupied Tulving and others is that of deciding which retrieval cues are most useful in reducing forgetting. In general terms, the answer seems to be that effective retrieval cues are those which help to re-create the original event or experience, or the context in which the event occurred. This appears to extend to a person's internal state: what is experienced in an alcoholic haze is best remembered in an alcoholic haze. The term "state-dependent retention" has been coined to refer to the finding that memory is at its best if learning and memory both occur when the individual is in the same internal state.

This phenomenon was amusingly illustrated in the film *City Lights*. Charlie Chaplin saves a drunk millionaire from an attempted suicide and is befriended in return. When the millionaire sees Charlie again he is sober, and does not recognize him. However, when the millionaire becomes drunk again, he catches sight of Charlie and treats him like a long-lost friend. He takes Charlie home with him; the next morning, when the millionaire is sober again, he forgets that Charlie is his invited guest and gets his butler to throw him out.

In a laboratory setting, Herbert Weingartner persuaded several people to drink about four and a half ounces of vodka mixed with six ounces of fruit juice. As expected, alcoholic intoxication made learning a lot slower than normal. But those who attempted recall four hours later in an intoxicated state remembered more than those who were by then sober, presumably because alcoholic euphoria helped in the re-creation of the learning experience. If you find yourself trying desper-ately hard to remember something important that you were told while drunk, then the phenomenon of state-dependent retention provides the ideal excuse to get in some more hard drinking!

Those who smoke marijuana or hash commonly report that they can-not remember events experienced while intoxicated by the drug until they take the drug again. Here too investigation has shown that infor-mation learned in a drugged state is better remembered under drugged than normal conditions.

State-dependent retention has not only been demonstrated with ex-treme states created by drink or drugs. Gordon Bower of Stanford Uni-versity used hypnosis to make people happy or sad, asking them to imagine a scene in which they had been delightfully happy or griev-ously sad. They then learned lists of words while happy or sad, and later recalled the words in one of those two emotional states. In one of the experiments, 78 percent of the words were remembered when the mood during learning and recall was the same, compared with only 47 percent when the mood was different. The practical application of this finding is that you may be able to reduce forgetting if you can re-create the emotional state you were in when the crucial event occurred. It goes without saying that you need to remember what the emotional state was in the first place.

Memory monitoring

Given the fallible nature of the memory system, is there any simple way in which it could be made to function more efficiently? One obvi-ous answer would be some kind of memory monitoring system that could tell us how likely it was that the information we were trying to remember was actually stored in the memory. Obviously, we would not waste time and effort trying to remember information not in the mem-ory store if there were a memory monitoring system to warn us that we were wasting our time; conversely, it would be useful to know that sought-for information can probably be found somewhere in the mem-ory if we try hard enough.

It may seem paradoxical that we can know that information has been stored even though we cannot locate it, but evidence suggests that we are in fact able to do just this; we do in fact have a memory monitoring system. The most dramatic example of the system in operation is the tip-of-the-tongue state, in which you know that a memory is on the verge of coming back to you. However, the system is not only in evidence in the tip-of-the-tongue state; it operates in a much more general and ubiquitous way.

An interesting attempt to assess the accuracy with which we monitor our memory store was made by J. T. Hart of Stanford University. He asked people general knowledge questions such as "Which planet is the largest in our solar system?" If they could not remember the correct answer, they were asked to indicate on a 6-point scale the extent to which they felt they knew the answer, even though they could not remember it at that moment. The accuracy of this feeling of knowing was assessed by giving them four possible answers for each question and asking them to guess which was correct. For the sample question, the four answers were: (a) Pluto; (b) Venus; (c) Earth; and (d) Jupiter.

When people felt very strongly that they knew the correct answer to a question, they turned out to be right 75 percent of the time; but they were right only 30 percent of the time if they were sure they did not know the answer. Thirty percent is, of course, very close to the chance figure of 25 percent. Clearly then, we can monitor our own memory system, and do so with considerable accuracy.

The most intense and even emotional form of feeling that you know something but can't recall it is the tip-of-the-tongue state. The greatest problem for psychologists studying this state is to work out a way of producing the tip-of-the-tongue state to order. Roger Brown and David McNeill of Harvard University came up with the ingenious idea of reading out the definitions of rare words and asking people to think of the word being defined. They were told: "If you are unable to think of the word but feel sure that you know it and that it is on the verge of coming back to you, then you are probably in a tip-of-the-tongue state."

This technique was successful in producing the tip-of-the-tongue state. Does this state indicate that we really are close to recalling what we are searching for? Brown and McNeill claimed, with good reason, that it does. The initial letter of the missing word was guessed correctly 57 percent of the time when someone was experiencing the tip-of-the-tongue state. The number of syllables in the missing word could also be approximated; if the word actually had one syllable, the average guess was one and a half syllables, and when it had five syllables the average guess was three and a half syllables. Furthermore, there was some ability to think of words that rhymed with the missing word, and these words usually had the stress on the same syllable as the missing word.

Among other things, Brown and McNeill have provided us with a plausible answer to the paradox of how we can feel sure that we know something in spite of being unable to find it in our memory. Their work tells us that the simple idea that we either recall a word in its entirety or not at all is wrong. It is entirely possible to recall some of the information about a word (such as its initial letter), and it is this partial retrieval of information that allows us to be so confident that we know what we are looking for. This is similar to the *modus operandi* of Sherlock Holmes, supremely confident that he was on the track of his quarry on the basis of a single hair or a broken twig.

A common example of partial recall occurs sometimes when one attempts to recall the name of an acquaintance who is not physically present and one obtains an image of his face prior to remembering his name. This can be studied by asking people to produce drawings of various objects which are defined (e.g., "a large, lighter-than-air craft used for transport in the 1930s"). Those who could recall an image but not the word drew pictures that were almost as accurate as the pictures drawn by those who recalled the word (which was "zeppelin").

In practical terms, you will find you remember more if you pay close attention to any fragments of information produced by your memory system. If the letter "D" occurs to you when you are trying to remember someone's name, don't assume that the information is wrong. Write the letter down and focus on it in an attempt to produce more fragments of information. Finally, take the memory monitoring system's advice—when it fails to indicate any feeling of knowing the required information, give up trying.

How anxiety affects memory

As a result of his extensive clinical experience, Sigmund Freud claimed that most forgetting was due to repression. By repression he meant forgetting motivated by the desire to prevent anxiety-toned ideas and episodes from intruding into our consciousness. Of course, clinical impressions are much less reliable as a source of information than the results of properly designed experiments, and so several experiments have been carried out to study repression.

Unfortunately, there is little likelihood of psychologists being allowed to induce in a laboratory setting the life-crippling traumas alleged to produce clinically observed repression. As a result, it has proved impossible to test the Freudian theory of repression in a satisfactory way. Nevertheless, there are plenty of informal indications that anxiety makes us forget things. Students are prone to explain poor examination performance by saying that anxiety caused them to forget a lot of the information they had painstakingly learned.

Irwin Sarason in the early 1970s tried to decide whether there was any validity to such claims or whether examinees merely try to rationalize or explain away their poor performance by blaming it on anxiety. After he had handed back some examination essays to his students, and discussed with them how easy it was to forget relevant material and become confused during the tense exam situation, he asked them: "Well, do you really think you would have performed any better under more relaxed circumstances?" Nearly all the students responded: "Of course."

As a result, Sarason started giving the students two tests instead of one. The arrangement was that if a student got a higher mark on the second test than the first, that would be the mark entered in the book; if the score on the second test was lower, there would be no penalty. He found that performance was indeed superior under the less anxiety-producing conditions of the second test. He also discovered that students who rated high scores on a test of anxiety showed four times as much improvement from the first to the second test as students who rated low.

Why does anxiety have this effect? The evidence does not really support Freud's theory of repression. Rather it looks as if anxiety involves a "stirred up" state of physiological arousal together with worry about oneself and one's level of performance (e.g., "I'm stupid," "I can't do this"). Worry appears to be the culprit: if you are thinking about your own problems, you obviously cannot focus properly on the task at hand.

Perfect memory: a mixed blessing

Most of us who have fallible memories must have wished at one time or another that we were blessed with a "photographic memory." This sort of memory (or "eidetic imagery" as it is usually called by psychologists) is a lot rarer than is generally supposed, probably occurring in fewer than 1 percent of Western adults, although there are reports that it is more prevalent in children and primitive groups. The reason for this difference may be that the majority of adults in Western societies rely more heavily on language than on visual imagery.

The most striking demonstrations of eidetic imagery were reported some ten years ago by Charles Stromeyer of Bell Telephone Laboratories. He investigated the powers of Elizabeth, a young and intelligent teacher at Harvard. She was a skilled artist and could readily project an exact image of a picture or scene onto her canvas.

In Stromeyer's experiments, the usual procedure was that two computer-generated stereograms were presented, each of which consisted of a 10,000-dot display. If you look at these patterns without the aid of a stereoscope, they appear completely meaningless. However, when viewed through a stereoscope, which presents one pattern to the right eye and the other pattern to the left eye, you see a three-dimensional figure.

In one early experiment, Elizabeth viewed one 10,000-dot pattern for one minute through her right eye. After a short rest of ten seconds, she looked at the other pattern with her left eye. When Stromeyer asked her to superimpose the eidetic image of the first pattern on the visible pattern, she unhesitatingly reported that she saw the letter "T" coming toward her. Amazingly, she had stored a detailed image of the precise arrangement of 10,000 dots.

In a later experiment using the same technique, Elizabeth was able to retain an exact image of a 10,000-dot pattern for twenty-four hours. On another occasion, she formed images of four 10,000-dot patterns presented to her right eye. The next day, she viewed a single pattern with her left eye, and recalled in turn each of the four eidetic images viewed by the right eye the day before. When these images were superimposed on the left-eye pattern, each created a different figure that was seen in depth.

It would be misleading to say that Elizabeth possessed a photographic memory. For one thing, her eidetic images were dynamic and fluctuating and, just like more commonplace images, they could be altered and manipulated voluntarily. They were not formed in the same rapid way that a camera takes a photograph. Instead, Elizabeth sometimes took several minutes to form an eidetic image of a complex pattern, moving her eyes around the various parts of the pattern.

She claimed that eidetic imagery had been less useful to her than might have been imagined. She had found it of some assistance when taking school and university examinations, but it was less helpful in her graduate work.

The most convincing evidence that phenomenal memory powers can be a mixed blessing was obtained by the Russian neurologist A. R. Luria. A man he referred to as S. appeared at his laboratory in the mid-1920s. S. was a newspaper reporter and had been sent to Luria by his editor, who had noted his apparently remarkable memory capacity. Now, most people occasionally combine experiences in different sense modalities (e.g., high-pitched sounds are associated with bright colors), but this tendency was very pronounced with S. He once commented to the psychologist Vygotsky, "What a crumbly yellow voice you have."

S.'s powers of imagery were so strong that, after only three minutes of study, he could reproduce a table of fifty numbers by calling out the numbers vertically, horizontally, or diagonally at great speed. He claimed to be able to see the table, so that he merely had to "read it off." On one occasion, he recalled a series of words accurately sixteen years after learning them.

These powers of imagery produced a variety of disadvantages for S. His compulsive tendency to turn everything into visual imagery often made it very difficult for him to think effectively at an abstract level. His imagery tended to be laden with vivid but irrelevant details, leading him to remark when trying to understand what someone was saying to him: "Each word calls up images; they collide with one another, and the result is chaos. I can't make anything out of this. And then there's your voice . . . another blur . . . then everything's muddled." In other words, the trouble with superb but uncontrollable imagery powers is that you cannot see the forest for the trees.

Conclusions

The main reason why we forget is that our environment does not always provide the appropriate cues to trigger off recollection of the missing information. It is often helpful, when trying to remember something, to be in the same internal state you were in when it entered your memory system. A state of anxiety can lead to increased forgetting. However, decay or fading of memory traces almost certainly plays a part as well.

In spite of the fallibility of human memory, we are lucky enough to have a memory monitoring system that gives us a reasonably accurate idea of whether we shall be able to remember forgotten information if we keep trying. Finally, it is not at all clear that an infallible memory system is really desirable; there is the danger that one's mind would be cluttered up with a vast quantity of indigestible information, just as happened with Luria's S.

16

Privacy and intimacy

When people meet each other, they find themselves thinking and feeling all sorts of things, some of which they are reluctant to give voice to. We tend not to say, "I find you extremely boring," or "I don't like you," or "You are an arrogant fool," except perhaps to our nearest and dearest. However, we often communicate such thoughts and feelings by means of non-verbal signals such as facial expression, gesture, posture, eye movements, and tone of voice. Looking at someone who is talking to you is an indication that you are paying attention to what he is saying; conversely, failure to look at the other person is sometimes an indication that you find his conversation boring. Similarly, if we dislike a person we tend to show it by standing some distance away from him and talking about totally impersonal topics.

At first glance, it seems strange that a complex set of non-verbal signals is required in everyday social situations. After all, the English language with its 500,000 words provides a very rich and powerful means of communication. Why has the "silent language" of non-verbal signals developed? Michael Argyle of Oxford University has suggested that language and non-verbal signals largely serve different functions, with non-verbal signals being used to establish and maintain personal relationships, and language being used to communicate information about events external to the speakers. The potential embarrassment of blurting out one's feelings about the person one is talking to can, it seems, be largely avoided by resorting to the much greater ambiguity of non-verbal signals.

Michael Argyle and his fellow workers were intrigued to know exactly what determines how we feel toward strangers; is it what they say or how they say it? They arranged for an attractive female to say things designed to express an attitude of superiority or inferiority. Her accompanying non-verbal signals conveyed either a superior attitude (un-smiling, head raised, loud dominating speech) or an inferior attitude (nervous deferential smile, head lowered, nervous eager-to-please speech). When there was a clash between what she said and the non-verbal signals she gave, feelings of friendliness, pleasantness, and so on toward her were far more affected by her non-verbal signals than by what she said.

One of the most fascinating aspects of non-verbal signals is that peo-ple are often influenced by them without being aware of it. Eckhard Hess found that emotional arousal produces enlargement of the pupil of the eye, and that men are more attracted by girls with enlarged pu-pils, though they are seldom aware that this is the cue to which they are responding. It is interesting to note that the drug belladonna, mean-ing literally "beautiful woman," produces enlarged pupils and was once considered a powerful weapon of seduction.

Touchers and non-touchers

An especially important form of non-verbal communication is touch-ing, which has been studied in detail by Sidney Jourard of the Univer-sity of Florida. He asked unmarried men and women between the ages of 18 and 22 to indicate which regions of their bodies had been touched by their mother, father, closest friend of the same and the op-posite sex, and which regions of these other people's bodies they had touched. With the obvious exception of touching between close friends of the opposite sex, there was some evidence of a touch taboo, possibly because touching in many Western societies normally has sexual con-notations.

Young men and young women reported about equal touching by their mothers, and on as many regions of their body. But young men did not touch their mothers' bodies in as many places as their mothers touched them, nor in as many as the young women touched their mothers. The young women touched their fathers on more regions than the young men did, and in return they were touched on more body areas by their fathers than were the young men. Indeed, several men reported that they were unable to recall any physical contact with their fathers at all. It seems that when it comes to touching within the fam-ily, it is the daughters who are the favored ones.

Jourard also found, not surprisingly, that physically attractive men and women are touched more by their parents and their friends than plain men and women. More puzzling was the finding that Protestant and Catholic girls reported being touched by their male friends on more parts of their bodies than Jewish girls.

Jourard concluded that touching is the primitive language of love and that extensive physical contact may act as nature's sedative or tranquilizer. However, while there are many therapy groups in California and elsewhere which engage in "feeling" and "groping," the results of increased physical contact are disappointingly variable.

Jourard was also interested in cross-cultural differences in touching. He watched pairs of people talking in cafés and coffee shops and counted the number of times that one person touched another at one table during one hour. In San Juan, Puerto Rico, the total number of touches was 180; in Paris, it was 110; and in London, it was 0. Maybe the notion that the English are cold and aloof has some truth to it.

Perhaps the most explored cross-cultural difference in non-verbal behavior has been the distance people like to keep between themselves and the person they are talking to. Germans, North Americans, and Swedes typically select greater distances than Latin Americans, Greeks, southern Italians, and especially Arabs. A comparison of Arabs and Americans revealed that the Arabs confronted each other more directly, got closer together, were more likely to touch and to maintain eye contact, and talked louder. Imagine the problems at international gatherings, with American and English delegates retreating backward pursued by Arabs and southern Europeans!

While there has been a lot of interesting work on non-verbal communication, most of it has explored one kind of signal at a time (touching; eye contact; physical distance). The work we are about to discuss provides important insights into the ways in which different aspects of non-verbal communication affect each other and suggests a useful theoretical framework.

Key experiment   Interpersonal intimacy (Michael Argyle and Janet Dean)

Michael Argyle and Janet Dean[1] of Oxford University took as their starting point the simple assumption that social interaction typically involves both approach and avoidance tendencies. On the one hand, the desire to be liked by another person and attraction for that person encourage intimacy; on the other hand, anxieties about revealing oneself or of being rejected by the other person discourage intimacy. According to Argyle and Dean, the net result is that there is a constant pressure between people to maintain a comfortable level of intimacy.

How is this comfortable balance between opposite tendencies arrived

*Intimacy being reduced to a comfortable level by turning away. Photo:
Multimedia Publications Inc. (Israel Sun).*

at? Argyle and Dean suggested that interpersonal intimacy is chiefly
reflected by a variety of non-verbal interactions, including the physical
distance between people, eye contact, smiling, and leaning. Standing
very close to someone, for example, is more "intimate" than standing
further away. But if someone stands too close to us, closer than we find
comfortable, the balance we are trying to establish is upset. While the
easiest solution would be to move away in order to restore the balance,
this is not always possible or socially acceptable. The alternative is to
compensate for the increased intimacy of one aspect of non-verbal
communication by reducing the intimacy of one or more other aspects.

Argyle and Dean explored some of these ideas in an experiment in
which various people were asked to take part in a study of conversations. When a participant arrived for the experiment, he or she was
introduced to another person who appeared to be another participant
but who was actually a confederate of the experimenter. The genuine
participant and the confederate then engaged in three conversations,
sitting 2 feet apart for one conversation, and 6 and 10 feet apart for
the other two; they also sat at 90 degrees to each other. They then
jointly made up stories on the basis of pictures suggesting different
themes. The confederate gazed continually at the participant, and two

observers behind a one-way screen looked directly into the participant's eyes without being seen.

The notion that people attempt to maintain a comfortable level of interpersonal intimacy suggests that Argyle and Dean's participants
should have restored equilibrium at the shortest physical distance (2
feet) by reducing the intimacy of other non-verbal reactions. As
predicted, the amount of eye contact which the participant had with the
confederate progressively decreased the closer together they sat. When
the participant and the confederate were of the opposite sex, eye contact occurred 58 percent of the time at 10 feet, 55 percent at 6 feet, but
only 30 percent at 2 feet. There were similar but less dramatic effects
when participant and confederate were of the same sex: eye contact
decreased from 72 percent at 10 feet to 55 percent at 2 feet. There was
much less eye contact overall with opposite-sex than with same-sex
pairs, presumably because there is more concern about being disliked
by strangers of the opposite sex and hence a certain amount of
wariness.

These findings seemed to Argyle and Dean to show that reduced eye
contact is one way of coping with the uncomfortable realization that a
stranger is sitting closer to you than you would like. However, there is
an alternative explanation. One of the reasons why we look at another
person is to gain information about their reactions to us. Now, the further away from us the other person is, the more difficult it becomes to
see the subtleties of his facial expression. In such a situation we need to
look more in order to find out what we want to know. Argyle and
Dean noted other manifestations of discomfort besides reduced eye
contact when confederate and participants were only 2 feet away from
each other: participants tended to lean backward, look down, shade
their eyes with their hands, narrow their eyes, scratch their heads,
smoke, and blow their noses far more than at 6 feet or 10 feet.

While many psychologists liked the basic idea that different aspects
of non-verbal behavior combine to produce an overall preferred level
of interpersonal intimacy, they were somewhat dubious about one or
two features of Argyle and Dean's study. For example, the participants
may have sensed that it was very unnatural to be stared at by the confederate throughout the whole of each conversation. And another
point, as the distance between the participant and confederate increased, so did the distance between the participant and the observers
behind the one-way screen who were recording eye contact. It must be
more difficult to tell whether or not the participant has direct eye contact with the confederate if he is sitting farther away. Nevertheless,
findings very similar to those of Argyle and Dean have been obtained
in other studies in which these problems were eliminated.

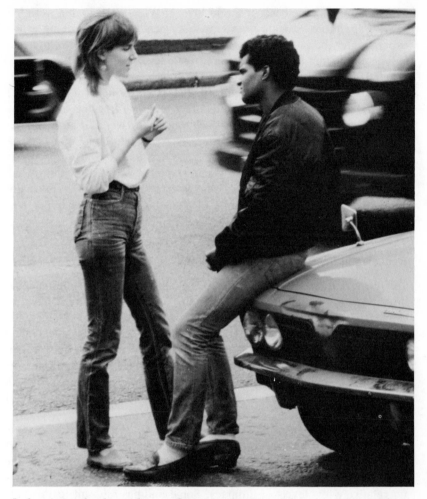

Is he sitting back on the car because she is standing too close? Photo: Multimedia Publications Inc. (Miki Koren).

Interaction of verbal and non-verbal signals

An interesting extension of the Argyle and Dean work concerns the way in which verbal and non-verbal intimacy affect each other. If someone is asked to talk about relatively intimate topics with a stranger, will this affect his non-verbal behavior? Richard Schulz and John Barefoot studied this question by getting people to answer questions varying between the fairly neutral (e.g., "What are your favorite subjects in school?") and the very personal (e.g., "Describe a person with whom you have been or are in love"). When participants were answering the more intimate questions they spent less time looking at the experimenter than when they were talking about neutral topics, presumably in an attempt to achieve a comfortable level of intimacy.

Schulz and Barefoot also found that participants gave shorter answers when they were sitting close to the experimenter (in this case 3 feet) and also engaged in less eye contact. A more puzzling finding was that participants smiled twice as much when they were close to the experimenter as when they were further away. Argyle and Dean had assumed that less smiling would occur if the desired level of intimacy was exceeded. However, smiling can mean a number of different things; the "come hither" smile of someone who knows she is attractive must not be confused with the forced smile of someone experiencing inner tension.

Reducing intimacy to a comfortable level

If we are in a social situation and feel that the level of interpersonal intimacy is too high, what aspects of our behavior are we most likely to change in an endeavor to restore the balance? Argyle has suggested that there is an important difference between the relatively unchanging characteristics of an interaction such as physical distance, body orientation, and posture, and its more variable and dynamic aspects such as eye contact, facial expression, and verbal intimacy. Adjustments in overall intimacy typically seem to involve the dynamic components of intimacy rather than the relatively stable ones.

As we all know from personal experience, people differ considerably in their preferred level of interpersonal intimacy in a given situation. It follows from some of the ideas of Argyle and Dean that those people who are especially worried about being rejected by others tend to prefer relatively low levels of intimacy. Some findings relevant to this particular question were obtained by Miles Patterson[2] of the University of Missouri. He placed a swivel chair several feet away from the experimenter's chair, and each participant was invited to "pull up a chair." People tended to put the swivel chair either about 3½ feet away from the experimenter's chair or about 14 feet away. Those who rated high on a test of social anxiety tended to put more distance between themselves and the experimenter than those who were not socially anxious.

The equilibrium model proposed by Argyle and Dean has obvious relevance to everyday social interaction. It also seems to shed light on the procedures typically adopted for religious confessions and psychiatric sessions, in which the sinner or patient is encouraged to say negative things about himself in the presence of another person (the priest or the psychiatrist) who avoids all eye contact. Since lengthy discussion of one's own inadequacies is an intimate topic of conversation, and liable to be embarrassing, any increase in interpersonal intimacy by means of eye contact would probably lead to reduced verbal disclosure (e.g., "I was rude to Mr. Smith last week" instead of "I dumped all my old grass cuttings in Mr. Smith's drive last week."

In spite of the obvious value of the Argyle and Dean theory, there are circumstances in which it predicts the exact opposite of what actually happens. In *The Thomas Crown Affair,* a film released in 1968, a wealthy criminal played by Steve McQueen and a young woman played by Faye Dunaway initially interact in a relatively neutral way. One evening, however, they play a game of chess. During the game, Faye Dunaway gently massages one of the chess pieces, gazes fixedly at Steve McQueen, and smiles enigmatically. According to Argyle and Dean, Steve McQueen should have moved his chair away from the chessboard and averted his gaze. In fact, he responded in the time-honored way and allowed himself to be seduced by his beautiful companion. Though this was a piece of acting rather than a slice of real life, it would probably be fair to say that preferred levels of intimacy between people are more flexible and more subject to change by non-verbal signals than Argyle and Dean implied.

Personal space

Another interesting and important aspect of non-verbal behavior, closely related to the behaviors studied by Argyle, is that of personal space. Robert Sommer of the University of California has argued that personal space refers to "an area with invisible boundaries surrounding a person's body into which intruders may not come." Others have likened personal space to a buffer zone which affords protection against perceived threats. In passing it is worth noting that many species seem to have their own personal spaces; for example, the minimum social distance for flamingos is about 2 feet, for subordinate male rabbits 1 foot, and for some kinds of monkey nothing.

One way of testing the importance of personal space is to see what happens when it is invaded. We humans feel threatened and worried by invasion and usually act defensively. A very simple attempt to observe reactions to invasion of personal space was made by Nancy Jo Felipe and Robert Sommer, who conducted one of their studies on the grounds of a large mental institution. The experimenter walked around the grounds and sat about 6 inches away from any man sitting alone and not engaged in a clearly defined activity. If the "victim" moved his chair or moved further along the bench, the experimenter moved the same amount to keep the space between them the same as before (i.e., 6 inches). The victim typically responded by facing away from the experimenter, placing his elbows by his sides, mumbling, laughing nervously, or talking delusionally. Half the victims took flight within nine minutes of the experimenter's sitting beside them, and only 8 percent stayed put, presumably because their personal space was not invaded.

Naturally enough, Felipe and Sommer wondered whether these striking results were due to the use of mental patients as subjects. In their next experiment, a female experimenter sat down very close to female college students in a relatively empty university library. Seventy percent of the students left the library within thirty minutes; 13 percent tolerated the close proximity of the experimenter and stayed put.

Some couples acquire a joint personal space. Note the identical posture adopted by this couple: folded arms, crossed legs, and identical direction of gaze. Photo: Multimedia Publications Inc. (Israel Sun).

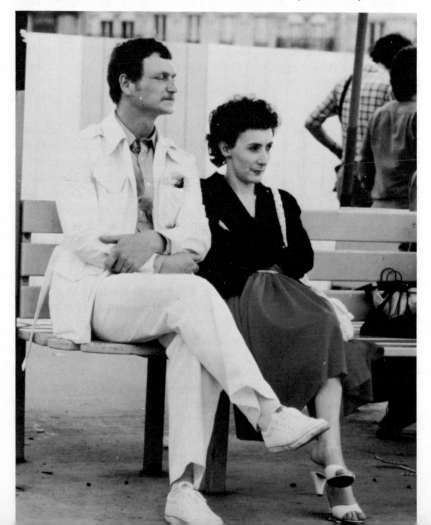

If someone enters our personal space and makes us feel uneasy, are we likely to ask the other person to move a little further away? Apparently not, according to the findings of Felipe and Sommer. They noted that only two of the mental patients and one out of eighty students asked the person invading their personal space to move away. This common reluctance to openly admit discomfort led Hall, one of the main investigators of human personal space, to write: "We treat space somewhat as we treat sex. It is there but we don't talk about it."

It has usually been assumed that invasion of personal space produces stress and tension, but there have been relatively few attempts to test this assumption. However, Dennis Middlemist and his colleagues at Oklahoma State University did so, using a three-urinal men's lavatory as the unlikely setting for their study. What they set out to prove was that stress or anxiety delays the onset of urination (decreased relaxation of the external sphincter, they argued, would cause increased intravesicular pressure and so shorten urine flow). They proved their point. When a man urinated alone, the average delay before urination was 5 seconds, compared with 8½ seconds when a confederate was standing in the adjacent urinal. The average duration of urine flow decreased from 25 seconds for men on their own to 17½ seconds for men standing next to the confederate. In these circumstances invasion of personal space did indeed produce a minor state of stress.

Gerald Koocher of Harvard Medical School was rather unhappy about this attempt to establish a psychology of the privy, pointing out that the boundary between drawing on everyday experiences and spying on people's intimate functions is a narrow one. Middlemist retorted that none of the participants in his urinal experiment had appeared in the least worried or concerned.

Do some people have a larger personal space than others? Some animal studies suggest that the answer is probably yes, and highlight the importance of dominance or status. For example, dominant male rabbits maintain an average of 3 feet between themselves and their subordinates whereas their subordinates are content with an average of 1 foot between themselves and others. In similar vein, the distance between a dominant chicken and a subordinate chicken is directly proportionate to the frequency with which the latter is pecked in the home coop.

In our own society, "important" people are usually given a larger personal space than other people—it would certainly seem strange if Queen Elizabeth or Prince Philip were jostled in the ribs at a public gathering. Larry Dean and his co-workers made observations on dominance-related personal space among personnel at the U.S. naval station in Long Beach, California. They discovered that interactions directed toward a superior typically took place at a greater distance than interactions directed toward a subordinate. Furthermore, this effect became more noticeable as the difference in rank increased.

Sex differences in personal space

Some interesting sex differences in personal space have also been discovered. Women choose to sit closer to other women than men do to other men, possibly because women are trained to express affection openly whereas men are trained to preserve "a stiff upper lip." Michael Ross compared the reactions of discussion groups of eight men or eight women sitting in an uncrowded room (13½ feet by 10 feet) or a crowded room (only 8 feet by 5½ feet). Men were generally happier with themselves and with the other members of the group in the relatively uncrowded room, whereas women were exactly the opposite and preferred the more intimate atmosphere of the smaller room.

A rather more puzzling sex difference was described by Jeffrey Fisher and Donn Byrne of Purdue University. In one study, the personal space of a male or a female student sitting in a university library was invaded by someone who sat down either immediately adjacent to

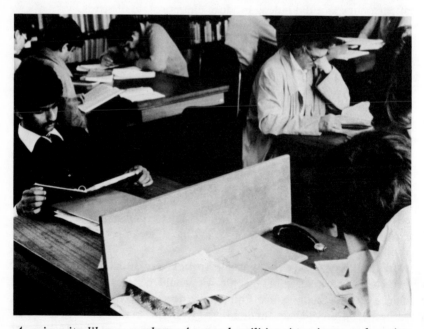

A university library, a place of mute hostilities, invasions, and capitulations. Photo: Multimedia Publications Inc. (Miki Koren).

them or directly across the table from them. Male students felt more uncomfortable with someone sitting opposite them than with someone sitting next to them, whereas female students were more upset by someone sitting next to them—the "Miss Muffet" reaction.

In a second study, Fisher and Byrne argued that students sitting alone in a library use books, coats, sweaters, and so on to mark off territory and erect barriers against intruders. Female students tended to erect barriers between themselves and adjacent seats, whereas male students erected barriers between themselves and the seat across the table.

We know that individuals generally sit face to face in competitive situations and side by side in cooperative ones. Since men are taught to be more competitive than women, it is possible that men view strangers who sit opposite them as a potential threat or challenge. In contrast, women are taught to be more friendly and cooperative than men and so might interpret a stranger coming and sitting next to them as an unwarranted demand for attention and friendship.

How we react when our space is invaded

Another example of invasion of personal space which will be familiar to most motorists is being stared at by the occupants of the next car while waiting at traffic lights. Most people who have had this experience will recognize it as subtly disturbing and will remember fidgeting, adjusting the car radio, starting talking to the passengers in the car, and so on. A less obvious reaction in this situation has also been noticed: drivers pull away from the lights more rapidly when they have been stared at. Can we interpret this as a form of escape response to a threatening situation?

A similar form of escape reaction was studied by Vladimir Konečni and his associates at the University of California. They found that pedestrians crossed the road rather faster when someone had been standing very close to them as they waited for the crossing signal. It is interesting to speculate on other possible reactions by pedestrians whose personal space is violated. Could it be that they regard the violator in a somewhat negative way? Konečni tested this notion by having a confederate stand either 1 foot or 10 feet from a fellow pedestrian while they both waited at the curb for the lights to change. When they were both on the crossing, the confederate "accidentally" dropped an object in front of the pedestrian. The question was whether the pedestrian would act in a helpful way—in other words, hand the object back to the confederate or call out to him saying, "Excuse me, you've dropped something." When the object was a cheap pencil, only 47 percent of pedestrians lent assistance in the 1-foot condition, compared with 80 percent in the 10-feet condition. A similar but less dramatic difference was obtained when the confederate dropped a key ring. It seems that we respond to invasions of our personal space by disliking the invader; this in turn makes us disinclined to lend a helping hand if required. However, this effect decreases as the value of the object lost increases (a key ring elicits more help than something trivial like a pencil).

Why do people respond in such subtle but consistently observable ways to invasion of their personal space? After all, being stared at or having a stranger stand very close to you usually involves no tangible threat, and yet we become embarrassed, attempt to escape, and are reluctant to help the person who has violated our personal space. One of the functions of personal space may be to keep aggression down to manageable proportions; the barriers we erect may be invisible but they are nonetheless a sort of safety zone in which others are unlikely to attack us and we are unlikely to attack others. Most people, for example, would find it easier to kill 10,000 people by dropping a bomb from a plane than to kill one person by stabbing him with a knife. Perhaps part of the reason for this is that personal space must be invaded in the mugging situation but not in the airborne situation (but see Chapter 3).

Interpersonal intimacy: liking and loving

All of us have seen people becoming anxious and embarrassed when another person's non-verbal behavior indicates a high level of interpersonal intimacy—invasion of personal space is one of the surest ways of causing embarrassment. But as Argyle and Dean pointed out, people typically cope with this situation by some kind of compensatory non-verbal behavior designed to restore the desired level of interpersonal intimacy.

Miles Patterson agreed that increased intimacy by one member of a pair may lead to a compensatory decrease in intimacy by the other, but he was dubious whether this notion adequately explains the behavior of couples falling in love. Increased non-verbal intimacy by one partner typically leads to increased non-verbal intimacy on the part of the other rather than to a decrease. In other words, lovers usually reciprocate intimate behavior rather than compensate for it.

Patterson argued that some kind of extension of previous theories was called for. He suggested that increased non-verbal intimacy on the part of one member of a pair produces physiological arousal and an associated emotional state. If the increase in non-verbal intimacy leads to negative emotional reactions (e.g., anxiety), then the other person will respond with compensatory behavior (decreased eye contact, greater physical distance, etc.). On the other hand, if a positive emotional state is created (e.g., love), then there will be a reciprocation of the original intimacy behaviors, leading to a new and different level of intimacy.

Why did Argyle and Dean and others highlight unpleasant emotional reactions to increased intimacy to the virtual exclusion of the pleasanter ones? According to Patterson, the answer lies in the fact that most experiments are not conducive to feelings of joy and euphoria. The pairs of people used in most experiments are total strangers to each other, the setting is usually fairly impersonal (e.g., a laboratory), and the participants are exposed to relatively extreme scenarios (e.g., being forced to sit almost on top of each other or having someone stare continuously at them for minutes on end). It is not surprising that people's usual reaction to such threatening, unsympathetic circumstances is discomfort or anxiety, followed by a definite decrease in non-verbal intimacy.

In striking contrast, there is the interaction between a mother and her baby within the home. John Bowlby reported that the more an infant smiles at his mother, the more likely she is to approach him, talk or sing to him, and pick him up and hug him. It is just as well that we sometimes respond to non-verbal intimacy with open arms rather than fight or flight. If we didn't, the human race would have died out long ago.

Conclusions

The most important function of non-verbal signals is to indicate the feelings one person has toward another. Members of couples highly attracted to each other like to stand closer together than members of couples who do not like each other. For any two people interacting with each other, there is likely to be a preferred level of interpersonal intimacy, and deviations from this level are disliked and where possible compensated for.

Invasion of personal space (or, for that matter, refusal to enter someone else's personal space) is a particularly powerful non-verbal signal. If a stranger stands much closer to us than we would like, clear signs of embarrassment manifest themselves, we become tense and anxious, and may even attempt to escape from the situation. While it is by no means clear why everyone has his or her own personal space, we are not alone in the animal world in finding some form of invisible barrier between ourselves and others useful. The importance of this barrier can be gauged by the strong emotions we experience when it is violated.

17

Justifying ourselves
to ourselves

It is a matter of everyday observation that people often become worried after making decisions in case they have made the wrong decision. Anyone who has bought a secondhand car will know the feeling. We all know, in our heart of hearts, that we only get what we pay for. So from the outset our common sense is at odds with our expectations. One way of resolving this conflict is to seek reassurance from friends and colleagues: "Not bad, is she, considering she's done 80,000 miles!" People are astonishingly forbearing in such situations; rather than give a hurtful but honest opinion: "You've got a heap which won't last five minutes," they give the only socially acceptable answer: "Yes, you've got a good bargain there." In other words, they play along with our need to feel comfortable about our actions and decisions.

Our constant need to justify our decisions, to produce consistency between our opinions and our behavior, inspired one of Aesop's best-known fables, the one about the fox and the grapes. An extremely hungry fox spies some luscious grapes several feet above him. His best efforts to jump up and pluck them are in vain, producing inconsistency between his energetic attempts to reach his goal and his failure to attain it. He then manages to reduce this inconsistency by convincing himself that the goal is not worth the effort anyway; he decides that the grapes are sure to be sour and inedible. Of course, this solution to the inconsistency would have been less appropriate had the fox spent the whole afternoon struggling to reach the grapes, since if the grapes were sour it would have made little sense to keep jumping up at them. But if he *had* tried all afternoon, unsuccessfully, our fox might have convinced himself that the exercise was good for him, enabling him to make nimbler escapes from farmers when they saw him making off with their chickens.

One of the most topical examples of major conflict between belief and behavior is the cigarette smoker who is well aware that smoking can cause cancer and other kinds of illness but nevertheless continues smoking. How do people handle this sort of conflict? Two obvious ways of reducing it would be to alter one's behavior (i.e., stop smoking) or else refuse to believe that smoking is dangerous. The causal link between cigarette smoking and cancer first impinged on the public consciousness in America in January 1964 in a report issued by the U. S. Surgeon General. Shortly afterward a survey was done to investigate its effects on smokers. It is, of course, well known that smokers find great difficulty in giving up smoking; and only 9 percent of the smokers interviewed had even attempted this conflict-reducing approach. Forty-one percent of heavy smokers (compared with only 11 percent of non-smokers) refused to accept that the link between cigarette smoking and cancer had been satisfactorily established. It thus appears that people will attempt to reduce disturbing conflicts in any way that is open to them.

Key experiment   Lying under pressure (Leon Festinger and James Carlsmith)

Leon Festinger and James Carlsmith[1] of Stanford University were extremely interested in the ways in which people coped with conflicts of the kind described above. In particular, they wondered how people's opinions would be affected by the unpleasant realization that they had been deliberately dishonest to someone.

In their experiment, every subject was required to perform two mind-numbing and utterly pointless tasks, each lasting for half an hour. The first task involved putting twelve spools on a tray, emptying the tray, refilling it with spools, and so on. The subjects were given a board containing forty-eight square pegs for the second task, and were asked to turn each peg a quarter turn clockwise, then another quarter turn, and so on.

After this hour of unrelieved tedium, the experimenter pointed out that he was interested in the effects of prior expectations on the performance of the tasks. Some subjects had been led to believe that the experiment was very enjoyable, a lot of fun, very interesting, intriguing, and exciting, the experimenter continued; he had given the job of misinforming the subjects to a student who had been hired specifically for the purpose. Unfortunately, the experimenter went on in a somewhat confused and embarrassed manner, this student was no longer available: would the participant be prepared to fill in for the missing student? In some cases he or she was offered $1, in others $20, for agreeing to perform this dishonest service and to be available in the future if a similar emergency occurred.

Nearly all the subjects agreed to do as the experimenter suggested and were then introduced to a girl who was the next subject. When the subject-stooge began talking in glowing terms about the experiment, the girl said she was surprised because a friend of hers had done the experiment a week earlier and had told her that it was boring and that she ought to try to get out of it. Most of the subjects dealt with this problem by trying to reassure the girl, saying something like "Oh, no, it's really very interesting, and I'm sure you'll enjoy it."

Finally, the experimenter took each subject to an interviewer, whose job was to evaluate this and other experiments so that they could be improved in the future. Among other questions, the interviewer asked each subject to rate how interesting and enjoyable the tasks were.

How do you think the subject's opinion of this boring experiment was affected by the amount of money offered to him as an inducement to be dishonest and claim that the experiment was very enjoyable? It would be natural to assume that people's attitudes toward the experiment would be made more positive by the large sum ($20) than by the small sum ($1), simply because it is more pleasant and rewarding to receive a large amount of money than a small amount. But in fact, the results were quite the opposite. Paradoxically, those subjects offered only $1 rated the experiment as much *more* enjoyable and interesting than those offered $20. The telling of a lie (pretending the experiment was much more interesting than it actually was) probably produces a state of conflict, because most people regard themselves as basically honest. Those offered $20 could justify their behavior by the large amount of money given to them: "Anyone would tell a lie if it was worth their while," but those offered only $1 could not square their conscience with their dishonesty so easily; the solution to their conflict was to convince themselves that they had not really been very dishonest, because the experiment had been genuinely interesting. In other words, the *less* money they were offered, the *greater* the conflict produced.

As sometimes happens in social psychology, the subjects were thoroughly deceived about several aspects of the experiment. The missing student who had been hired to tell subjects that the experiment was very interesting did not exist, the female subject was actually a confederate of the experimenter, the interviewer was employed by the experimenter, and, worst of all, the subjects were asked at the end of the experiment to give back the $1 or $20. Many psychologists are concerned about the ethics of such large-scale deception.

Cognitive dissonance

However, whatever the rights and wrongs of this experiment, Festinger's findings enabled him to propose that the first crucial step in persuading people to change their opinions is to produce a state of "cognitive dissonance." This is an unpleasant state which exists whenever an individual simultaneously holds two ideas or opinions that are inconsistent with each other. For example, in the Festinger and Carlsmith experiment, the participants may have said to themselves, in almost the same breath, "I have just been dishonest" and "I am a basically honest person." Since basically honest people do not go around telling lies, it is the conjunction of these two thoughts which produces cognitive dissonance.

Festinger then went on to argue that, since the occurrence of dissonance is relatively unpleasant, individuals are motivated to reduce it by whatever means are available. One way to do this is by adding extenuating ideas or thoughts; thus, those offered $20 for lying could think about the large sum of money involved and persuade themselves that, under those particular circumstances, lying was justified. Alternatively, dissonance can be reduced by changing one or both of the dis-

A woman in a traditionally male occupation. She may minimize dissonance by wearing men's overalls, and her male colleagues may reduce dissonance by reasoning: "She may be a woman, but she knows her job." Photo: Multimedia Publications Inc. (Israel Sun).

sonant ideas or beliefs so that they fit together better. Those offered only $1 for lying could not readily justify their behavior in terms of money, and so were unlikely to change their minds about being basically honest. Thus, the only way in which they could easily reduce their dissonance was by changing the thought "I have just been dishonest." This they did by convincing themselves that the experiment had been quite interesting, in which case they had not told much of a lie.

Festinger also proposed that the amount of dissonance created would be highest when the dissonant ideas are of great importance to the individual. One of the reasons for the amount of opinion change observed by Festinger and Carlsmith is probably that most individuals' self-concept includes the belief that they are basically honest. Finally, Festinger proposed, the amount of dissonance experienced depends on the number of ideas that are consonant or dissonant with an action or decision.

The money angle

Festinger's theory of cognitive dissonance obviously provides a plausible explanation of the results he and Carlsmith obtained. However, psychologists are skeptical by nature, especially when confronted with counter-intuitive findings, and one point that bothered many of them was the amount of money offered to the participants. Some suggested that those offered $20 probably didn't change their opinion of the experiment just because of the money—after all, $20 doesn't buy very much; others suggested that some of the participants were so disconcerted by the sum of $20 that their judgment was grossly distorted.

Neither criticism, however, turned out to have much validity. Arthur Cohen persuaded Yale students to write essays favoring the repressive actions of the New Haven Police Department in quelling a student riot by offering them $1 or 50 cents. Those offered the smaller sum came to believe in the truth of what they had written to a greater extent than those offered the larger sum.

Are people always most likely to change their opinions, when persuaded to do something unpleasant, for a small rather than a large bribe? Festinger's basic idea that people will justify their own actions in any way available suggests that there might be exceptions to this tendency. For example, if participants can be persuaded to tell lies about the enjoyableness of an experiment, the thought "I was compelled to tell lies" might provide just the justification they need for their dishonesty; again the result would be reduction of dissonance. Under such circumstances, Festinger found, there was an exact reversal of the usual picture: those who had been given $1 said they found the experiment more enjoyable and rewarding than those who had been given 50 cents, or half that amount.

Dissonance can also be reduced if the confederate who is told that the experiment is very interesting refuses to be convinced ("Well, you're entitled to your opinion, but I don't think I've ever enjoyed an experiment and I don't think this one will be much fun"). When that happens, the participant can justify his dishonesty ("Since it had no effect, it didn't really matter that I lied"), and his feelings about the experiment are unaffected by the size of the reward.

The mechanism of self-justification

All of the available evidence suggests the following basic rule of thumb for working out what will happen when people act in a way inconsistent with their own opinions: if their behavior can be readily justified for some external reason (offer of a lot of money, lack of choice, no bad consequences), then their opinions change very little; if their behavior cannot be justified in any other way, there will be an opinion shift to bring their opinions and their behavior into line.

Festinger's ideas have been related to an enormous variety of other situations. For example, Philip Zimbardo wondered how highly disliked foods, fried grasshoppers for example, could be transformed into a prized delicacy. He argued that if people were asked to eat fried grasshoppers by someone who acted in a pleasant and friendly way, they might just do so and justify their behavior by arguing, "I did it as a favor because he's a nice guy." On the other hand, if the person doing the persuading was snobbish, tactless, bossy, cold, and hostile, they could not use the "nice guy" justification for tackling their plate of grasshoppers, and so dissonance would be created. Then the easiest way to reduce dissonance would be to convince themselves that they really liked grasshoppers. Zimbardo actually put these ideas to the test and found that approximately half his participants agreed to eat at least one fried grasshopper, but that it was only those who were persuaded to eat by an unpleasant person who consistently came to like the thought of eating grasshoppers (e.g., "They taste like shrimp"). The non-eaters actually went the other way, expressing even greater repugnance for grasshoppers as a dish.

There is one important part of Festinger's approach that has received less attention than it deserves, and that is the notion that dissonance is experienced as a state of discomfort and tension. In one study most of the students who had agreed to write essays in favor of compulsory military service experienced dissonance and changed their true opinions in the direction of the attitudes they were asked to express. They did this to reduce the feelings of tension produced by dissonance. What if other students were given an innocuous drug before essay writing but were told it would produce feelings of tension? Would they be able to attribute any tension they felt to the temporary effects of the drug and therefore not experience any need to change their opinions? This is exactly what happened; it was found that the usual dissonance effect of opinion change did not occur after an allegedly tension-inducing drug had been given.

Social implications

We have seen that opinions change much more when there is insufficient justification for our actions than when there are good reasons for behaving in a certain way. It has been argued that most of the history of medicine can be explained in terms of cognitive dissonance!

Most forms of medical treatment used to be thoroughly unpleasant, ranging from putting cholera patients into scalding-hot water to bleeding patients with leeches. If medical treatment is disagreeable, time-consuming, or embarrassing, then there is potential dissonance between the two thoughts "I have consented to a repulsive method of treatment" and "I am still as ill as before." The dissonance can be eliminated, and the treatment fully justified, only if the patient can convince himself that he is actually getting better. When people say, "It tastes so awful it must be doing me good," they are being more perspicacious than they realize. (Of course, many illnesses do not permit this kind of self-delusion.)

A similar kind of analysis can be applied to the cost of medical treatment. As doctors discovered a long time ago, raising the price of a treatment can augment its healing powers by increasing the need for the patient to justify the expense involved ("I'm paying a lot of money, so I must be getting the best possible treatment").

Dissonance theory has also been applied to the important issue of molding children's behavior to fit the moral values of the society they live in. It is relatively easy to stop a child from behaving inappropriately if you threaten him with punishment. However, if the socialization process is successful, the child must also learn to behave properly in the absence of direct pressures or sanctions, and this is a much more difficult task.

Applying the dissonance theory, it is better to stop a child from performing an antisocial act by means of a mild rather than a strong threat of punishment. Why should that be so? If the child stops doing something he wants to do, i.e., throwing stones, because of a strong threat of punishment, then his justification is "I was forced to stop but I still want to go on throwing stones." If he stops throwing stones in response to a mild threat, however, he is likely to justify himself by saying, "I didn't really want to throw stones anyway."

The realization that strong pressure can be counterproductive has dawned on generations of parents. All too often, the more pressure parents put on teenagers not to associate with disreputable members of the opposite sex, the more enamored of them they are likely to become ("If I want to keep on seeing him in spite of my parents' disapproval, he must be important to me").

Support for the notion that mild threats can be much more effective than strong threats was obtained by Elliot Aronson and James Carlsmith. They told 4-year-old children not to play with a preferred toy, such as a battery-powered fire engine, under conditions of mild threat ("If you play with it, I'll be annoyed") or severe threat ("I'll be very angry. I'll take all the toys away and go home and never come back again. . . . You're behaving like a baby"). While both threats were effective in stopping the children from playing with the toy while the adult was out of the room, mild threat led to decreased liking for the forbidden toy, whereas severe threat didn't.

The cognitive dissonance principle has also been applied to the question whether individuals think more highly of a club or organization that goes in for an embarrassing or rigorous initiation than one that has only mild initiation procedures. Since most people do not like being embarrassed, one might think that an organization that provides unpleasant experiences would be disliked. According to dissonance theory, however, the two ideas "I have agreed to join this organization" and "I have allowed myself to be embarrassed for the sake of membership" cause dissonance, and this can only be reduced by exaggerating the positive aspects of the organization.

Elliot Aronson and Judson Mills at Stanford University tested these ideas by requiring female college students to undergo an initiation in order to become members of a group discussing the psychology of sex. The mild initiation involved reading aloud non-obscene words related to sex (e.g., prostitute, virgin, petting), whereas the severe initiation involved reading aloud obscene words (cock, fuck, screw) and then reading aloud two vivid descriptions of sexual activity from contemporary novels. After this initiation, they listened to a very boring and banal group discussion of secondary sex behavior in the lower animals. The girls who underwent the severe initiation condition evaluated the tedious discussion much more favorably than those who underwent the mild one.

Nevertheless, other explanations have been offered for the above findings. Perhaps girls who underwent the severe initiation became sexually aroused rather than embarrassed, and this produced pleasure and increased the attractiveness of the discussion group. However, incidental observations indicated that the girls did become embarrassed (hesitating, blushing, looking at the floor). Another possibility is that these girls felt relief from sexual anxiety when they found the group discussion innocuous instead of embarrassing, and this increased their positive evaluation of it.

However, explanations in terms of sexual arousal or sexual anxiety are not applicable to a later study, in which those who underwent a series of severe electric shocks in order to gain admission to a dull discussion group rated the group more favorably than those who experienced only mild shocks.

The religious dimension

The effects of cognitive dissonance have also been observed in various religious sects. In an investigation by Festinger and his co-workers, a number of psychologists managed to infiltrate a sect called the Lake City group. A woman belonging to the group received written messages from a number of "guardians" who lived in outer space, and these extraterrestrial beings informed her that on a given date, just before dawn, a cataclysmic flood would cover most of the North American continent. The activities of the group received considerable publicity when one of its members was asked to resign from his job as physician at a student health center because of his beliefs.

In the face of much taunting and sarcasm from non-believers, the members of the sect attempted to keep a low profile while they prepared themselves for evacuation before the flood. Four days before the flood was due, they were told, a flying saucer would land in the back garden of one of their houses, at four in the afternoon, to pick them up. Although they waited hopefully with coats in hand, the saucer did not arrive. They were then informed that the flying saucer would come at midnight, and they waited in vain for many hours on a cold, snowy night. Eventually, after several more false alarms and the non-appearance of the flood, there was a message from God to say that He had saved the world and stopped the flood for the sake of this one small group and the light and strength they had spread throughout the world.

How did these people cope with the conflict produced by the failure of their predictions? While abandonment of their beliefs might have been possible if their commitment to the cause had been lukewarm, many members of the sect had given up their jobs and discarded precious possessions in readiness for evacuation from this planet. The only way in which they could reduce dissonance was to convert as many other people as possible in order to provide themselves with more social support; this they did enthusiastically, replacing their earlier secrecy with an avid desire for publicity.

However, different reactions were found among the members of the Church of the True Word, a group which accepted the message of the Bible in a literal sense. From the Book of Revelations they calculated that one-third of the earth's population was about to be obliterated by nuclear warfare, and they expected to play a divinely inspired role in healing and converting survivors. Over one hundred members of the group prepared for this emergency by moving to a remote area of the southwestern United States, where they set to work building bomb shelters.

Upon receipt of a prophetic message, "The Egyptians are coming," 103 of the devout spent forty-two days underground awaiting a nuclear attack that never came. When they reemerged into the sunlight, they reduced dissonance by claiming that God had used them to warn a non-vigilant world and had tested their faith. They all decided that they had passed the test and were thus especially worthy in the sight of God. However, they did not busily try to convert others as the Lake City group had done. Probably the difference between the behavior of the two groups was due to the fact that the True Word group was larger and more cohesive than the Lake City group and therefore had more social support in its hour of discomfiture. The True Worders were fairly benevolently treated by the surrounding community, which helped to prevent the buildup of dissonance and conflict.

Doubts about dissonance

So far all the examples of dissonance we have discussed have been relatively straightforward—there is little doubt that the strong conflicts were produced by inconsistent ideas. However, it is not always so easy to be sure whether or not dissonance is created. Suppose you have told all your friends that a particular contemporary artist is your favorite painter, and it then transpires that he is a chronic alcoholic. This may well not cause dissonance, because you can always argue that artists are a law unto themselves. On the other hand, you would probably experience some dissonance if you discovered that a very prominent and well-respected member of the church had been an alcoholic for many years and consistently ill-treated his wife.

What determines whether dissonance is felt? Generally speaking, dissonance is likely to occur only when an expectation is violated. We have a definite expectation that churchmen will avoid the perils of drink, but no clear expectation about artists and alcohol.

Another difficulty which rather undermines the dissonance approach is that we all have different opinions about ourselves. Lying, as in the Festinger and Carlsmith studies, produces dissonance only if the liar regards himself as basically honest. If the liar regards himself as a callous psychopath he may actually relish the thought of deceiving others and experience no guilt or dissonance at all.

The implication is that dissonance theorists must pay more attention to the individual's self-image. For example, successful performance of a task would not usually be thought likely to produce dissonance; however, people who expect to fail have been found to become rather anxious when they actually succeed in something.

Finally, it would be potentially disastrous if we always did our utmost to reduce dissonance; that would be like weaving a permanent cocoon around ourselves. We would continually be justifying our own actions, never admitting that we make mistakes, to the point where we would be unable to profit from our mistakes. Let us take as an example a group of students who decided to take essay-type examinations rather than multiple-choice-type examinations. Many of them then chose to read articles explaining why essay examinations are more difficult and anxiety-provoking. Their reading would presumably increase dissonance, but the usefulness of the information so obtained was worth the price.

Conclusions

The dissonance theory suggests that man is a rationalizing animal rather than a rational one. We attempt to justify our behavior and appear rational both to ourselves and to others. This need for self-justification is a powerful one, and can be seen in the field of medicine, in the acquisition of moral values, in the behavior of religious sects, and in countless other aspects of life.

Because we are so eager to justify ourselves, we sometimes behave in strange and apparently unpredictable ways. However, largely as a result of the pioneer work of Leon Festinger and his colleagues, psychologists are beginning to understand how people deal with inner conflict.

SECTION E

The uses of psychology

Psychologists are often attacked for living in ivory towers. We study trivial academic problems, our accusers tell us, which have no rele- vance to broader social issues. There is an element of truth in the charge, especially with respect to the activities of some psychologists, whose motto seems to be "Publish or perish." Regrettably most of them opt for the former rather than the latter alternative.

It would, however, be a big mistake to imagine that psychological research is broadly irrelevant. An increasing number of professional psychologists are making significant contributions to society in the occupational, clinical, and educational fields. Indeed, the junior author of this book was surprised to discover at the annual convention of the American Psychological Association held in Toronto in 1978 that academic experimental psychology accounted for just one out of more than thirty sections of that association.

Common sense suggests that psychology ought to be of immense benefit to society at large. After all, it deals with the understanding and prediction of human behavior, and the whole functioning of society ultimately depends on the ways in which people behave and interact. For example, psychology is of primary relevance to court proceedings. A major aspect of the trial procedure consists of lawyers' attempts to uphold or destroy the evidence of eyewitnesses. The light which psychology can shed on the accuracy of such testimony was discussed in Chapter 13.

One of psychology's greatest contributions to human welfare has been in the treatment of mental illness—a variety of mental disorders can now be successfully treated. As we saw in Chapter 6, animal experiments carried out by psychologists have suggested appropriate methods of treating various human neuroses.

Bringing up children is difficult at the best of times, but parents today have to cope with a lot of conflicting "expert" advice as well. Should they choose the permissive approach or the more "old-fashioned" disciplinary approach? The merits of both are discussed in Chapter 18, but important new research indicates that both these extreme positions are wrong. There is, it seems, a saner middle way.

It is ironical that education—to which psychological principles and findings are especially relevant—has benefited little from psychological insights. The main reason for this is that major changes in educational practice are typically made by people who are influenced more by ideological preconceptions than by the available evidence.

As we point out in Chapter 19, it is particularly unfortunate that most educationalists have the mistaken view that all children are likely to react in the same way to any given instructional method. In fact, some children learn better when taught by one method rather than another. Clearly, a satisfactory educational system would be one which fully catered to individual differences between children.

In Chapter 20 we discuss some of the exciting possibilities of "biofeedback." Biofeedback is a psychologically based method of treating certain physical disorders and it has attracted enormous publicity in recent years. The basic idea is that problems which have a clearly defined physiological basis can be cured if the physiological abnormalities are rectified. Patients can help to treat themselves if they are provided with information about their success (or otherwise) in altering their physiological state. Biofeedback can help toward a cure, or at least control, of a host of problems, including hypertension, migraine, a peripheral circulatory ailment known as Raynaud's disease, and certain sexual disorders. But close examination of the effects of biofeedback suggests that it is very far from being the "wonder cure," as some best-selling authors have suggested.

The incidence of crime, especially violent crime, has increased in virtually all Western countries. Is there anything we can do about it? It is argued in Chapter 21 that the first step is to understand the factors which lead some people to become criminals and others to remain relatively virtuous. There is some evidence that a long period of punishment-based conditioning can lead to the development of a "conscience." It may be that the permissiveness of contemporary society is reducing the number of such conditioning experiences and thus indirectly contributing to an increase in crime.

There are encouraging signs that psychological methods of treatment may prove effective in reforming some, if not all, criminals. Various conditioning techniques have been used to induce both juvenile delinquents and adult offenders to adopt more socially desirable attitudes.

As we shall see in Chapter 22 psychology also has important applications to political and social thought, from Communism to Fascism. Over the centuries, many people have distinguished between "left-wing" and "right-wing" attitudes; now psychologists have identified a radical-conservative dimension which corresponds to this distinction. However, some radicals (i.e., left-wingers) are tough-minded and others tender-minded, and the same goes for conservatives; this has led to the introduction of a tough-minded/tender-minded dimension within broad ideological categories.

Why do different people have different social and political attitudes? Common sense suggests that such attitudes are determined environmentally by family, friends, and other social contacts. However, there is exciting new evidence that heredity plays a substantial role and that personality also helps to determine which political attitudes are accepted and rejected.

In sum, psychology is of ever-increasing significance to society. There are very few areas of life in which it has no contribution to make.

18

How not to bring up children

Most parents worry how best to bring up their children. In their anxiety, some of them turn to psychologists or psychiatrists, or even psychoanalysts. This may not be a wise move; professionals and so-called experts have a poor track record in advising worried parents. J. B. Watson, the father of the behaviorist movement, was the first of the best-sellers on bringing up children; his influential *Psychological Care of the Infant and Child* sold more than 100,000 copies within a few months. Bertrand Russell, a man not easily duped, became a strong supporter of Watson's beliefs. But professional psychologists were decidedly critical; some felt that the book damaged his status as a serious scientist. Watson's message was a simple one: children should be brought up on a scientific, rather than an emotional or traditional basis. He advocated that one should not mollycoddle one's offspring, show them too much affection, or even kiss and cuddle them, for to do so encourages a dependent mentality; feeding should be on schedule, not on demand. Watson tried this regime on his two sons; one committed suicide, and the other, to Watson's intense annoyance, became a psychoanalyst. In the end, Watson regretted writing his book, not, he said, "because of its sketchy form but because I did not know enough to write the book I wanted to write."

After the tough, anti-loving, non-permissive Watson the pendulum swung back, as pendulums do, and we got his very opposite, the psychoanalytic Dr. Spock with his extremely permissive, feeding on demand not on schedule, hugging and kissing prescription. *Baby and Child Care* was outsold only by the Bible. Mothers everywhere gratefully relapsed into a more emotional relationship with their children, something Watson had warned explicitly against. But both the permissive and scientific child-rearing models were based on too narrow a view. Spock finally acknowledged that his recommendations had been wrong. Bringing up children his way failed to bring the results he had hoped for.

Both Watson and Spock, in their different ways, illustrate the evil of giving advice, supposedly scientific in nature, on the basis of preconceived opinions instead of firmly established scientific theories grounded in fact. The truth is that psychologists simply do not know enough about the upbringing of children to assume the role of omniscient advisers.

Watson relied on the narrow basis of a fundamentalist behaviorism, Spock on the narrow and insubstantial basis of the Freudian credo. Neither of their systems is supported by sufficient facts to bear the weight of the superstructure they and other writers erected on top of them. We know very little about the upbringing of children, but we do know enough by now to realize that Watson and Spock both gave advice that was wrong for most children—the one being too tough, authoritarian, and unemotional, and the other too soft, permissive, and lovey-dovey. Most mothers would have brought their children up more successfully if they had never read either. Beware of psychologists bearing advice—this is one gift horse into whose mouth it would pay parents to look most carefully.

Can we then offer nothing to parents who ask our advice? In fact, we can . . . a little. Interesting and important studies have been carried out in recent years which do suggest a few guidelines. The first—and most obvious, since few mothers need reminding of it—is that children are all different and that there is no one way of bringing them up. Each child should be treated as an individual. The second is that heredity is very important, both for intelligence and for personality; parents are not presented at birth, as Watson maintained, with some shapeless mass of putty which they can mold into any shape they like.

The difficulties of child research

A lot of money and energy has gone into child research; why is it that in spite of all this effort we still know so little? There are two interlinked reasons. The first is that research in this field is very difficult; it is usually thought unethical to expose children to regimes which might provide us with control data because experimental methods are believed to be more useful, successful, and advantageous. (This is a universal difficulty in medical research as well as in applied psychology. To take just one example, when intensive-care units were introduced for the treatment of cardiac arrest, this very expensive method of care was believed to have many advantages over looking after patients in their homes; demands for controlled comparisons between the two methods were brushed aside with the argument that it would be unethical to continue to expose patients to the dangers of old-fashioned care—it was cavalierly assumed that the new methods were better. Nevertheless, the experiment was done, and the result was unequivocal: the old-fashioned method was better!)

The second difficulty is that psychologists have preconceived ideas, which they are often unwilling to expose to experimental proof lest they be proved wrong. Psychologists (and psychiatrists and psychoanalysts) are only human, and subject to all the usual human foibles— they can be just as wrongheaded, obstinate, aggressive, and downright perverse as anyone else, and child rearing is a topic which seems to bring out the worst in them.

Here is a typical example. Imagine a psychologist (or a sociologist, psychiatrist, or psychoanalyst) who wishes to investigate the hypothesis that beating children as a punishment does not improve their behavior but makes them behave worse. Imagine him setting up an experiment in which he studies an experimental group of children whose parents do not beat them at all, or who at most beat them only occasionally, and then compares them with another group, a control group, of children whose parents beat them often and mercilessly. He then investigates the adult careers of these two groups of children and finds that those who were beaten tend to grow up into aggressive, hostile, often vicious adults (the correlation is not very high in the studies that have been done, but the trend is unmistakable). And his conclusion? He will claim that he has proved his point, that beating children is bad. But is this really true?

Obviously he may be right. The data do not contradict such a hypothesis, but neither do they confirm it. There are alternative hypotheses which explain the facts equally well, without implicating parental punishment. For example, it is possible that the genetic constitution of the parents, which causes them to behave in this brutal fashion toward their children, is inherited in part by the children and causes them, too, to behave in a brutal fashion when they grow up, regardless of the punishment they have suffered. In fact, without punishment they might have been even more aggressive and brutal! There is much evidence for the importance of heredity in aggressive and hostile behavior, so this alternative hypothesis is a genuine possibility.

A third possibility would be that some children are by nature so badly behaved, and so uncontrollable, that they can be held in check only by severe beatings; but as they grow up, their original behavior, no longer curbed by physical correction, manifests itself again in vicious and unruly conduct. There is also a lot of evidence to show that the behavior of parents is often provoked by the behavior of their children. In other words, parents react to what their children do, rather than the other way around. Thus we have another explanation for the original findings of our hypothetical psychologist.

This example neatly illustrates a fundamental fallacy in much modern sociological and psychological research into upbringing, namely the fallacy of interpreting observed correlations as causes and effects. The unruly behavior of the children as they grow up *is* correlated with brutal treatment handed out by parents, so researchers assume that the former is the result of the latter, but they have not proved it. In Copenhagen there has been a continuous decline in the number of babies born over the past thirty years; similarly there has been a decline in the number of storks nesting in the city; but this does not prove that the storks bring the babies. This "sociological fallacy," as it has been called, because it is a fallacy sociologists are particularly prone to wander into, vitiates a large number of research studies in this field and makes it very difficult to come to any logical conclusions about real causes and effects.

There are two ways of getting around this difficulty. One is to do a genetic study which weeds out genetic from environmental effects. Thus we might study identical and fraternal twins, their spouses, and their children, to obtain information on different genetic relationships and different environmental relationships which lend themselves to proper statistical analysis. The drawback of such studies is that they require large numbers of twins and are difficult and expensive. With few exceptions, psychologists have avoided experiments of this kind and concentrated instead on observing the effects of given forms of treatment on randomly selected experimental and control groups of children.

A good example of this second kind of approach to child research was a study done by Mary Gribbin.[1] She was interested in the effects of "permissive" and "old-fashioned" upbringing on preschool children.

Key experiment   Preschool play groups (Mary Gribbin)

This experiment looked at differences in play patterns between children attending two different preschool groups, one the formal, old-fashioned sort and the other run on new, permissive lines. Both groups consisted of boys and girls between 2 and 4 years of age, and the author was particularly interested in patterns of aggressive play ("agonistic behavior"). Both groups had a similar social background, so that any differences between them were unlikely to arise because of socioeconomic or other social factors. As Gribbin says, "differences between the groups' overall behavior must be largely a result of the different play environments."

What were the differences between the two groups as far as do's and don'ts were concerned? In the new-style group, children were forbidden to bring any guns or violent toys to play with, a prohibition presumably based on the hypothesis that playing with guns leads to antisocial and violent behavior. In the old-style group, children were allowed to bring any toys they wanted; more often than not they chose guns, tanks, and similar weapons.

The second difference was that in the new-style group there was a lavish supply of climbing bars, creative toys, and an outdoor play area. There was also little direct supervision of play. In the old-style group, however, which was restricted to an indoor hall with less equipment, the behavior of the children was more closely supervised. Supervision included strict rules of acceptable behavior, and transgressors were confined to a "sin bin" for serious misdemeanors (such as biting another child). Antisocial behavior in the new-style group was looked upon by the supervisor as a sign that the naughty child needed love and understanding, which he or she received, often at the expense of the victim, who was virtually ignored while the social problems of the aggressor were dealt with.

Thus the two groups provide a clear contrast between the permissive and the restrictive organization of society at large. We shall see later whether the lessons learned from this small-scale experiment can indeed be extended to society as a whole. But before going on to a discussion of the actual results of the experiment, readers are invited to guess for themselves what the effects of these two styles of treatment were on the children involved.

First, let us look at the amount of aggressive and antisocial behavior in the two groups. Gribbin defined "agonistic interaction" (aggressive play) in terms of a variety of behaviors, ranging from mild abuse, accompanied by verbal and non-verbal threats, at one end to actual physical violence at the other. Boys in the old-fashioned group showed 5 instances of aggression, but in the progressive group there were 89 instances! Girls showed no instances of aggression at all in the old-fashioned group, but 42 in the progressive group. For the two sexes combined, the totals were 5 instances of agonistic behavior in the old-fashioned group, 131 in the progressive group. The 5 incidents in the old-fashioned play group were all simple verbal personal abuse. In the progressive play group something like 65 percent of incidents led to blows being exchanged, often with scratching and biting. Thus there was a tremendous difference between the two groups, with the "no guns" permissive group showing vastly more agonistic behavior than the old-fashioned disciplined group.

Gribbin asks the question: "Are the children who have no violent toys, lots of sympathetic understanding, few restrictions on play within the group, and a slightly more 'affluent' society in terms of available toys, more able to cope with social interactions and cooperative behavior? Far from it." As she goes on to point out, one of the most interesting features of her study was that the children in the "no guns" regime were busily engaged in making guns, tanks, and swords out of harmless Lego kits. "The forbidden fruit clearly tastes sweeter, especially when the results encouraged an adult response along the lines of 'Now, Nigel, that isn't a gun you're making, is it?'" In the old-style group, by contrast, even the violent toys were generally treated by the children simply as comforting reminders of home and seldom used for any "violent" or even mock-violent purposes.

There were many other differences between the two groups. The children in the old-style group played in bigger units (three or four individuals) than those in the new-style group, where children played mostly in pairs. Inevitably this meant that there were more mixed groups of boys and girls playing together in the old-style than in the permissive group. These and many other differences are discussed by Mary Gribbin in her paper, but the most important difference she left to the end: "We also formed the distinct impression (admittedly a subjective interpretation, but still one based on hours of watching at each group) that the children in the old-fashioned group were just plain happier than those in the progressive group." This bears out the observation frequently made by psychologists that children actually prefer a structured environment and feel lost and unhappy when such structure is not provided by adults or older children. Chaos, even if labeled permissive, does not make for happiness.

This experiment strongly indicates the importance of the environment for the behavior of children. The different treatments given the two groups overrode even the most basic biological difference of all, namely that between the sexes; in both groups boys were more aggressive than girls, but this sex difference fades into insignificance compared with the much greater difference between old-fashioned and progressive types of behavior.

This is hardly the result that would have been predicted by the advocates of progressive teaching, who in the last seventy years or so have turned our preschool groups, kindergartens, and elementary schools into permissive places of no work and all play, from which all socializing and restraining influences have been banned. The motives no doubt were good, but the effects were not. The hoped-for improvement in the happiness and mental health of our children did not happen; progressive methods have not helped them to grow into well-adjusted, socialized human beings. Gribbin's experiment is not the only one, of course, to demonstrate the adverse effects of permissiveness, but it does show how complex social interactions can be studied experimentally.

Academic achievement

Let us turn to another, larger study undertaken to investigate the influence of secondary schools on the accomplishments and behavior of children. Here too there has been much poorly informed discussion, in which the permissive climate of opinion and the erroneous views of "experts" have played havoc with our educational system. Some of the background of this troubling story is worth retelling.

In 1966 James Coleman published a very influential report in the United States entitled *The Equality of Educational Opportunity*. He conducted a large-scale survey of the achievements of some 645,000 students in 4,000 secondary and elementary schools. He believed that the results showed that educational attainment was largely independent of the schooling a child receives, and this conclusion was supported by Christopher Jencks in *Inequality: A Reassessment of the Effect of Family and Schooling in America* in 1972. Jencks concluded his complex statistical analysis by stating that "equalizing the quality of high schools would reduce cognitive inequality by 1 percent or less" and that "additional school expenditures are unlikely to increase achievement, and redistributing resources will not reduce inequality."

In the United Kingdom, the Plowden Report of 1967, which was in many ways comparable with the Coleman study, concluded that home influences far outweighed those of school. Altogether there was widespread pessimism about the extent to which schools could exert any influence on children's development. This view was well expressed by Basil Bernstein when he said, "Education cannot compensate for society" (meaning presumably that where education has failed, revolution must take its place).

These conclusions, so contrary to common sense, were largely based on statistical and theoretical fallacies (experts in education are generally as fallible as experts in child upbringing). For example, Coleman compared two factors which supposedly promote achievement at school, the environment provided by parents and the environment provided by the school. But such a comparison is meaningless because it takes no account of genetic differences in intelligence among children. Whatever precise figure we use to index the contribution of genetics, no

serious student has come up with a figure below 50 percent, and the
majority would rate it much higher than that; 70–75 percent is probably the most accurate estimate available at the moment.

By leaving out this extremely important factor, Coleman in fact con-
founded it with the environmental influences exerted by family background, socioeconomic status, and so on, thus increasing the hypothetical importance of these factors out of all proportion. If his
analyses are repeated with the proper introduction of genetic factors
into the equations, the picture alters completely, and schools can be
shown to be very important indeed in producing differences in achievement. How so many "experts" could overlook Coleman's error and ac-
quiesce in his conclusions is a mystery.

Compared with these studies of very large numbers of schools and
pupils, a recent book by Professor Rutter and colleagues, *Fifteen
Thousand Hours,* deals only with a small group of secondary schools
and their effects on children.[2] But the small size of the study in no way
detracts from its value—quite the contrary. Large-scale studies are usually conducted at too great a distance from the actual details of children's behavior and activity. Close contact is a powerful corrective,
and Rutter's book is far better factually than any of the large-scale ex-
ercises. Here we only have room to discuss Rutter's conclusions, but interested readers should read his book for themselves—not a difficult
task because the book is short, full of properly researched facts, and
written in clear, incisive English (Rutter eschews the atrocious jargon
that normally afflicts educationalists).

What then are his major conclusions? The first is that secondary
schools in Inner London differ markedly in the behaviors and attain-
ments shown by their pupils. This was evident from the children's behavior during school hours (as observed by the researchers as well as
reported by teachers and by the pupils themselves), from the regularity
of their attendance, from the proportion who stayed on at school beyond school-leaving age, from their success rate in public examinations,
and from their delinquency rate.

The second finding was that although schools differed in the proportion of behaviorally difficult or low-achieving children they admitted,
these differences did not wholly account for the variations between
schools and their pupils' later behavior and attainment. Children were
more likely to show good behavior and good scholastic attainment if
they attended some schools than if they attended others. The implication is that experiences at school do influence children's progress. It
was also found that variations between schools in terms of post-school
success or failure were reasonably persistent over periods of at least
four or five years.

Rutter's third conclusion was that individual schools performed fairly consistently on all the various measures of "outcome"; that is to say, schools which did better than average in terms of their children's behavior in school tended also to do better than average in terms of examination success, post-school success, and so on.

The fourth, and particularly important, finding was that these differences in outcome between schools were not due to such physical factors as the size of the school, the age of the buildings, or the amount of space available. Differences in administrative status or organization were also irrelevant.

The fifth conclusion was this: "The differences between schools and outcome *were* systematically related to their characteristics as social institutions. Factors as varied as the degree of academic emphasis, teacher actions in lessons, the availability of incentives and rewards, good conditions for pupils, and the extent to which children were able to take responsibility were all significantly associated with outcome differences between schools. All of these factors were open to modification by the staff rather than by fixed external constraints."

The sixth conclusion was that outcomes were also influenced by factors outside teachers' immediate control, such as academic balance in pupil intake. Examination success tended to be better in schools with a substantial nucleus of children of at least average intellectual ability, and delinquency rates were higher in those with a heavy preponderance of the least able. The intake factor was most marked with respect to delinquency, and least important in the case of observed behavior in the classroom and elsewhere about the school.

Lastly, Rutter observes: "The association between the *combined* measure of overall school process and each of the measures of outcome was much stronger than any of the associations with individual process variables. This suggests that the *cumulative* effect of these various social factors was considerably greater than the effect of any individual factors on their own. The implication is that the individual actions or measures may combine to create a particular *ethos,* or set of values, attitudes and behaviors which will become characteristic of the school as a whole." In conclusion he writes: ". . . to an appreciable extent children's behavior and attitudes are shaped and influenced by their experiences at school and, in particular, by the qualities of the school as a social institution."

These conclusions, we believe, follow pretty directly from the facts recorded in the book and are of considerable importance to teachers, administrators, politicians, and particularly parents. They may seem obvious to most people with some experience in the field, but as Rutter and his colleagues comment: "One of the common responses of practitioners to any piece of research is that it seems to be a tremendous amount of hard work just to demonstrate what we knew already on the basis of experience or common sense. . . . After all, it is scarcely surprising that children benefit from attending schools which set good standards, where the teachers provide good models of behavior, where they are praised and given responsibility, where the general conditions are good, and where the lessons are well-conducted." Perhaps so, but as they go on to say: "It might have been equally obvious if we had found that the most important factors were attending a small school in modern, purpose-built premises on one site, with a particularly favorable teacher-child ratio, a year-based system of pastoral care, continuity of individual teachers, and firm discipline in which unacceptable behaviors were severely punished. In fact *none* of these items were significantly associated with good outcomes, however measured." This point is well taken, and it certainly justifies the length of time and hard work spent amassing, recording, and analyzing the data. The book is an example of how such research should be done and puts to shame the much more ambitious efforts of Coleman, Plowden, and the like.

New realism

May one hope that those in authority will pay some attention to the results, sack teachers who set a bad model, and promote those who influence children in a positive way? The last twenty years have seen an ideological preoccupation with unrealistic theories, poorly done research, invalid conclusions, bad statistics, unwarranted conclusions, and a firm desire to depart from reality in favor of utopian ideals of very limited appeal to parents anxious for the future of their children. Mercifully this period seems to be drawing to a close, and reality is again moving into conjunction with the educational process.

Some readers may feel that we are advocating a return to Victorian rules of discipline and classroom organization. This is not so. As Rutter and his colleagues point out, "firm discipline in which unacceptable behaviors were severely punished" was not associated with particularly favorable outcomes—as we saw in Chapter 17. Imposing too harsh a discipline and too severe punishments is just as misguided as being too permissive; as usual, wisdom lies in moderation. Both extremes have their advocates, of course, but the evidence solidly opposes them. Setting a good example, maintaining good discipline with the minimum of punishment, and trying to achieve an ethos which leads to the children's being socialized almost unconsciously seem to be the best way of achieving goals which most parents and teachers would agree on.

To conclude, recent empirical studies do offer helpful advice to parents on how to bring up children. The answer seems to be to avoid the extremes of Watsonian and Spockian ideology, and to create an ethos at home which reinforces cooperative and socialized behavior. Antisocial and agonistic behavior should be discouraged rather than absolutely vetoed. The task for parents and teachers alike is not an easy one, but the evidence shows that we can produce children who are reasonably happy and well adjusted, provided we reject irrational prejudices, harmful ideology, and the advice of "experts" who fail to back their preaching with sound research.

19

Realizing
educational potential

For thousands of years man has been attempting to improve his means
of achieving certain social objectives. In education, politics, the penal
system, and many other areas of life numerous theories have been put
forward and many new methods tried in order to improve existing
practices. Looking back over the centuries, or even just over the past
few decades, a fairly uniform pattern of progress is discernible. A new
theory is born, and received with the usual doubt and scorn by reac-
tionaries, but thanks to the powerful advocacy of its enthusiasts finally
gets accepted and implemented on a large scale; for a while, success
seems to attend the new method, but then it is found that it is not, after
all, much better or much worse than previous methods, and is abandoned. Why is it that our attempts to improve our dealings with our
fellow men are so unsuccessful?

This is an interesting and important question. After all the "progress" we have seen in education, are our methods today really better
than those of Socrates? Have we really learned anything in the last two
thousand years? Are children today taught any better than they were in
ancient Greece and Rome? Are we more successful at discouraging
crime and violence? One would have to be an incurable optimist to say
yes to all these questions. Frankly, our educational practices, to compare them only with those prevalent thirty or fifty years ago, do not
seem to produce results which are better than or even as good as those
achieved before the introduction of the various new methods. Why do
we keep on failing?

There are two main reasons, one of which is very simple. In science,

Traditional kindergartens and elementary schools tend to favor ex-troverted children. Photo: Multimedia Publications Inc. (Israel Sun).

most ideas that are put forward are erroneous; very few survive experimental testing. In matters psychological, and particularly in matters of social import, experiments are relatively rare; social policies are adopted on the basis of political or social ideology. One would not therefore expect many new ideas to be good or useful, and history bears this out. There should always be an intermediate stage between the enthusiast conceiving an idea and society implementing it, namely a stage of small-scale experimentation in which scientists neither favorable nor hostile to the idea try it out to see whether it contains anything that might be useful in the long run. Only after such a preliminary analysis and empirical testing should full-scale implementation of any system be attempted.

The second reason for the consistent failure of new social policies is perhaps less readily accepted. It involves an almost universal assumption about human nature which is demonstrably wrong, but is held by practically all social innovators, be they politicians who approve new ideas or those who actually implement them. This assumption is that a method which is useful and helpful for Jimmy must also be useful and helpful for Harry and James and Ida and Margaret. In other words, the assumption is that all human beings react similarly to similar stimuli, conditions, methods of teaching, and so on. This assumption is quite wrong. What is more, it disregards human individuality and personality.

Suiting the method to the pupil

We have already seen (in Chapter 10) that human beings are very different from one another, and that these differences are much more profound than most people realize. Furthermore, they are based on firm genetic predispositions which, while they can be modified by environmental influences, nevertheless strongly determine a person's behavior and conduct. So it seems very likely that certain methods of teaching might prove useful and helpful for extroverts, say, but exactly the opposite for introverts.[1] Thus if we compare a new method of teaching with an old-established method, and find that the new method is neither better nor worse than the old, this may indeed mean that there are no differences between the two methods. But it may also mean, and this is much more likely, that the new method is *better for some people* and *worse for others*. The new method only appears neither better nor worse than the old because the two effects, one positive, one negative, appear to cancel each other out.

Take the relationship between personality and academic achievement: it has often been found that extroverted children do better than introverted ones in primary school and in the early years of secondary school; but in the later years of secondary school and in college, introverts do considerably better than extroverts. This seems to be largely due to the fact that the relatively free and easy methods of teaching adopted in most primary schools suit extroverted children, who thrive on informality and like to flit from topic to topic fairly quickly. Introverts prefer the formal teaching atmosphere of the later secondary school. They like to get their teeth into a topic and persevere with it, and generally do better than extroverts at college and university in later years, where the emphasis is on specialism.

In other words, one simply cannot say that one method is "better" than another; all we can say is that one method suits the extrovert, another suits the introvert. Perhaps introverted children would do better at primary school if a more formal system were adopted. Similarly extroverts might do better in the later years of secondary school and in college, if courses were less specialized and allowed their interest to range wider.

But is there any evidence that different personalities react to different methods of teaching in different ways? The answer is yes. Many different interactions between teaching method and personality have been discovered. Unfortunately the variety of these interactions is such that it is virtually impossible to demonstrate the superiority of any one method over another.

Passive versus active learning

One of the traditional great divides in teaching theory is that between the "discovery" method and the direct instruction method. The essence of the discovery method is that the child is not told the law or principle underlying a phenomenon but has to discover it for himself by experiment (he is, of course, given the wherewithal to conduct his experiments). This is very different from the usual "reception" type of teaching, in which the child is presented with whatever generalizations can be made and simply has to learn them. Reception learning has been criticized because it tends to make the pupil a passive recipient of wisdom; discovery learning has been praised because it enables the child to find out for himself. On the other hand, critics have pointed out that most children are too young and immature to discover complex laws for themselves, and that they may actually prefer to do their work and their experiments in the context of knowledge transmitted to them by the teacher. Who is right?

Key experiment   (Professor G. O. Leith)

Comparisons carried out to study the relative superiority of discovery learning over reception learning or vice versa have usually failed. Professor G. O. Leith[2] examined the possibility "that the greater readiness of extroverts to become bored by routines but likely to respond to stimulus variation, and of introverts to be disturbed by changes of set but able to maintain attentiveness to a highly prompted task, would result in a method $\times$ personality interaction."

Leith arranged for teaching materials for a course in genetics to be carefully prepared to give equal amounts of discovery learning and instruction learning in randomly chosen groups of students. "The materials were so chosen as to cover a range of personal discovery, tolerance for uncertainty and error-making as well as of differences which may be described as plunging into the deep end or stepping into the shallow end of the pool." Two hundred students took part in the experiment, and were tested one week after the course and again five weeks later. They were also tested for introversion/extroversion.

The major finding was a highly significant interaction between personality and method. On both testing occasions introverts and extroverts learned equally well *on average;* in other words, there was no overall superiority of one method over the other. But extroverts learned much better with the discovery method than introvérts, while introverts learned much better with the direct teaching method than extroverts.

At the final count, introverts had a mean score of 17 using the discovery learning method, but a mean score of 26 using the traditional reception learning method. Extroverts had a score of 24 using the reception learning method, but one of 30 using the discovery learning method. Leith's experiment illustrates very clearly the danger of comparing different methods of teaching without also measuring personality and looking for the different reactions of different personality types to the methods of teaching being investigated.

Another illustration of the interaction between personality type and teaching method is provided by a study conducted by Leith and E. A. Trown in 1970.[3] They studied the optimal placing of rules in school learning tasks, i.e., whether rules abstracted from a program of learning were better given befòre or after sections of the program containing practice examples. In general the evidence suggested that it was better to have the rules following practice, but again there was a significant interaction with personality. For extroverts the "rules before" program was significantly less helpful than the "rules after" program. There was no significant difference between the programs for introverts, although if anything "rules before" was slightly more helpful.

Paired learning

Another interesting area of education in which personality interaction is particularly marked is that of paired learning, i.e., where learners work in pairs. Leith (1974) has reported one such study, in which pairing was arranged on the basis of neuroticism (pairs being similar, stable-stable or anxious-anxious, or opposite, stable-anxious) and also ability. Thus, pairs matched or mismatched for neuroticism were also homogeneous (similar) or heterogeneous (different) for ability, giving a total of ten pair categories. The improvement shown by the different pairs was very different indeed, depending on the personalities of the two people involved. Opposite anxiety pairs showed something like a 100 percent superiority over same anxiety pairs on the test used! So, if we want to raise the achievement of the children making up the pairs, we should put together a high neuroticism scorer and a low neuroticism scorer, rather than two lows or two highs. This was true regardless of whether the ability of each pair was homogeneous or heterogeneous.

Quite a different picture emerged when extroversion/introversion

Paired learning boosts achievement if pupils are matched for ability but mismatched for anxiety. Photo: Multimedia Publications Inc. (Miki Koren).

and ability were made the basis of pairing. In this situation homogeneous pairs performed better than heterogeneous pairs, regardless of whether the pair was made up of two extroverts or two introverts. It is clear, then, that we could greatly assist the learning of our children by pairing them, according to their personalities, in ways which produce significantly higher achievement. As we have seen, the pairing of heterogeneous children, one anxious, one stable, would be one way of combating the negative effects of anxiety.

Supportive and exploratory teaching strategies

Another way was suggested by an experiment done by Trown and Leith in 1975,[4] in which nearly 500 boys and girls took part. The experiment was designed to contrast the effects of "supportive" and "explorative" strategies in mathematics teaching in four junior schools (the average age of the children involved was 10 years and 6 months). As Trown and Leith reported: "In the case of the supportive strategy, the sequence employed over each of the twelve sections of learning material was that of teacher-provided statements of organizing principle, followed by related pupil activity with mathematical models, and subsequent restatement of principle by the teacher. Such statements were both spoken and written on the blackboard.

"The same activities, with models, were used in the exploratory strategy, but this time at the beginning of each section of the learning sequence. Each statement of principle by the teacher was now delayed until pupils had been given the opportunity to perceive the relationship themselves and had been encouraged to attempt an appropriate generalization."

Differences in neuroticism (anxiety level) produced clear differences in performance in the learner-centered exploratory situation; some children profited from it, others were handicapped by it. Mean scores in the test for remembering what they had learned were almost twice as high for low-anxiety as for high-anxiety children. However, when they learned in the supportive situation, there were no differences between low- and high-anxiety children. Again, overall differences between the two teaching strategies were minimal when the personalities of the children were ignored.

The lesson is clear: had the experimenters failed to take the children's personalities into account, they would have come to the quite erroneous conclusion that both strategies were identical in their effects. Both extroversion and neuroticism play a part in a child's reaction to these different methods of teaching. No method is good or bad in itself; its usefulness or otherwise depends very much on the personality of the child it is applied to. The stable extrovert child flourishes in discovery and exploratory situations, whereas the introverted child, particularly when unstable, is heavily penalized. He or she does much better with supportive strategies and reception learning.

Matching teaching methods to personality—a way forward

Leith summarized the conclusions he believes can be drawn from his many studies in this field as follows: "The evidence presented . . . does not lead to definitive conclusions which can be applied immediately with confidence in classrooms. It can be claimed, however, that the repeated findings of interactions between personality (as measured by neuroticism and extroversion scales) and instructional methods (defined in terms of both global differences and experimentally manipulatable variations) require that educationalists pay serious attention to the need for adapting learning situations to learners."

An examination of the interaction between personality and teaching methods shows that extroverts are not intrinsically poorer students.

They have simply been disadvantaged by methods more suitable for teaching introverts. In an age of educational innocence, this may have been tolerable, but today it begins to look more like discrimination. Much more research should and must be undertaken.

If future research should turn out to support the findings of Leith and others, what should be done? Certainly it would be wrong to track on the basis of personality and/or ability. The type of teaching system which treats class units as relatively homogeneous blocks of children is administratively convenient, not educationally enlightened. A teaching system which fully recognized personality differences is more likely to be based on the methods used in many infant schools; in other words, it would provide a variety of approaches, and tailor those approaches to individual children by closely monitoring their progress. Investigations into cooperative learning were a step toward finding ways of giving individual instruction in de-tracked, comprehensive-type classes. Cooperative learning would provide not only learner-centered activities but continuous feedback, progress checks, and the means to make the most of the social environment of school.

Teachers please note

Above all, prospective teachers (and practicing ones, too) need to be taught the facts of personality structure and the interaction between personality and teaching strategies and systems. At the moment the kind of psychology taught to teachers is almost entirely useless as far as dealing with children in classrooms is concerned. It consists of irrelevant Freudian shibboleths and similar snippets of misinformation which may make teachers think they understand the psychology of the teaching situation but which are unhelpful in practice. Given some knowledge of the behavior patterns of extroverted and introverted, stable and unstable children, and provided with questionnaires to test their pupils in order to spot extremes, teachers should be able to work out the best methods of motivating and instructing children of different ability and personality. To go on pretending that all children are alike is unrealistic, and most teachers realize it. But at the moment little help is given to them in their professional training, although enough is already known to make better teaching possible, and detailed instructions on how best to apply existing knowledge are already available (Wakefield, 1979). Lecturers in training colleges have no excuse for avoiding what should be a central task in the preparation of teachers for their job. It is time that the facts became more widely known and were applied to the better and more successful instruction of our children.

What has been said here in relation to education is equally true in relation to all other aspects of psychology—experimental psychology, social psychology, clinical psychology, industrial psychology, and so on. In all these fields practitioners and experimentalists alike refuse to face the fact that individuals differ greatly in their reaction to any kind of experimental or social situation, and that a person's reaction is powerfully determined by his personality. Just as the physicist does not expect mercury to behave like gold, or aluminum like iron, so it is completely irrational to expect an introvert to behave like an extrovert, whether in the laboratory or in social situations. Similarly, an emotionally unstable person reacts quite differently from an emotionally stable person and recognition of this fact is an absolute necessity in the study of psychology generally and its application to specific areas.

So far we have dealt only with academic, abstract learning, but of course the task of the teacher goes far beyond mere scholastic attainment. There is a tradition, particularly in English schools, of "character building," which insists that children should not only possess a knowledge of the three R's but should also be educated to become well-integrated, honest members of society. We have already cited experiments (Chapter 6) to show that this can be accomplished through a process of conditioning, and that the great innate differences in conditionability produce great differences in socialized or antisocial behavior. But there are other ways in which personality subtly interacts with education.

Exam nerves and school phobia

Most people have heard of examination anxiety, and most of us have, in some degree, experienced how debilitating it can be. We feel too nervous to give of our best in the examination room. Examination anxiety is quite widespread; so is school phobia, a fear of going to school so strong that the child absolutely refuses to go, plays truant, and may become a very real problem to his parents, his teachers, and himself.

Examination anxiety and school phobias tend to occur mainly in children who are characterized by a high degree of emotionality or neuroticism, i.e., who are innately predisposed to feel strong emotions of fear in situations they perceive as threatening. Fortunately these minor neuroses are fairly easy to clear up, by means of a method of therapy called "desensitization." In desensitization, the patient is trained in methods of physical relaxation, relaxation being as incompatible with anxiety as tenseness is with euphoria.

During the actual treatment session, the child is first completely relaxed, and then he is asked to imagine a scene, such as getting up in the morning and getting ready to go to school. This normally produces some anxiety, but not enough to overwhelm the anti-anxiety properties of the relaxation; consequently the child learns to tolerate a small degree of anxiety. In other words, he becomes conditioned to respond with "non-anxiety" to a previously threatening situation.

Gradually the therapist builds up to situations which normally evoke more and more anxiety, always being careful not to overstep the mark where relaxation is a sufficient countervailing force against the anxiety provoked. The patient is led through a number of imaginary scenes, from getting up in the morning and getting ready for school, to actually walking out of the house, down the street, boarding the bus, seeing the school in the distance, seeing other schoolchildren, approaching the school building, walking into it, and so on. When all this can be done in imagination without producing undue anxiety, the therapist gets the child, again in a condition of complete relaxation, to go through these stages in real life, accompanying him all the time. Gradually the child becomes "desensitized" and manages to go to school. The success rate of this treatment is almost 100 percent, and the treatment does not take long.

Examination anxiety can be treated in the same way, again with practically 100 percent success. The child is taught to relax, and then imagines himself in examination situations, progressing from low-anxiety situations to actual examination conditions.

Both treatments are now very widely used with children. Teachers are not usually trained in these methods, but there would be no difficulty in training them. Examination anxiety and school phobia are such frequent problems that it would be worthwhile introducing treatment methods into teacher-training courses.

Even more worthwhile would be prophylaxis—preventing the problems in the first place. To do this it would be necessary to identify those children most likely to suffer from examination anxiety or school phobia. Fortunately this is relatively easy; questionnaires of neuroticism and introversion could be given, and children scoring high on both would be singled out as the most likely to succumb to examination anxieties or school phobias. The teacher (or therapist) could then "inoculate" the children by the desensitization method just described before they showed signs of phobia or anxiety. In American schools special school psychologists are employed to do this kind of work, and it might be a good thing if British schools were to follow suit. Unfortunately, there is never much money for prophylactic schemes. Governments tend to wait until things have gone wrong and then spend money putting them right, even though it would have cost much less if the trouble had been prevented in the first place.

Much the same is true at the university level. Again America has been much more adventurous in providing psychological treatment centers, staffed by clinical psychologists, in most universities; nothing of the kind is known in Britain or on the Continent. These centers deal with the manifold emotional and other problems experienced by students, and the well-known fact that there are quite large numbers of suicides at universities in Britain and Europe tends to suggest that these problems are very real and widespread. By a mixture of prophylaxis and treatment a great deal can be done to save valuable and highly intelligent young people from the undesirable consequences—failure, suicide, nervous breakdown—of their temperamental peculiarities.

Conclusions

We have mentioned the fact that at both school and university level children and students with high neuroticism-instability-emotionality scores tend to do much less well than more stable students. A great deal can be done to help them to make the most of their talents. Education should not be understood in the narrow sense only. High academic achievement is not all that counts. It is just as valuable to learn how to manage the overly strong and unstable emotions which interfere with learning and application. School teachers and university staff should be familiar with these facts, should have some insight into personality dynamics, particularly where neuroticism and extroversion are concerned, and should be able either to help directly or to refer their pupils to a psychologist capable of dealing with their problems. It is unnecessary cruelty to allow emotionally unstable people to suffer breakdown, failure, and anxiety when the remedy is available and usually works. A society is judged by the efforts it makes to look after the deprived, the unfortunate, and the unlucky. Our society could certainly do better than it has done in the past.

20

Biofeedback:
mind over matter?

If you were asked to walk with a simulated limp, putting more weight on one leg than the other, you might think it bizarre but you would have no doubts about your ability to do so. On the other hand, if you were asked to make more blood flow through one of your ears than through the other, you would think it even more bizarre and consider it physically impossible.

It is a matter of common knowledge that we have voluntary control over many activities, such as walking, thinking, and speech, but the workings of our internal organs (heart, liver, stomach, kidneys, and so on) are outside our conscious control. Physiologists refer to these internal organs as the "viscera."

There are good reasons why we do not need to exert voluntary control over, for example, the stomach. It would be most tiresome if we had to stop doing everything else after a meal in order to supervise the stomach's digestive processes. But while it is clearly a great convenience for us that our internal organs look after themselves in our day-to-day lives, there are occasions on which the ability to control them would be extremely welcome. The man with a hangover or the seasick traveler would dearly love to be able to discipline his protesting innards.

The general notion that bodily activities can be divided up into those that are voluntary and those that are involuntary has a long history. Two thousand years ago, Plato drew a distinction between the superior rational soul in the head above and the inferior souls in the body below. More recently it has been argued that voluntary behavior is pos-

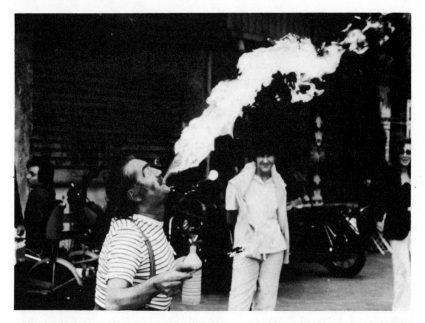

Fire-eating, a dramatic demonstration of mind over fire. Photo: Multimedia Publications Inc. (Israel Sun).

sible only for skeletal responses produced by the cerebro-spinal nervous system, whereas involuntary behavior characterizes the visceral and emotional responses of the more primitive autonomic nervous system.

This simple distinction held sway for a very long time among philosophers, psychologists, and physiologists. However, there are several intriguing examples of voluntary control over apparently "involuntary" responses which suggest that this view may be oversimplified. The famous memory man S., who had an exceptional capacity to imagine vividly, was able to control his heart rate and temperature. Merely by visualizing himself as asleep or vigorously active, S. was able to alter his heart rate abruptly over a range of nearly 40 beats per minute (the average beat per minute is 70). Even more dramatically, S. could raise the skin temperature of his right hand by imagining that it was on a hot stove, while at the same time lowering the temperature of his left hand by imagining that it was holding an ice cube. He was able to cash in on his unusual skills by changing his profession from newspaper reporter to professional mnemonist. (See also Chapter 15.)

The most famous example of someone who capitalized on similar special abilities was the illusionist and escapologist Harry Houdini.

Whenever he performed one of his famous escapes, his clothes and body were searched beforehand by several skeptical spectators. When they had satisfied themselves that the Great Houdini was not concealing any keys, he was encased in chains, padlocks, and handcuffs.

In spite of the careful scrutiny to which he was exposed, Houdini escaped from his shackles every time. The method he used was to hold a key suspended in his throat and to regurgitate it when he was unobserved. Since the natural unlearned reaction to having an object stuck in one's throat is to gag, it is not surprising that no one thought of Houdini's throat as a possible hiding place for keys. Houdini's real trick was that he had learned to control his gag reflex; this he had achieved by practicing for hour after hour with a small piece of potato tied to a length of string.

Amazing claims have been made about the powers of Indian yogis, including the ability to make their hearts stop beating. It is difficult to evaluate most of these claims, and undoubtedly some yogis have been motivated by the desire to part the gullible from their money. However, a serious attempt to study yogis scientifically was made by Dr. Bal K. Anand, the chairman of the Department of Physiology at the All-India Institute of Medical Sciences in New Delhi. He has tested over 400 yogis under carefully controlled laboratory conditions. Though most of them proved disappointing, a handful demonstrated unusual abilities. One yogi was able to reduce his heartbeat to half the normal rate by blocking the action of the so-called cardiac pacemaker, and another yogi could make his forehead break out in perspiration without moving a muscle. Two more yogis were able to slow down their metabolism until they were functioning at less than half their normal waking metabolic rate—approximately *five times* as great a drop in metabolic rate as occurs in very deep sleep!

The first really thorough attempt to see whether the internal organs or viscera can learn in the same way that rats learn to press a lever for food was made by the distinguished American psychologist Neal Miller. His painstaking research in the 1960s helped initiate today's scientific interest in "biofeedback."

Key experiment   Can the internal organs learn? (Neal E. Miller and Leo DiCara)⁻

As Neal E. Miller[1] of Rockefeller University, New York, stared intently at his own reflection in the bathroom mirror of his weekend house in Guilford, Connecticut, he saw a stocky, energetic man, bald except for a white fringe behind the ears, with a firm jaw, broad nose, and deep-set green eyes. However, the focus of his gaze was his ears, because he was trying to teach himself to wiggle his right ear without moving his left ear. He believed that all learning requires the appropriate use of reward or reinforcement. Accordingly, he was looking carefully for the faintest indication that he was beginning to master the trick of wiggling one ear on its own so that he could reward this elusive wiggle with a burst of self-congratulation.

He tried various techniques, including imagining that the left side of his face was cold or numb, so that the ear on that side would be unable to wiggle; they all failed. He finally discovered that standing in front of the mirror and approaching the task little by little was the best strategy. He explained his technique in the following way to Gerald Jonas of *The New Yorker:* "I'd start by trying to produce the most minute independent movement with my right ear. Then I'd try to increase it a little bit each day. If my left ear started to move at any time, I'd drop back until I was sure that only the right one was moving. Then I'd start increasing the movement again, little by little. Eventually . . ." At this point in his conversation with Jonas, Miller paused and seemed to be concentrating deeply. His right ear began to twitch while the left ear remained motionless. After a while, he relaxed and broke into a wide grin, indicating that success is its own reward.

This story illustrates the way in which people can learn to do strange and unusual things if they are suitably rewarded and if they receive direct information or feedback about the success or otherwise of their efforts. Could heart rate voluntarily be lowered or raised if constant information about the speed of functioning of the heart were available? Miller felt this ought to be possible, and argued that it could occur in two very different ways: (1) directly through actual visceral learning; (2) indirectly through voluntary control of skeletal activities such as exercise or breathing (e.g., if you take long, slow, deep breaths your heart rate will tend to slow down).

Miller regarded the alteration of heart rate by indirect, non-visceral means as "cheating" and pointed out that an impressive demonstration of genuine learning by the internal organs required the elimination of the possibility that skeletal activities were responsible. The technique he chose was to use injections of curare, a drug which causes virtually complete paralysis of the skeletal muscles, including those involved in breathing, but which permits the internal organs to function fairly normally.

Curare was originally obtained by South American Indians from the roots, stems, and bark of jungle plants, and they used it to envenom the darts they used against other tribes, having discovered that their targets died within minutes from respiratory failure. Later on curare was used as an anesthetic during surgery. Since the patients remained completely immobile, it was generally assumed that they felt nothing during the operation. Although the patients screamed, as soon as the effects of the curare had worn off, that they had suffered excruciating agony with every cut of the surgeon's knife, their complaints were at one time dismissed as hallucinations.

The basic contention of Miller and his co-workers was that if the visceral responses of curarized animals could be manipulated by reward or reinforcement, this would show conclusively that the internal organs are capable of learning. Since there are obvious dangers in using a powerful drug like curare on humans, and because it might have been difficult to find people prepared to submit themselves to temporary paralysis, Miller decided to use rats in most of his experiments. Since curarized rats cannot breathe unaided, their breathing had to be maintained by artificial means.

Miller decided that the major reason why the internal organs do not normally seem to show much learning is that we are not normally aware of their activities. In order to facilitate the learning of heart rate changes in their rats, Neal Miller and Leo DiCara[2] arranged a complicated system to provide the rats with information about their heart rates. Each rat was initially given an operation in which electrodes were sewn under its skin in such a way that they could be attached to an electrocardiograph, a machine which records and monitors heart rate. The apparatus was set up so that a small spontaneous increase in heart rate (usually a 2 percent rise) was followed by reward. As time went by, the rat had to increase its heart rate by larger and larger amounts in order to obtain reward.

How on earth do you reward a rat that is totally paralyzed? Miller and DiCara got around this tricky problem by giving their rats brief electrical stimulation of that part of the rat's brain which acts as a kind of "reward center." They found that by rewarding progressively greater increases in heart rate with brain stimulation they could increase the curarized rat's heart rate by 80 beats a minute in just 1½ hours of training. Thus it looked as if the internal organs *could* learn by the reward method in spite of a widespread belief at the time (mid-1960s) that such a thing was impossible.

Could rats learn to alter the functioning of other internal organs? Miller found that curarized rats could learn to increase or decrease intestinal contractions; they could also learn to vary the amount of blood in the stomach wall, and they could even control the rate of urine formation.

Miller was still not satisfied that he had shown visceral learning to be the same as the learning of skeletal responses such as pressing levers for food. For instance, "normal" learning is usually remembered reasonably well. To prove that visceral learning is also remembered Miller tested rats who had spent 1½ hours learning to increase or decrease their heart rates three months earlier, and found that they did indeed remember how to control heart rate.

Finally, Miller argued that "normal" learning of, say, the skills involved in a sport shows a progressive improvement in the precision with which movements are made. Does visceral learning show the same precision? Apparently so, because curarized rats were able to make more blood flow through one ear than the other when rewarded for so doing.

Why has nature endowed us with the capacity for visceral learning if it is so little used that most people believe that we do not even possess it? As Miller himself pointed out, it would be very strange if evolution had created a mechanism that had "no normal function other than that of providing my students with subject matter for publications."

The answer to that puzzle may be related to the fact that most aspects of our internal environment (e.g., temperature, blood flow) need to be kept fairly stable all the time; this is known as "homeostasis." Unlearned control systems usually suffice to maintain homeostasis, but

An experiment in which the subject tries to exert voluntary control over heart rate. Her pulse rate is played back to her over headphones. Photo: Multimedia Publications Inc. (Israel Sun).

Biofeedback used to help a patient control tension. Photo: Multimedia Publications Inc. (Israel Sun).

visceral learning may be available as a supplementary mechanism if the internal environment is seriously threatened.

An ironical footnote to this work of Miller's is that back in the 1930s he and his mentor Clark Hull had vigorously promulgated the notion that all forms of learning, whether of the skeletal or the visceral variety, depended on reward or reinforcement. Miller now finds it remarkable that none of Hull's research associates seriously investigated visceral learning all those years ago: "With so many other people insisting that it couldn't be done, even the smallest positive result would have been a terrific coup for the theory. . . . I may have dodged this particular application of Hull's theory because I felt that it might be refuted here, and I was unconsciously reluctant to face this possible outcome."

The greatest irony about the research carried out by Neal Miller is that in spite of his well-merited reputation as a meticulous experimenter, it has proved rather difficult to replicate his findings. Researchers at other institutions have had some success, but Miller himself, in collaboration with Barry Dworkin, has not been so lucky.

Whatever the ultimate scientific value of Miller's research, there is no question at all about the huge influence of his work. In particular, the entire development of biofeedback as a medical tool in the treatment of several human problems would never have occurred without Miller's seminal work.

Medical use of biofeedback

At the level of ideas, Miller's work has apparently shown that the difference between man's reason and his emotions may be less extreme than previously believed, since both can be controlled in the same way. At the more practical level, the notion that man can control his internal organs opened up new vistas for the treatment of a wide range of complaints, ranging from migraine headaches to heart irregularities. Of course, Miller did most of his work with rats, but since people are more intelligent than rats they ought to be able to train their internal organs at least as well.

Some support for this general position was obtained by Lee Birk of Harvard Medical School, who volunteered to be injected with curare. After the injection, he could not lift his head from the chair, nor was he able to lift any extremity, open his eyes, swallow, or utter intelligible sounds. Even in this state, he continued to show evidence of remembering a visceral response learned previously while not curarized.

The media have devoted a lot of attention to "biofeedback," the new "wonder cure" stemming from the work of Miller and others. The term simply refers to a technique in which biophysiological instruments provide the patient or other person with information about changes in bodily functioning of which he is usually unaware. The patient's "reward" is to observe his increasing control over the workings of a part of his own body, and the apparatus is set so as to gradually "shape" the visceral response in the desired direction.

Case histories

One of the most spectacular success stories for the biofeedback approach was reported by Peter Lang and Barbara Melamed of the University of Wisconsin. They treated a 9-month-old boy, A.T. His birth weight was 9 pounds 4 ounces, and at 6 months his weight had gone up to 17 pounds. However, he had suddenly started regurgitating and vomiting most of his food within ten minutes of each feeding, so that at 9 months of age his weight was down to under 12 pounds. He was in an advanced state of dehydration and malnutrition and was being fed directly to his stomach. He was not expected to live.

Psychoanalysts have argued that such symptoms in children are due to a disruption of the mother-infant relationship in which the mother's inability to fulfill an adult psychosexual role prevents her from providing warm and loving care for her child. The infant reacts by seeking its own gratification from within by regurgitating its food and retaining it in the mouth. Unfortunately for this idea, the prescribed remedy of very warm and intensive nursing had no effect whatsoever on the vomiting.

Lang and Melamed measured the muscle potentials along A.T.'s esophagus and discovered that the first wave of reverse peristalsis just preceded regurgitation. They arranged things so that the infant received unpleasant electric shocks that started whenever the esophagus started to back up and continued until the vomiting had stopped. After only a few meals, the infant stopped vomiting. One month after discharge from the hospital his weight had more than doubled to 21 pounds, and he had become a healthy toddler.

Biofeedback has also been applied to the treatment of male sexual problems. In spite of the claim by the well-known sexologists Masters and Johnson that "erections develop just as involuntarily, and with just as little effort, as breathing," penile tumescence can be trained and controlled. In one early study, Raymond Rosen found that penile tumescence could be greatly increased when there was information about the rate of progress and when financial incentives were offered. However, he remained skeptical of the alleged ability of some experienced yogis to withhold the ejaculation of sperm during orgasm.

Rosen applied his biofeedback technique to the treatment of Mr. W., a 45-year-old school janitor who had been married for twenty-two years. Mr. W. was arrested in a supermarket parking area for exposing himself while dressed as a woman. Rosen's first step was to videotape a thirty-minute sequence in which Mr. W. masturbated to orgasm in his usual female attire.

For the treatment sessions, Mr. W. was fitted with a mercury-in-rubber gauge which measures even momentary changes in penile blood flow. At first when Mr. W. viewed the videotape of himself he showed consistent and protracted erections on the gauge. In order to prevent this from happening, an amplified recording of Mr. W.'s alarm clock was played whenever his penile tumescence exceeded a particular level, and the volume of the recording was regulated according to the degree of erection. Mr. W. was told to try to prevent the recording (and himself) from coming on; by the twelfth session there was total suppression of the penile response to the videotape.

On the more positive side, Mr. W. manifested great penile tumescence to a typical heterosexually oriented stag film, and this reaction was encouraged. According to Rosen, "Mr. W. is a relatively inhibited, naïve lover whose sexual repertoire is currently being expanded," which makes him sound like a music-hall entertainer getting his act to-gether! At home all was well for a time. Sexual relations with his wife improved, and Mrs. W. started to have orgasms. She also agreed with some reluctance to wear more erotic articles of clothing during sexual contact. Unfortunately, Mr. W. resumed his transvestite activities and was arrested and imprisoned for again exposing himself while dressed as a woman. Thus the apparent success of his biofeedback treatment was only temporary.

Is it possible that biofeedback produces sexual arousal simply be-cause the individual "thinks dirty"? In one study, the vaginal blood flow of two sexually experienced unmarried women in their twenties was examined while they thought of the most erotic fantasies possible, based either on their own experiences or on activities they imagined to be erotic. Interestingly, only the more sexually experienced of the two women showed an increase in vaginal blood flow while fantasizing. In contrast, both women showed a substantial increase in vaginal blood flow when fantasy was combined with biofeedback which indicated whether the flow was increasing or decreasing. So in this case biofeed-back had an effect over and above that of sexually oriented thinking.

Voluntary control of blood pressure

One of the most important applications of biofeedback has been in the treatment of hypertension. There has been a dramatic increase in degenerative disorders such as coronary heart disease and hypertension in the complex and fast-moving societies of the Western world. Esti-mates of the prevalence of hypertension vary from 10 percent to as high as 30 percent of the total adult population, depending on the definition of what constitutes high blood pressure. More than 90 per-cent of all cases are of unknown cause, and so fall into the category of "primary" or "essential" hypertension. Hypertensive individuals are at greater risk than others of succumbing to such disorders as myocardial infarction, congestive heart failure, stroke, and damage to kidneys, eyes, and other organs.

Hypertension is normally treated by various drugs, including tran-quilizers. However, many drugs have undesirable side effects, and biofeedback might be a preferable method of treatment. Treatment of essential hypertension has most often used the "constant cuff" method, which permits continuous, beat-by-beat feedback of blood pressure. A crystal microphone is mounted inside a standard pressure cuff and placed over the brachial artery. The cuff is inflated and set at a con-stant pressure close to the patient's average systolic or diastolic blood pressure. Biofeedback in the form of a light and/or sound signal is given if the patient manages to achieve a slight reduction in blood pressure.

Biofeedback training with hypertensive patients has often been successful in achieving reductions of about 10–15 percent in systolic blood pressure and slightly less in diastolic blood pressure. This sounds quite impressive but it turns out that if one simply asks hypertensive patients to attempt to reduce their blood pressure, without telling them how to do it and without using the elaborate equipment of biofeedback, one can obtain blood pressure reductions nearly as great as those achieved by means of biofeedback! It may be that biofeedback works simply because the patient is being attended to and feels that something constructive is being done about his problem.

The most serious doubt about the efficacy of biofeedback in reducing blood pressure is that its beneficial effects have typically only been demonstrated in the laboratory. No one has any clear idea of whether the reductions in blood pressure can be maintained under the more stressful conditions of everyday life, and there are some grounds for pessimism. Peter Seer reviewed all the work on the use of biofeedback to treat hypertension at the end of 1979 and felt compelled to conclude: "At present we have no convincing evidence that essential hypertension can achieve clinically relevant and persistent blood pressure reductions through blood pressure feedback training."[3]

Other applications of biofeedback

Biofeedback techniques have also been applied to the treatment of migraine headaches. These headaches typically involve increased blood flow in the head, resulting in painful dilation and distension of the cranial arteries. There are several substances available, such as Benzedrine, caffeine, and ephedrine, which cure migraine by producing vasoconstriction. However, these drugs can have unfortunate side effects.

It is known that people suffering from migraine tend to have cold extremities, and it has been argued that if blood flow to the peripheral regions were increased, this would decrease the blood flow to the head and so ease the migraine headache. When biofeedback has been used to increase finger temperature, there has usually been a modest reduction in the incidence of migraine headaches, but it is not clear whether this is caused by the increased blood flow to the periphery or not.

A further application of biofeedback is to a peripheral circulatory ailment known as Raynaud's disease. This disease is sometimes treated surgically by means of a sympathectomy, but the effects are permanent and irreversible, and not always desirable. Biofeedback has been able to produce an increase of about 9° F. in hand temperature and shows some promise as a method of treating circulatory ailments.

A more psychological application of biofeedback has been to use it to increase the amount of alpha-wave activity in the brain in order to create the "alpha experience." This state of consciousness is usually described as being a pleasant, relaxed, and serene state, characterized by a loss of body and time awareness and an absence or reduction of thought. The pleasantness of the alpha experience is apparently so great that many people have shown an extraordinary enthusiasm for spending large sums of money on the necessary biofeedback equipment. But the evidence indicates convincingly that these people are wasting their money. The feeling (whether justified or not) that one can control one's brain waves, combined with the power of suggestion, produces the alpha experience. If people are fooled into believing that alpha is increasing even when it is not, they report the usual strong alpha experience.

So far biofeedback has turned out not to be the medical cure-all promised by best-selling authors. But why is it that rats have a greater capacity for visceral learning than humans? One of Miller's findings offers a clue. He discovered that curarized rats showed much better visceral learning than undrugged rats, and speculated that curare helped to eliminate the various sources of distraction that interfere with learning. In other words, human patients may also need to be paralyzed in order for biofeedback to work properly!

Conclusions

In spite of a prevalent belief that the internal organs are incapable of learning, there is now strong evidence that they can learn and, moreover, acquire very specific kinds of skills. This suggests that a rethinking of the old division of mind and body, or reason and emotion, may be called for.

These exciting new discoveries have helped to generate interest in treatment by means of biofeedback. Unfortunately, the medical use of biofeedback, while much trumpeted, has proved extremely disappointing so far.

21

Can criminals be cured?

Ever since Charles Darwin, in *On the Origin of Species by Means of Natural Selection* (1859), published his theory of evolution, and established that human beings share a common ancestry with the lowliest of animals, all students of the human sciences have had to take into account our inheritance from our animal ancestors. This inheritance applies as much to the human brain, the seat of reason and sensation, as to any other part of our physical and psychological structure.

The well-known American neurophysiologist P. D. McLean[1] has used Darwin's theory of evolution in his work on the brain. The human brain is clearly divided into three parts—they can be distinguished quite easily when the brain is dissected, even without a microscope. McLean calls it the "triune" brain—three brains in one, each of which descends from a different stage in evolutionary history.

At the bottom is the brain stem and the lower part of the brain, what McLean calls the "reptile brain." It is the most ancient from the point of view of evolution and descends to us from our reptile ancestors. Superimposed upon this, and enveloping it, is the paleocortex, or limbic system, a brain structure which developed later and which governs the expression of the emotions. Superimposed upon both these structures, and enveloping them in turn, is the neocortex, the gray matter that above all else distinguishes man from his animal relatives. It is the neocortex which enables him to reason logically, use language, and break the bounds of biological evolution. Man inherits more than genes; he inherits the complex cultures he creates as well. Of course, there is some degree of intercommunication between the three parts of the brain; nevertheless, they all have their separate functions, and no attempt to account for human nature can be successful unless it allows for these differences.

The growth of the neocortex has made possible the interlinked functions of reasoning and language; but because they derive from a "separate," later structure, reasoning and language have little power over the limbic system of the paleocortex and the emotions which it governs. However, the limbic system also has a language; but it is the language of Pavlovian conditioning. Most people will be familiar with Pavlov's famous experiment, in which he conditioned dogs to salivate to the sound of a bell by pairing the bell with food on a number of occasions; after a certain number of pairings the dogs salivated to the sound of the bell, even though no food was forthcoming. The importance of Pavlov's experiment is often forgotten. It was important because it showed that emotions and physical reactions can be conditioned in the same way (see Chapter 6). This is what makes conditioning theory relevant to the manipulation of human behavior.

The sociological and the psychoanalytic approach

Conditioning is particularly relevant to the treatment of criminal conduct. In fact, it is not too sweeping a generalization to say that an adequate theory of criminality, like an adequate theory of neurosis, is crucially dependent on Pavlov's conditioning experiments. But let us briefly mention two alternative theories first, neither of which, in our considered opinion, really accounts for criminal behavior.

The first of these is the sociological theory, which links criminality with such factors as poverty, inequality of wealth, capitalism, poor housing, and so on. During the past thirty years or so all these factors have been growing weaker in the major European countries and in the United States. In Europe and the United States there is greater equality, better housing, and a higher standard of living. So, on the sociological hypothesis, crime should have decreased; in fact the evidence is conclusive that it has increased, in some cases manyfold. This seems to disprove the notion that it is economic deprivation which causes crime. True theories should predict consequences accurately.

The second theory is the psychoanalytic, according to which criminal behavior is a subspecies of neurotic behavior caused by infantile complexes and curable by psychoanalytic treatment. We will merely mention two studies which contradict this hypothesis. The first is the Cambridge-Somerville study in which large numbers of potentially criminal youths in Boston, Massachusetts, were divided at random into two groups. The experimental group received a great deal of psychoanalytic guidance, interpretation, and treatment; the control group received no such treatment. The hope was that the psychoanalytic treatment would act as a preventive. But after the groups had been followed up over a period of thirty years, the outcome proved to be the opposite of what the theory predicted. Such differences as were found favored the control group; the group that had received psychoanalytic treatment committed, if anything, more crimes than the controls.

Along similar lines, Grendon Underwood Prison in Britain was created to give prisoners psychotherapeutic treatment along psychoanalytic lines. Recidivism at Grendon was compared with that of a typical old-fashioned prison (Oxford), and the results showed that recidivism was exactly equal for the psychoanalyzed group and the unpsychoanalyzed group. There is a lot more evidence to show that the psychoanalytic interpretation of criminality does not conform to the facts and that psychoanalytic treatment is irrelevant in reducing criminal conduct.

Crime = bad or inadequate conditioning

The conditioning theory of criminality, however, accords much better with the facts. For the sake of brevity we have had to state the theory much more dogmatically than we would like, and readers are referred to a book entitled *Crime and Personality* (Eysenck, 1977) for a more detailed statement. The first point to be made is that moral conduct is not the result of rational decisions and is not influenced very much by rational considerations. Very few of those who commit crimes are caught and punished; that is a widely known fact. Anyone who organizes his life along purely rational lines might choose a life of crime as more likely to advance him materially than a blameless life full of virtue. The real question, then, is: why do relatively few people commit crimes when the rewards are so immediate and so obvious and the probability of punishment so remote?

The answer, we suggest, lies in the concept of "conscience," conceived not as a religious mechanism implanted by God, but rather as a conditioned response implanted by a long period of "Pavlovian" conditioning. Consider the events that take place when a young child grows up. He naturally misbehaves, is selfish and antisocial and dishonest. Whenever he behaves in such a fashion, he is punished by his parents, his teachers, his peers, or whoever else happens to be around. Such punishment, whatever it is—a box on the ear, standing in the corner, going to bed without supper—is painful and disagreeable. We thus have a regular chain of events. First comes the *conditioned stimulus,* the sound of the bell in the Pavlovian experiment, but in the case of the child his or her intention to commit an antisocial act and the actual carrying out of that act. The *unconditioned stimulus,* corresponding to the appearance of food in the Pavlovian experiment, is the punishment meted out by parents, teachers, or peers. The *unconditioned response,* corresponding to the salivation of Pavlov's dogs, is the pain, anxiety, and fear which the punishment causes in the child. According to Pavlovian principles, the conditioned stimulus should become associated, after a number of reinforcing episodes, with the unconditioned response, so that after a time antisocial intent or behavior should become connected with the anxiety typically resulting from punishment. This anxiety, coupled with the intention of carrying out some antisocial activity, is what we commonly call "conscience," and it effectively prevents most people from indulging in antisocial and criminal activities, even though these might be undetectable and very much to their advantage.

To many people this account may seem to endow conditioning with a far greater force than seems credible, and they may reject the theory on these grounds. However, there is experimental evidence to suggest that conditioned responses are extremely powerful in producing socialized behavior. We have, for example, the work of R. L. Solomon and his colleagues,[2,3] which was carried out both with very young children and with puppies. Here we will merely recount briefly their work with puppies, but their results with young children were equally impressive.

Key experiment (R. L. Solomon)

Essentially, Solomon's experiment was carried out as follows. The puppies, starved for one whole day, are brought into a room which contains the experimenter sitting on a chair, a plate full of boiled horsemeat (which the puppies like very much) to the right of the chair, and a plate full of commercial dog food (which the puppies don't like very much) to the left of the chair. The experimenter holds a folded newspaper in his right hand and whenever the puppies try to eat the horsemeat, the eating of which he has arbitrarily decided is an antisocial activity that must be discouraged, he slaps the puppy over the rump with the folded newspaper. Note that this "punishment" is exceedingly mild and does not really hurt the dog or cause it any degree of pain; it simply signifies the displeasure of the experimenter. After a few attempts to eat the boiled horsemeat the dog goes and eats the commercial dog food, in a rather disgruntled fashion. That concludes the experiment for the day, and it is repeated the day after, and the day after that, until the end of the week.

The next stage of the experiment begins at the start of the following week. This time the experimenter is absent when the twenty-four-hours-hungry puppies are brought into the room; instead he surveys the scene through a one-way glass screen. The boiled horsemeat is there for the dogs to eat if they want to, and there also is a very small portion of commercial dog food. The interest, of course, is in what the puppies will do now that they are free of the presence of the experimenter and apparently free to disregard the "socializing" influences set up by the experimenter. In other words, will the conditioned "conscience" make the dog act counter to his desires and instincts? The answer is that for most of the puppies this was indeed the case; they circled the boiled horsemeat and looked at it yearningly, but ate the commercial dog food and left the horsemeat untouched. A few succumbed to temptation, but the great majority did not. After half an hour the puppies were taken back to their kennel, starved for another twenty-four hours, then brought out again, and the same procedure was repeated. This time a few more decided to eat the boiled horsemeat, but the majority still resisted the temptation. To cut a long story short, it seemed that many of the puppies would rather have died of starvation than act counter to the conditioned "conscience" implanted in them by the experimenter (or course, the experimenter did not allow this to happen, and the puppies were fed long before they starved). But note that the very mild "punishment," the unconditioned stimulus, set up a sufficiently strong conditioned response for many of the puppies to prefer death to the simple act of doing what their newly acquired "conscience" forbade. Much the same result was obtained with young children, so we cannot comfortably dismiss the experiment as only applicable to animals.

From puppies to people

This, of course, is only one illustration of the "conscience" theory. There is an enormous mass of experimental material to indicate that this theory is, if not 100 percent correct, then at least along the right lines. It suggests two things. One is that the reason we have seen such a tremendous increase in crime since the war may simply be that over the past thirty years the general climate of "permissiveness" has reduced the number of "conditioning" experiences children receive at the hands of parents and teachers. In other words, the amount of social conditioning has decreased. This would automatically reduce the strength of the child's "conscience" and make him much more likely than his prewar counterparts to indulge in antisocial or criminal activities. Again there is much observational material to support this hypothesis; there seems to be no doubt that schools where greater "permissiveness" is practiced have a higher delinquency and criminal record among their

"Conscience" is less a result of psychoanalytic treatment or appeals to reason than of social conditioning. Photos: Multimedia Publications Inc. (Israel Sun).

pupils than schools where the atmosphere is more formal, "old-fashioned," and less permissive (Rutter et al., 1979[4]). We do not have time here to go into all the experiments and studies supporting this view; we simply mention it.

The second point about the "conscience" theory is that it can be related to the treatment of criminals, whether children, juveniles, or adults. It suggests ways in which their antisocial and criminal conduct might be changed, so that they become socialized human beings with a proper "conscience." What is needed is not psychoanalytic treatment of non-existing complexes and neuroses, or verbal appeals to reason and the "better nature" of the wrongdoers. What is needed is simply a supply of what has been lacking in their upbringing, namely a suitable number of occasions for conditioning to take place.

Token economies

There are many ways in which reconditioning can be done, and one of them is the so-called token economy. This was originally introduced by an English penologist whose work was done over a century ago, Maconochie of Norfolk Island. Norfolk Island was a penal colony off the coast of Australia, to which all of Britain's worst offenders were sent. When Maconochie arrived there he discovered that the treatment of the prisoners was inhumane, cruel, and bestial; Norfolk Island, far from having any reforming influence, produced a high degree of recidivism (see Eysenck, 1973).

Maconochie introduced a system of points which prisoners could earn by working hard, by not fighting, and by generally behaving in a socialized manner; punishment was the withdrawal of points. Very soon the effect of this regime was very noticeable; prisoners began behaving much better than when they had been brutally punished. Equally noticeable were the aftereffects. From the universal testimony even of his critics, it appears that Maconochie succeeded in inculcating in his prisoners concepts of socialized behavior which lasted well beyond their stay in prison. Unfortunately his efforts at revolutionizing the prison system were constantly attacked and ultimately thwarted by the British Home Office, which finally relieved him of his post.

In more recent years token economies of this kind have been tried out by American psychologists with many different groups, mainly juvenile delinquents. Research into outcomes is, of course, difficult, and many more years of follow-up will be required before we know the full extent of the success or otherwise of these trials. Nevertheless, it can already be said that token economies, properly implemented, can reduce the recidivism rate of young offenders by something like 50 percent over a period of three years after they are released from custody. This is, of course, nothing like a complete 100 percent success. Even so, being able to halve the number of recidivists is one of psychology's most useful contributions to criminology. If the decrease could be extended over the whole prison population the saving in money alone would repay the cost of the enterprise thousands of times over (Ayllon and Azrin, 1968;[5] Sarason, 1978;[6] Stumphauzer, 1973, 1979[7,8]).

Recent research has tended to move away from treating criminals in institutions like Borstals or prisons, for the very simple reason that in institutions peer groups are a strong countervalent against reconditioning procedures; in such settings all attempts at reconditioning tend to reinforce and even strengthen the criminal inclinations of the inmates. There seems to be no doubt that the process of "de-institutionalization" has much to be said for it: it is also much cheaper. In some of the experiments done in the United States it has been found that new psychological methods of treatment, administered outside institutions, not only cost as little as one-third of the cost of traditional treatment, but are much more successful in preventing recidivism as well. One would think that cost-conscious governments would consider this an excellent argument for introducing new psychological methods of treatment, but European countries as a whole have shown little interest in these developments in spite of their great promise.

We do not wish to exaggerate the success already achieved. What has been done so far may not work with all types of prisoners; what has worked in America may not work in Britain or Germany. It is already clear that personality interacts with treatment to determine which offenders will benefit most from certain types of conditioning. In all honesty, though, there are a multitude of caveats which deserve mention; unfortunately space prevents us from discussing them in detail. What we would like to suggest, however, is that small-scale research trials should now be made with suitable offenders, particularly juveniles, to test these methods and see to what extent the successes of the Americans can be copied elsewhere.

Is there a criminal personality?

The picture we have painted so far lacks certain important features. The first of these is related to the problem of personality. It has often been suggested that criminals are characterized by particular personality profiles, and there is now solid evidence to support this view.

Secondly, different people have different predispositions to form conditioned responses quickly and strongly. Pavlov observed this in his dogs; some dogs formed the association between bell and salivation after only 5 exposures to the bell-food connection, whereas others took 100 or even 200 or 300 exposures before forming the conditioned response.

Theory suggests, and experiments demonstrate, that introverted humans form conditioned responses much more readily than do extroverts (see Chapter 6). People who are sociable, impulsive, happy-go-lucky, and generally outgoing in their behavior find it rather more difficult to form conditioned responses, whereas people who are shy, unsociable, and retiring and who think before they act form conditioned responses readily and strongly.

An experiment done with human subjects, illustrated the marked difference between extroverts and introverts. The experiment used the eyeblink reflex, i.e., the closure of the eyelid when a puff of air is directed against the cornea. Subjects wear goggles which are penetrated by a nozzle connected through a rubber hose to an external air supply; a stream of air can then be directed against the cornea of the eye. The conditioned stimulus is a tone relayed over earphones, and the experiment consists of measuring the closure of the eyelid in response to the tone. At first there is no reaction, but as the tone is repeatedly followed by a puff of air, the subject gradually becomes conditioned to respond to the one with closure of the eyelid (this closure is not a voluntary reaction; voluntary reactions are much slower than conditioned ones, and can therefore be clearly differentiated from them).

It turns out that introverts are markedly quicker at learning to blink than extroverts; in other words, they are "conditioned" more easily. So we would expect extroverts to be more difficult to condition in other respects, and consequently, other things being equal, to be more likely to indulge in antisocial behavior. There are many studies which have shown that this is so, the subjects of these studies including schoolchildren, adolescents, and adults.

Other personality traits shared by criminals and by people who indulge in antisocial behavior are strong emotionality, or what is technically called neuroticism, i.e., overresponsiveness of the limbic system (based in the paleocortex), which controls the expression of the emotions. There are other personality traits also associated with criminality,[9,10] but it is not necessary to go into detail here in order to make the point that antisocial behavior is strongly associated with certain personality types.

This association is found not only in Western European countries and in the United States; similar relationships have been found in Communist countries like Hungary and Czechoslovakia, and in Third World countries like India. In other words, the association is not culturally determined, as some Marxist thinkers have believed, but is of universal validity.

The genetic component of criminality

It is now well established that the personality dimensions in question here are strongly rooted in the genetic constitution of human beings, with genetic factors accounting for something like three-quarters of the total amount of variability encountered, and environmental factors accounting for something like one-quarter. This suggests strongly that criminality, like intelligence, has a genetic component, and indeed the evidence fully supports this view.

One line of evidence comes from studies of identical and fraternal twins. In investigations of this kind the psychologist goes into a prison to look at the records of all the inmates in order to find out which of them are twins. He then looks for the other twin, to find out whether he is an identical or fraternal twin, and whether he too is "concordant" for criminality (i.e., whether he too has broken the law). As identical twins share 100 percent heredity, as against an average of only 50 percent for fraternal twins, one would expect identical twins to show greater concordance than fraternal twins if heredity is at the root of criminal behavior. There are now some ten studies of this sort, carried out in many different countries. And the universal finding is that identical twins show concordance about four times as frequently as fraternal twins do. In other words, the brother of a criminal twin is four times as likely to be a criminal himself if he is an identical rather than merely a fraternal twin.

The other line of evidence comes from studies of adopted children. Children adopted early in life receive their genetic baggage from their true parents, and their environment from their adoptive parents. The question now arises: which of the two is stronger in determining criminal or non-criminal behavior as they grow up? The answer, again judging by several studies done in different countries, seems to be that the genetic component is much the more important. Adopted children tend to behave very much as their true parents did, rather than as their adoptive parents brought them up to behave. Here too environment can be shown to be less important than heredity, although of course it would be foolish to stress heredity to the exclusion of environment. Both are important and both play a part in causing antisocial behavior; we have stressed the genetic aspects here because in the past fifty years there has been a tendency to overstress environment to the exclusion of genetic causes.

We can now see why it has been found so difficult in the past to change human behavior, to manipulate motivation and conduct, and to persuade criminals to become law-abiding citizens. There is a strong genetic factor, working through a rather primitive part of the brain (the paleocortex), which speaks a language quite different from, and alien to, the language of reason appreciated by the neocortex. What we have tried, usually, has been to communicate with the criminal as if he were a rational being capable of appreciating appeals to reason. This approach has failed, just as better housing and better social conditions have failed, just as psychoanalytic appeals to the subconscious have failed. If we want to succeed we will have to learn to speak the language of the paleocortex and discover how to apply the laws of conditioning to the problems posed by criminality.

The when and the how of reconditioning

This is a daunting task, but a beginning has been made, and success, even if limited, has already been achieved. The point we want to make here has often been misunderstood. People tend to jump to the conclusion that the theory of conditioning we have described justifies savage correction. It doesn't. A great deal is known about the effects of punishment, and what stands out above all else is that severe punishment increases the emotional responsiveness which is already part of the criminal's innate character, and may make things worse rather than better (Walters and Grusec, 1977[11]). Remember that in Solomon's experiment with puppies (described earlier) the punishment—a light slap with a folded newspaper—was very mild, so mild as hardly to constitute a punishment. It is only when relatively mild punishments or rewards are administered under closely controlled conditions that the desired results are obtained. The conditioning theory gives no justification for particularly harsh treatment of criminals, although it does not justify mollycoddling either.

Another of Solomon's findings from the puppy experiment may be of interest, and indeed of practical importance. Conditioning the puppies to develop a strong "conscience" was far more successful if the experimenter was also the person who, before the experiment, had fed them and looked after them. In other words, a previous personal bond between man and animal made the conditioning process much more effective. This suggests that the effective inculcation of a "conscience" in human beings must be the task of the parents rather than anyone else, and that any punishment handed out must be handed out against a general background of love and affection if it is to have the desired result.

From the point of view of preventing delinquency and crime it is vitally important that this message is brought home to parents generally. In this era of permissiveness many parents evade their duty to transmit the social message of their culture to their children; it is only by reeducating parents to accept and perform this duty that we can prevent our whole civilization from deteriorating even further.

In advising parents, teachers, and others in authority about the need to establish a "conscience" in children by a process of conditioning, it is important to bear in mind one final finding of Solomon's.

He found that the *timing* of the slap with the folded newspaper was extremely important in determining how the puppies would behave later on. If the slap occurred as the puppy approached the boiled horsemeat and before it started eating, it had the effect of a deterrent. The puppies learned not to approach the meat and eat it, which is of course what the "conscience" training was supposed to accomplish in their case. However, if the slap came later, after they had begun to eat, the result was dramatically different. Left to themselves, the puppies approached and ate the meat, but thereafter showed strong evidence of guilt (by avoiding the experimenter, slinking into corners, and generally behaving as if they were aware of having done something naughty). In other words, untimely or wrongly applied conditioning can lead to guilt feelings rather than avoidance of antisocial behavior, and this of course is not the desired result. There is little point in making people feel guilty once the antisocial act has been performed; the aim must be to prevent performance of the act in the first place.

Dealing with "tough nuts"

There is one further personality trait which is extremely important in relation to antisocial behavior and criminality. This trait relates to psychotic and psychopathic behavior and consists essentially of egocentric, hostile, aggressive, and selfish types of conduct, associated with a lack of empathy and care for others' rights and privileges, placing personal satisfaction and gratification before all else. This trait, which might be called "tough-mindedness" or "thinking tough," has also been found to be strongly heritable. As one might expect, it is related to masculinity —males show it far more frequently, and to a much stronger degree, than females. This accords well with the fact that most crimes are committed by males, that males are much more aggressive than females and also much more impersonal in their social relations. Tough behavior is probably causally related to testosterone secretion (i.e., the amount of male hormone characteristic of a person). When present to an extreme degree tough-mindedness leads to psychopathic behavior and even to psychotic (mainly schizophrenic) disorders.

Tough-mindedness is particularly related to crimes which have a vicious and aggressive element; crimes against the person—muggings, sexual crimes, and bodily harm—are the criminal acts most often associated with this personality trait. And it is crimes of violence which are particularly destructive to society, and they are increasing more than any other sort of crime, particularly in the Western world. Here again it seems likely that permissiveness has been the crucial factor, with parents and others failing to restrain children from acting tough.

Tough-mindedness is also important from the therapeutic point of view because it has been shown many times that tough-minded individuals are much less receptive to psychotherapy, behavior therapy, or indeed any method of treatment. It might almost be said that the degree to which a person's behavior can be altered by any kind of social interference is determined largely by his degree of tough-mindedness; the more tough-minded he is, the more difficult it is to alter his behavior. The only known way of affecting the tough-minded person is by way of token economies (strict conditioning programs) or by administering phenothiazines and other antipsychotic drugs which temporarily reduce their tough-mindedness and make them amenable to treatment. Unfortunately phenothiazines have a feminizing effect; male patients who take them over any period of time may start growing breasts, etc.

Whether society is justified in using drugs for the purpose of reducing a prisoner's tough-mindedness to make him more amenable to a course of conditioning or psychotherapy is an ethical point which we cannot discuss here; it must be left to experts in the fields of ethics and political science. In this instance we are merely concerned with setting down the facts rather than making recommendations.

One last point: it would be a gross oversimplification to say that criminals form a homogeneous group, or that any generalization ever applies to all prisoners. In our work we have found that there are a whole range of crimes which can be committed by persons of different personality structure. As we have already said, prisoners high on tough-mindedness are much more likely to have committed crimes of violence. But murder within the family, the most common kind of murder in the Western world outside America, is usually associated with introversion. Potential murderers tend to be rather mild, introverted people who allow resentment and hatred to grow until an explosion occurs which leads to murder. Confidence tricksters, on the other hand, are extremely extroverted, but low on neuroticism and tough-mindedness. This again makes sense, because a confidence trickster relies on making a good impression, and abnormal behaviors such as those associated with neuroticism and tough-mindedness would not impress his "clients" favorably.

Conclusions

Treatment must always depend on the personality of the prisoner; none of the methods discussed here would be suitable for all criminals. The broad outlines are fairly clear, but much detailed work still needs to be done to discover the best methods for different personalities. In addition to personality, age and sex may form important subgroups for deciding on the best treatment. Such research has hardly begun, and until far more resources are devoted to it we shall not be able to say with any degree of certainty what is the best way of rehabilitating any individual criminal.

However, all the evidence so far suggests that while the traditional methods are almost completely ineffective, modern psychology holds out a promise that effective methods can be worked out for manipulating attitudes and behaviors in a direction favorable to the survival of society. More than that we cannot claim at the moment, but we feel certain that if society were to invest in research along the lines we have suggested, its investment would be amply repaid. The rehabilitation of criminals is not a visionary or impossible task, but one well within our means.

22

Personality politics

To most people today the word "ideology" (not coined incidentally until 1817) has strong overtones of struggle, terror, and violence, and with good reason. Political violence has found twentieth-century defenders in leaders like Hitler, Mussolini, and Stalin and in philosophers like Sorel, Fanon, and Sartre. As the British sociologist M. Cranston has pointed out: "It is characteristic of ideology both to exalt action and to regard action in terms of a military analogy. Some observers have pointed out that one has only to consider the prose style of the founders of most ideologies to be struck by the military and war-like language that they habitually use, including words like struggle, resist, march, victory, and overcome; the literature of ideology is replete with martial expressions. In such a view, commitment to an ideology becomes a form of enlistment so that to become the adherent of an ideology is to become a combatant or partisan."

Is there not a suggestion here that perhaps personality traits play a powerful part in defining the ideologue, the person who believes in an ideology, adheres to it, and becomes identified with it? Such a person, according to Cranston's suggestion, would be aggressive, violent, physically active, and "committed." At this point this can be no more than a suggestion; but we shall see later that there is empirical evidence to support such a view.

A narrow definition of ideology would confine it to fairly recent political systems like Communism and Fascism, but there is a case for following J. Plamenatz, the American sociologist, in defining it as "a set of closely related beliefs or ideas, or even attitudes, characteristic of a group or community." This definition would allow us to regard as ideologies the religious and nationalistic beliefs, ideas, and attitudes characteristic of groups and communities in eras of history preceding ours. It also has the advantage that the attitudes, beliefs, and ideas which constitute particular ideologies can be presented for approval or rejection to groups of people, in the form of tests. In other words, ideologies can be studied systematically by psychological methods. It is our belief that ideologies have played and are playing such an important part in the politics of the modern world that it is the duty of psychologists to examine this particular phenomenon.

Psychologists have from the earliest days of attitude measurement proposed a dimension around which attitudes can be structured, namely that of radical-conservative or progressive-reactionary, or left-right . . . there are many names for this dimension, but they all amount to much the same thing. Furthermore, this dimension embodies a theory which stretches back over the centuries and which is almost universally accepted by politicians as well as by the mythical man in the street.

Following the custom of the French Revolution, when moderates and conservatives sat on the right and the Jacobins and other militants sat on the left of the Assembly, political parties favoring the working classes, such as the Labour Party and the Communist Party in Great Britain or the Social Democratic Party in West Germany, have been called "left-wing," and the political parties favoring the middle classes, such as the Conservative Party in Great Britain and the Christian Democratic Party in West Germany, have been called "right-wing." Even in America, supposedly less class-ridden than European countries, there has been a tendency for the Democratic Party to be relatively "left" and the Republican Party to be relatively "right."

Investigation of this radical-conservative dimension has formed a large part of psychopolitical research, but there have been many difficulties to overcome. In the first place, there are many different kinds of "conservative." One may be conservative when it comes to socialist proposals for the nationalization of industry, but radical in one's aesthetic preferences in music or painting—many millionaires, by definition "conservative," like Picasso. Different scales have been constructed for the measurement of "conservatism," but they correlate poorly. In the second place, parties of the extreme left (like the Communists) or the extreme right (like the Fascists) create difficulties. Is it really true to say that Communists are more left than orthodox Labour Party members? The Labour Party is opposed to the death penalty, but respect for individual human life has never been characteristic of Communism. Is it really true to say that Fascists are more right than Italian or German Conservatives? Mussolini appealed powerfully to the Italian working classes, and Hitler included the word "socialist" in the name of his party (Nationalsozialistische Deutsche Arbeiterpartei).

E. Shils, the well-known American sociologist, has argued that modern world history has repeatedly demonstrated the inadequacy of the notion that ideologies fit into a simple left-right continuum ranging from Liberalism to Conservatism.[1] As he points out, Italian and German Fascism were not consistently right-wing in nature, nor has Soviet Communism been consistently left-wing. Fascism introduced such policies as government control of private enterprise. In the name of Communism, Stalin conducted purges, reintroduced patriotism as official policy, and repressed national and religious minorities. Welfare legislation has often been used to sugar the pill of political repression. Hostility to private property has coexisted with racial and ethnic prejudice. Shils expressed all this clearly when he wrote of the similarity between Fascism and Communism: "Their common hostility towards civil liberties and political democracy; their common antipathy for parliamentary institutions, individualism, private enterprise; their image of the political world as a struggle between morally irreconcilable forces; their belief that all their opponents are secretly leagued against them, and their own predilection for secrecy; their conviction that all forms of power are in a hostile world best concentrated in a few hands; and their own aspirations for concentrated and total power—all these show that the two extremes have much in common."

F. A. Hayek, Nobel laureate economist, has tried to combine this notion of the similarity between Fascism and Communism with the opposition between right-wing and left-wing.[2] As he points out: "The picture generally given of the relative position of the three parties (Conservative, Liberal, Labour) does more to obscure than to elucidate their true relations. They are usually represented as different positions on a line, with the Socialists on the left, the Conservatives on the right, and the Liberals somewhere in the middle. Nothing could be more misleading. If we want a diagram, it would be more appropriate to arrange them in a triangle with Conservatives occupying one corner, with the Socialists pulling towards the second, and the Liberals towards the third." We can see, then, that there are empirical problems involved in making models of attitude relationships. We must tread very carefully if we are to reach a proper understanding of modern ideologies.

The first psychologist to suggest explicitly that there might exist a dimension in the field of social attitudes other than the right-left or conservative-radical one was the prewar German writer and experimentalist Professor E. R. Jaensch of the University of Marburg.[3] He is perhaps best known for his work on eidetic imagery (the ability to imagine absolutely clear and lifelike images—see Chapter 15), but for our purposes it is his book *Der Gegentypus* which is the most relevant. As Jaensch makes clear, the *Gegentypus* (literally, "against type") person is opposed lock, stock, and barrel to the philosophy underlying Hitlerian national socialism; he is characterized as liberal or even extreme liberal in his attitudes. As we shall see, the *Gegentypus* is the opposite, in many ways, of the *authoritarian personality* of Adorno and others.[4]

Now, Jaensch was an avowed follower of Hitler long before the Nazi movement came to power. T. W. Adorno and the other authors of *The Authoritarian Personality* (1950), however, were victims of Hitler's persecution and strongly anti-Fascist. Our understandable revulsion at Hitler's appalling crimes makes it almost impossible for us not to side with the Adorno group and oppose Jaensch. But in the interests of truth we must resist partiality. At worst we can learn from our enemies; at best we must realize that Jaensch, however misguided, was on to something very important.

In the writings of Jaensch the attitudes held by the *Gegentypus* person are intimately linked with the description of personality. It is this relationship which constitutes the original part of Jaensch's book, and we will return to it later. For the moment let us note that the *Gegentypus* has attitudes which are somewhat radical, though his main characteristics might be typified as "extreme liberal." In many ways the *Gegentypus* is the exact opposite of the authoritarian personality, which is tilted toward the conservative side, but which is conservative in a very specific, authoritarian manner. The precise meaning and position of these two theoretical concepts can best be understood by looking at Figure 1.

Diagram A shows the traditional single dimension from Communism on the left to Fascism on the right; B shows the hypothetical contrast between Liberals on the one hand and Communist-Fascist ideologies on the other. In our theory these two single dimensions are combined in a two-dimensional framework, diagram C. Note that the radical-conservative dimension is supplemented by another dimension ranging from authoritarian at one end to democratic at the other.

We would also suggest that authoritarianism is characterized by a particular type of personality structure which may be called "tough-minded," while the democratic attitude is characterized by a particular personality structure which may be called "tender-minded." Again this is a concept we shall be returning to later.

The authoritarian personality and the *Gegentypus* do not lie along either of the two dimensions proposed in diagram C. As shown in Figure 2, the authoritarian is tough-minded, but tilted toward the conser-

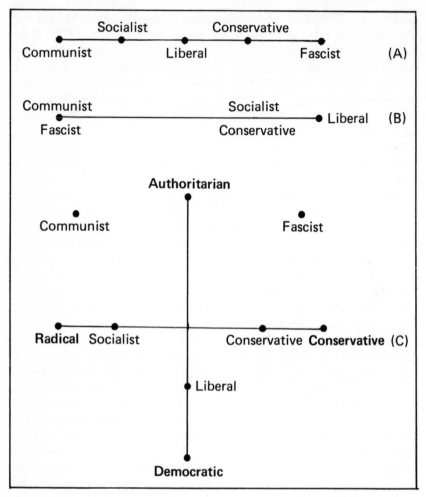

Figure 1

vative side, whereas the *Gegentypus* is tender-minded but tilted toward the radical side. Many critics have pointed out this tilt, which is not really in accordance with the data and which arose primarily from the political biases and preferences of the authors of the books dealing respectively with the *authoritarian personality* and the *Gegentypus;* what we shall be concerned with in this chapter is the tough-minded versus tender-minded axis, or the T axis rather than the radical-conservative or R axis.

A hypothesis such as that developed here naturally requires empirical proof, and this can only be given by a correlational analysis of endorsements or rejections of attitude statements relevant to these dimen-

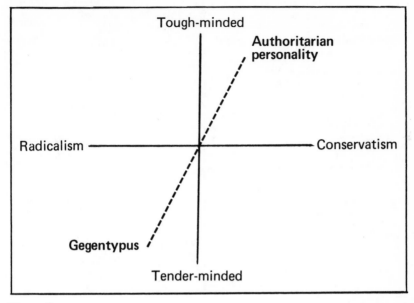

Figure 2

sions made by large samples of the population. Many such studies have been reported. Figure 3, for example, shows data from the original studies which inspired *The Psychology of Politics* (Eysenck, 1954[5]). The tough-minded/conservative quadrant contains attitudes we would now tend to regard as Fascist, while the tough-minded/radical quadrant contains attitudes commonly identified with Communist beliefs. Tender-minded attitudes are identified with Liberalism. This is merely an interpretation of the data. However, many empirical studies have demonstrated that members of the Communist and Fascist parties, as well as members of the Socialist (Labour), Liberal, and Conservative parties, hold attitudes which assign them to the particular parts of the two-dimensional framework to which theory has confined them in Figure 1, diagram C. Descriptively, therefore, the two-dimensional system of attitude measurement we propose offers a reasonably accurate picture of the position of the two major modern ideologies, and their relationship to the more ordinary social attitudes and beliefs held by members of the traditional parties.

Key experiment   (Thelma Coulter)

The crucial experiment which investigated these various relationships, as well as the connection between ideology and personality which will be discussed later, was carried out by the Canadian psychol-

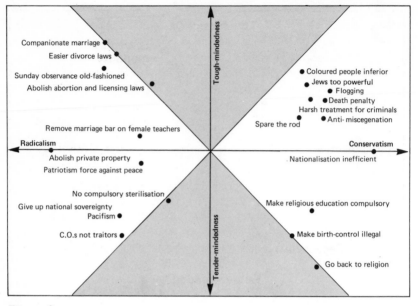

Figure 3

ogist Thelma Coulter. She administered many attitude and personality questionnaires and tests to members of the Communist and Fascist parties, not, let us note, to student members but to working-class members of long standing (with a sprinkling of middle-class members, also of long standing). This point is important because students are apt to join extreme parties and leave them again after a very short while; therefore they cannot be considered "committed" exponents of either ideological dimension (Eysenck and Coulter, 1972[6]).

Coulter had many difficulties in getting her subjects, all of them male, to take part in the experiment. Ideologues tend to be very suspicious, even paranoid, and regard anyone who is not with them as against them. In the interests of research, therefore, she was forced to join both parties at the same time, a very daring and indeed dangerous procedure. Fortunately she was never found out, and went to meetings, canvassed, sold newspapers for both parties, and joined them in other activities without the one ever getting to know of her affiliation with the other. With her as a party member, both Communists and Fascists were more willing to take part in the testing, and her thesis records what must be one of the most adventurous as well as one of the most interesting social-psychological investigations ever carried out.

The differences and similarities between the two groups were striking, and the personalities of members of both parties were remarkably similar, as we shall see presently. The study was done in the fifties, when there was still a Fascist party in England; nowadays no such party officially exists, although the National Front has taken over many of its policies. It would be interesting to repeat the study with a new generation of Fascists and Communists, perhaps using American, German, and other national samples as well as English ones.

What were the main personality traits of Coulter's Fascists and Communists? She noted strong hostility and aggressiveness, very much as Cranston's description at the beginning of this chapter would have led one to expect. Another marked similarity which differentiated both ideological groups from a normal control group was the rigidity of their attitudes; Fascists and Communists were much more rigid in their mental processes than were the controls. They were also much more emphatic in their attitudes; whatever they believed in they felt very strongly about, and interpreted criticism or denial as hostility. They were intolerant of ambiguity, i.e., they could not tolerate doubt or uncertainty, and demanded immediate decision and action. Dogmatism and dominance were other traits which emerged, the former more associated with the Fascists, the latter more with the Communists. Altogether, there were marked similarities between the two ideological groups compared with the controls, but also a few differences; the Communists displayed less direct aggression than the Fascists. On the whole, though, the similarities far outweighed the dissimilarities.

Jaensch originally postulated a close relationship between personality and the social attitudes characteristic of the *Gegentypus:* "In our long-continued investigations of the fundamental differences of human beings, we have again and again come upon a type which in our circle we called 'the type of dissolution and destruction.' . . . This type, in its most clear-cut and definite form, is characterized by extreme liberalism. For this type, there are no ties, and this general failure to relate, to be tied, is firmly grounded in biological reality. . . . In our work, we have tried to construct a bridge between empirical and experimental psychology on the one side, and cultural psychology and philosophy on the other. . . . Extreme liberalism is not only a political, but a much more all-embracing, biological-psychological fact, which is primarily, and in extreme form entirely, found in the dissolution type. . . . Psychophysics has shown by experiment that liberalism has a biological basis, and thus goes far beyond a simple political doctrine."

Adorno and his colleagues also attempted to link personality with the concept of *authoritarianism,* making much use of psychoanalytic concepts in the process. With them, as with Jaensch, the rigor of the experimental studies was rather weak, and many criticisms have been made of their work. Let us merely note that both the concept of gegentypism and that of authoritarianism have been linked very closely with personality by their authors, and that a genetic basis has been implied, at least by Jaensch, for this connection. Is there any evidence for a genetic determination of R (radicalism-conservatism) and T (tough- and tender-mindedness)?

The majority of writers on social attitudes have not even considered the possibility that attitudes are anything but the product of environmental influences. To date the only empirical study concerned with evaluating the possibility of genetic determination of attitudes is one reported by Eaves and Eysenck.[7] This study used the Eysenck questionnaire for the measurement of R and T, illustrated in Figure 3, and also measured an additional variable called "emphasis," which is simply the sum of the degrees of extremity shown in the endorsement of the various items (items are judged on a 5-point scale from Agree Very Strongly through Agree, Doubtful, and Disagree to Disagree Very Strongly; the emphasis score adds together the number of very strong agreements and disagreements, disregarding the direction of the endorsement).

This questionnaire was administered to a total of 708 twins, 451 of whom were monozygotic (identical) and 257 dizygotic (fraternal). The results were analyzed using the new and very powerful biometrical genetical methods of analysis pioneered by the Birmingham School of K. Mather and J. L. Jinks. These methods have enabled us to construct a model of genetic action which gives us not only the heritability of the trait involved but also information about other aspects of genetic architecture.

Only the briefest summary of these results can be given here. First, for the R factor (radicalism-conservatism) heritability was 65 percent; for the T component (tough-minded/tender-minded) heritability was 54 percent. For emphasis, heritability was 37 percent. These values are much higher than one would have expected on *a priori* grounds, and certainly disprove the widely held notion that attitudes are determined by environmental factors alone. Such a belief in the potency of the environment never had any empirical support in any case—it was purely a manifestation of the *Zeitgeist*.

In the Eaves and Eysenck study mentioned above, personality inventories were also obtained. It was known from previous work done by both researchers that personality factors show strong genetic determination, and the same effect was observed again in this study. The personality traits investigated were E (extroversion/introversion), N (neuroticism/stability), and P (tough-mindedness). The nature of some of these personality dimensions and their biological determinants were discussed in Chapter 10. Here let us merely repeat that extroversion/introversion refers to the opposition of sociable, impulsive, physically active traits and non-sociable, non-active, non-impulsive behavior patterns. Tough-mindedness is a personality dimension which is characterized by cold indifference, hostility, aggressiveness, disregard for social conventions, non-conformity, and a certain degree of paranoia. Neuroticism is characterized by emotional overreactivity and the persistence of emotional reactions long after the occasion for them has passed. Eaves and Eysenck hypothesized that extroversion would be correlated with tough-mindedness, and also that P would be even more powerfully correlated with authoritarianism. Statistical analysis of the results of the twin studies confirmed both hypotheses: "Our study confirmed the correlation between E and T, showing that it has a genetic, rather than an environmental basis. There is also a significant genetic correlation between P and emphasis. This suggests that individuals who achieve high P scores share the strong conviction of being right which is characteristic of some psychotic behavior." There was an even more significant tendency for high P (tough-mindedness) scores to be associated with authoritarianism, very much as expected.

Eaves and Eysenck have since conducted several further studies, involving familial relationships and adopted children; these have strongly supported the major conclusions derived from the original work quoted above.

To summarize, there seems no doubt that there are relationships between personality and authoritarianism, that these relationships have a genetic basis, and that consequently it is impossible to discuss ideologies simply in terms of rational beliefs.[8] Endorsement of these belief systems is determined very largely by genetic and hence philosophically irrelevant factors.

The relationship between the emphasis score and P on the one hand, and authoritarianism on the other, is of particular interest. The general bellicosity of ideologies noted at the beginning of this chapter, and the "commitment" involved, are shown in the emphatic endorsement given to statements by tough-minded subjects and by the generally aggressive nature of the high P scorers. Further evidence for these relationships comes from the Eysenck and Coulter (1972) study of avowed Communists and Fascists, who clearly showed these personality traits to an extreme degree. The evidence now points very strongly to a relationship of the kind predicted in *The Psychology of Politics* (Eysenck, 1954).

Our theory seems to leave open the most fundamental question of all, namely why do ideologies arise in the first place? We can suggest what sort of person is likely to fall prey to ideologies; we can predict the sort of ideologies which are consistent with right-wing or left-wing political ideals; and we can show how the dynamism of certain ideologies fits the personality features of the people who adopt them. The question of origin requires an answer which must go beyond psychology, although it inevitably must also include certain psychological principles.

In outline, what we would suggest is this. Right-wing and left-wing political ideas, capitalism and socialism, contain within themselves contradictions which inevitably lead to conflict, change, and dissolution. The contradictions of capitalism have been pointed out by many writers, including of course Marx; unless restrained by government action and trade-union pressure capitalism leads to monopoly and the enrichment of the few at the expense of the many. The contradictions of socialism have been pointed out by F. A. Hayek, K. Popper,[9] and many others. The egalitarian principle underlying socialism is in conflict with biological reality and can only be enforced by dictatorship. In other words, full-blooded capitalism and full-blooded socialism can only be maintained by repression and denial of human rights. Ideologies are, by definition, coercive. Capitalism, however democratic in intent, requires Fascist-type dictatorship to preserve its privileges. Socialism, however democratic in intent, requires Communist-type dictatorship to enforce its policies.

Neither the enforcement of social ideals nor the maintenance of privilege is, of course, successful. Fascism only preserves the empty shell of capitalism, shorn of all real power, and Communism only preserves the empty shell of socialism, shorn of all its ideals. In practice both right-wing and left-wing ideals need to be restrained by government action, otherwise they end in impasse. But government action finally congeals into government control, dictatorship, and loss of freedom. The only valid alternative is to compromise, to give up right-wing and left-wing ideals in favor of a middle-of-the-road position which reconciles both capitalist and socialist doctrines, which allows for both a private sector and a state-run sector of industry.

Why is this compromise so often disregarded in favor of extreme and militant ideological postures? The answer may lie largely in the "principle of certainty" enunciated by the British psychologist R. H. Thouless on the basis of his work on religious beliefs. He defined the certainty principle as follows: "When, in a group of persons, there are influences acting both in the direction of acceptance and of rejection of a belief, the result is not to make the majority adopt a lower degree of conviction, but to make some hold the belief with a high degree of conviction, while others reject it also with a high degree of conviction." This observation applies closely to political beliefs too.

One of the authors of this book did a study in which he tabulated the distribution of 22,208 votes, on a 7-point attitude scale, on a variety of social and political questions where there were clearly "influences acting both in the direction of acceptance and of rejection" of the beliefs in question. The result showed a distinct tendency for extreme values (+3 and —3) to be more frequent than intermediate values. It was also found that when the different groups which took part in the study were compared, there was a marked tendency for the more extreme groups to be more certain of their opinions, which leads one to speculate that in any society which contains haves and have-nots (in effect, all but the most small and primitive societies), conservative and radical attitudes would be found among the inhabitants partly as a reflection of their social status and partly as a reflection of their personality. These attitudes would be held with varying degrees of conviction, again depending on the personality of the holder. P+ personalities would have a high degree of conviction, P— personalities low conviction.

Given a particular form of social organization, whether capitalist or socialist, the internal contradictions of that organization would bring about its eventual breakdown unless those who were strongly convinced of its essential rightness ensured its survival by physical force and the suppression of civil rights. Ideologies would arise as a natural consequence of two factors, the internal contradictions of existing political systems and the "principle of certainty" which makes it difficult for many people to hold their beliefs with a low degree of conviction although a low degree of conviction would certainly be appropriate to our lack of knowledge of the consequences of social actions.

Repression, of course, begets rebellion, as inevitably as action begets reaction in Newtonian physics. Thus one ideology begets its opposite ideology. The political process further exacerbates the tensions created by the "principle of certainty"; the conviction that he is ultimately right drives the ideologue farther and farther away from the possibility of compromise, and leads him finally to genocide, to the murder of whole classes or races and to other obscenities which recent history chronicles only too well. The principles outlined briefly here are, of course, likely to have wider applications. We need only substitute Catholic and Protestant for capitalist and socialist and we immediately see the same picture, with minor changes to fit the religious content. There are inner contradictions in religious systems just as there are in political systems, and the "principle of certainty" operates with equal force for any set of beliefs one chooses to name. As another example, we might consider the struggle between the *Optimates* and the *Populares* in ancient Rome, a depressing period of cruelty, murder, and repression.

In conclusion, we contend that it is impossible to study modern or ancient ideologies properly without paying close attention to psychological principles, and in particular to the relationships between ideology and personality. As yet our scientific implements have only scratched the surface of this absorbing and complex set of problems. Nevertheless, the results are significant enough, and coherent enough, to suggest that in due course we will understand the springs of ideology far better than we do at present.

Epilogue

In this book we have discussed some of the most fascinating and important discoveries ever made by psychologists. But we have not covered even a tenth of all the major areas of research in which psychologists are active. It would take many weighty volumes to do that. Psychology is concerned with human behavior and is therefore relevant to almost any activity involving man.

Let us review quickly a few of the areas we have had to omit. Take architecture. Most people feel that buildings should be designed to be pleasing to look at and comfortable to live in. Psychologists have a valuable contribution to make at this man-building interface.

Overpopulation, one of the major nightmares of recent years, is another important field for the psychologist. In twenty or thirty years from now the world's population will have grown explosively, causing starvation and social strife on a gigantic scale, unless, of course, successful birth control programs can be implemented, and implemented now. While it is tempting to leave the problem to politicians to deal with, it is not they who will directly supervise such programs or advise on effective advertising campaigns. It is the psychologist.

Another important area in which psychology is of universal value is ergonomics, the interaction of men and machines. If you think about it, the entire organization of our work environment is increasingly influenced by occupational and industrial psychologists. The problems posed by decaying industries, poor worker morale, low productivity, and technological change all basically call for answers at the psychological rather than the political level.

Psychology pervades many facets of our daily lives. Some people find this vaguely sinister; they suspect that the insidious horrors of George Orwell's *1984* lurk just around the corner. The authors of this book totally reject such a pessimistic view. Apart from anything else it is quite unfounded. As we have been at pains to show, the richer understanding of human nature which psychology provides is already revolutionizing major aspects of society (our education and penal systems, the treatment of mental illness) in ways which are wholly beneficial.

What of psychology tomorrow? It is, of course, foolhardy to attempt to predict the future. However, we are prepared to risk making the following three forecasts (call them informed guesses if you prefer) as to the ways in which psychology will develop in the future.

First, psychology will be perceived as being more and more relevant to social problems, and to an increasing number of them, than is the case today. For example, most general practitioners have little knowledge of, or interest in, psychology. They simply treat the physical symptoms of the patients who visit their offices. Yet many of their patients are more in need of psychological attention than of pills and potions. The "placebo effect" (patients recovering rapidly even when given dummy drugs) strongly suggests that physical illness and recovery can be caused and aided by psychological processes. Hopefully there will be a more fruitful marriage of psychological and medical knowledge in the future.

Second, some of the experiments in modern psychology which have hit the headlines have done so because of the ethical issues they pose. If we look into the future, it seems highly probable that research psychologists will be under increasing pressure to justify their work in moral terms. Our only wish is that a proper balance be struck between the concern of the psychologist to carry out relevant and useful research, and the duty of administrators, politicians, and the general public to protect the rights and dignity of those who take part in psychological experiments. It would be a tragedy if a witch hunt were started against psychologists, leading to a total shackling of their research endeavors.

Third, major advances in any science often occur as a direct consequence of important technological breakthroughs. The radio telescope was one such breakthrough; the whole scope of astronomy was dramatically widened by its invention. In similar fashion Allan and Elaine Hendrickson's exciting new discoveries about intelligence would not have come about had new ways of measuring brain-wave activity not been devised.

If the future is anything like the past, then the crucial research of the 1980s and 1990s will depend on further technological developments.

We cannot know just what these developments will be, but we confidently predict that there will come a time when our present attempts to unravel the mysteries of the human mind will seem like the uncertain steps of a baby learning to walk.

Notes

Chapter 1

1. Darley, J. M., and Latané, B. "Bystander intervention in emergencies: Diffusion of responsibility," *Journal of Personality and Social Psychology,* 8 (1968), 377–83.
2. Latané, B., and Darley, J. M. *The Unresponsive Bystander: Why Doesn't He Help?* New York: Appleton-Century-Crofts, 1970.

Chapter 2

1. Efran, M. G. "The effect of physical appearance on the judgment of guilt, interpersonal attraction, and severity of recommended punishment in a simulated jury task," *Journal of Research in Personality,* 8 (1974), 45–54.
2. Bercheid, E., and Walster, E. "Physical attractiveness," *Advances in Experimental Social Psychology,* Vol. 7. New York: Academic Press, 1974.

Chapter 3

1. Milgram, S. "Behavioral study of obedience," *Journal of Abnormal and Social Psychology,* 67 (1963), 371–78.
2. Milgram, S. *Obedience to Authority.* New York: Harper & Row, 1974.

Chapter 4

1. Zimbardo, P. G. "On the ethics of intervention in human psychological research: With special reference to the Stanford prison experiment," *Cognition,* 2 (1973), 243–56.
2. Zimbardo, P. G. "Transforming experimental research into advocacy for change," in M. Deutsch and H. A. Hornstein (eds.), *Applying Social Psychology: Implications for Research, Practice, and Training.* London: Halstead, 1975.

Chapter 5

1. Rosenhan, D. L. "On being sane in insane places," *Science, 179* (1973), 250–58.
2. Rosenhan, D. L. "The contextual nature of psychiatric diagnosis," *Journal of Abnormal Psychology, 84* (1975), 462–74.
3. Spitzer, R. L. "On pseudoscience in science, logic in remission, and psychiatric diagnosis: A critique of Rosenhan's 'On being sane in insane places,' " *Journal of Abnormal Psychology, 84* (1975), 442–52.

Chapter 6

1. Baum, M. "Rapid extinction of an avoidance response following a period of response prevention in the avoidance apparatus," *Psychological Reports, 18* (1966), 59–64.
2. Carlson, N. J., and Black, A. H. "Traumatic avoidance learning: Note on the effect of response prevention during extinction," *Psychological Reports, 5* (1959), 409–12.
3. Page, H. A., and Hall, G. F. "Experimental extinction as a function of the prevention of a response," *Journal of Comparative and Physiological Psychology, 46* (1953), 33–34.
4. Polin, A. T. "The effects of flooding and physical suppression as extinction techniques on an anxiety motivated avoidance locomotor response," *Journal of Psychology, 47* (1959), 235–45.
5. Rachman, S. J., and Hodgson, R. J. *Obsessions and Compulsions.* New York: Appleton-Century-Crofts, 1980.

Chapter 7

1. Terrace, H. S. *Nim.* New York: Alfred A. Knopf, 1979.

Chapter 8

1. Harlow, H. F. "The nature of love," *American Psychologist, 13* (1958), 673–85.
2. Harlow, H. F., and Mears, C. *The Human Model: Primate Perspectives.* Washington, D.C.: Winston, 1979.

Chapter 10

1. Eysenck, H. J. (ed.). *A Model for Personality.* New York: Springer, 1980.
2. MacArthur, R. S. "An experimental investigation of persistence and its measurement at the Secondary School level." London: Ph.D. thesis, 1951.
3. Zubin, J., Eron, L. D., and Schumer, F. *An Experimental Approach to Projective Techniques.* New York: Wiley, 1965.
4. Eysenck, H. J. "Graphological analysis and psychiatry: An experimental study," *British Journal of Psychology, 35* (1945), 70–81.
5. Fulker, D. W. "The genetic and environmental architecture of psychoticism, extraversion and neuroticism," in H. J. Eysenck (ed.), *A Model for Personality.* New York: Springer, 1980.

6. Eaves, L., and Eysenck, H. J. "The nature of extraversion: A genetical analysis," *Journal of Personality and Social Psychology, 32* (1975), 102–11.

Chapter 11

1. Sperry, R. W. "Hemisphere deconnection and unity in conscious awareness," *American Psychologist, 23* (1968), 723–33.
2. Gazzaniga, M. S., and LeDoux, J. E. *The Integrated Mind.* New York: Plenum Press, 1977.

Chapter 12

1. Schachter, S., and Singer, J. "Cognitive, social, and physiological determinants of emotional state," *Psychological Review, 69* (1962), 379–99.
2. Marshall, G. D., and Zimbardo, P. G. "Affective consequences of inadequately explained physiological arousal," *Journal of Personality and Social Psychology, 37* (1979), 970–88.

Chapter 13

1. Clifford, B., and Bull, R. *The Psychology of Person Identification.* London: Routledge & Kegan Paul, 1978.
2. Loftus, E. F., and Palmer, J. C. "Reconstruction of automobile destruction: An example of the interaction between language and memory," *Journal of Verbal Learning and Verbal Behavior, 13* (1974), 585–89.

Chapter 14

1. Cherry, E. C. "Some experiments on the recognition of speech with one and with two ears," *Journal of the Acoustical Society of America, 25* (1953), 975–79.
2. Kahneman, D. *Attention and Effort.* Englewood Cliffs, N.J.: Prentice-Hall, 1973.

Chapter 15

1. Eysenck, M. W. *Human Memory: Theory, Research, and Individual Differences.* Oxford: Pergamon, 1977.
2. Tulving, E. "Cue-dependent forgetting," *American Scientist, 62* (1974), 74–82.
3. Tulving, E., and Psotka, J. "Retroactive inhibition in free recall: Inaccessibility of information available in the memory store," *Journal of Experimental Psychology, 87* (1971), 1–8.

Chapter 16

1. Argyle, M., and Dean, J. "Eye-contact, distance, and affiliation," *Sociometry, 28* (1965), 289–304.
2. Patterson, M. L. "An arousal model of interpersonal intimacy," *Psychology Review, 83* (1976), 235–45.

Chapter 17

1. Festinger, L., and Carlsmith, J. M. "Cognitive consequences of forced compliance," *Journal of Abnormal and Social Psychology, 58* (1959), 203–10.

Chapter 18

1. Gribbin, M. "Granny knows best," *New Scientist, 84* (1979), 350–51.
2. Rutter, M., Maughan, B., Mortimer, P., and Ouston, J. *Fifteen Thousand Hours.* London: Open Books, 1979.

Chapter 19

1. Eysenck, H. J. "The development of personality and its relation to learning," in S. Murray-Smith (ed.), *Melbourne Studies in Education,* pp. 134–81. Melbourne: University Press, 1978.
2. Leith, G. O. "Individual differences in learning: Interactions of personality and teaching methods," in *Personality and Academic Progress, Conference Proceedings,* pp. 14–25. London: Association of Educational Psychologists, 1974.
3. Leith, G. O., and Trown, E. A. "The influence of personality and task conditions on learning and transfer," *Programmed Learning, 7* (1970), 181–88.
4. Trown, E. A., and Leith, G. O. "Decision rules for teaching strategies in primary schools: Personality-treatment interactions," *British Journal of Educational Psychology, 45* (1975), 130–40.

Chapter 20

1. Miller, N. E. "Learning of visceral and glandular responses," *Science, 163* (1969), 434–45.
2. Miller, N. E., and DiCara, L. "Instrumental learning of heart rate changes in curarized rats: Shaping, and specificity to discriminative stimulus," *Journal of Comparative and Physiological Psychology, 63* (1967), 12–19.
3. Seer, P. "Psychological control of essential hypertension: Review of the literature and methodological critique," *Psychological Bulletin, 86* (1979), 1015–43.

Chapter 21

1. McLean, P. D. *A Triune Concept of the Brain and Behaviour.* Toronto: University of Toronto Press, 1973.
2. Solomon, R. L. "Punishment," *American Psychologist, 19* (1964), 239–53.
3. Solomon, R. L., Turner, L. H., and Lessac, H. S. "Some effects of delay punishment on resistance to temptation in dogs," *Journal of Personality and Social Psychology, 8* (1968), 233–38.
4. Rutter, M., Maughan, B., Mortimer, P., and Ouston, J. *Fifteen Thousand Hours.* London: Open Books, 1979.

5. Ayllon, T., and Azrin, N. *The Token Economy.* New York: Appleton-Century-Crofts, 1968.

6. Sarason, I. G. "A cognitive social learning approach to juvenile delinquency," in R. D. Hare and D. Schalling (eds.), *Psychopathic Behavior.* New York: Wiley, 1978.

7. Stumphauzer, J. S. *Behavior Therapy with Delinquents.* Springfield, Ill.: Charles C Thomas, 1973.

8. Stumphauzer, J. S. *Progress in Behavior Therapy with Delinquents.* Springfield, Ill.: Charles C Thomas, 1979.

9. Eysenck, H. J. *Psychology Is about People.* London: Allen Lane, 1972.

10. Eysenck, H. J. *Crime and Personality.* London: Routledge & Kegan Paul, 1977.

11. Walters, G. C., and Grusec, J. E. *Punishment.* San Francisco: W. H. Freeman, 1977.

Chapter 22

1. Shils, E. "Authoritarianism: 'Right' and 'Left,'" in R. Christie and M. Jahoda (eds.), *Studies in the Scope and Method of "The Authoritarian Personality,"* pp. 24–49. Glencoe, Ill.: Free Press, 1954.

2. Hayek, F. A. *The Constitution of Liberty.* London: Routledge & Kegan Paul, 1960.

3. Jaensch, E. R. *Der Gegentypus.* Leipzig: J. A. Barth, 1938.

4. Adorno, T. W., Frenkel-Brunswick, E., Levinson, D. J., and Sanford, R. N. *The Authoritarian Personality.* New York: Harper & Row, 1950.

5. Eysenck, H. J. *The Psychology of Politics.* London: Routledge & Kegan Paul, 1954.

6. Eysenck, H. J., and Coulter, T. "The personality and attitudes of working-class British communists and fascists," *Journal of Social Psychology, 87* (1972), 59–73.

7. Eaves, L., and Eysenck, H. J. "Genetics and the development of social attitudes," *Nature* (London), *249* (1974), 288–89.

8. Eysenck, H. J., and Wilson, G. D. *The Psychological Basis of Ideology.* Lancaster: Medical & Technical Publishers, 1978.

9. Popper, K. *The Open Society and Its Enemies.* 2 vols.; London: Routledge & Kegan Paul, 1945.

Index